Going Native

A Bike Journey From Austin To Argentina!

Ezra Teter

Copyright © 2024 by Ezra Teter

All rights reserved.

ISBN: 979-8-89324-275-1

Special Thanks to Chris W for taking my travel journal and pictures and putting this book together as a birthday present!

Dear reader, I am so honored that you have taken an interest in my adventures. If you have any questions, comments, or feedback, please feel free to contact me using the email address provided below. I would love to hear from you and will do my best to respond in a timely manner.

Goingnative123@gmail.com

Cheers!! - Ezra Teter

"Bicycling is a metaphor for life.
Well, for me, bicycling is my life. Sometimes in
life you have to overcome obstacles to continue on.
Every hill, headwind, or flat tire is only a temporary
obstacle on the way to reaching my goal. I am now
stronger and wiser for having dealt with this adversity.
Humanity thrives on adversity. It is what forced us
to adapt to new environments. I am confident
that I can conquer any obstacle in my path."

-Ezra T.

PREFACE

I wrote this book, Going Native, as a journal of my two-year bicycle trip from Austin, Texas to Buenos Aires, Argentina and then to São Paulo, Brazil where I lived for ten years. My (mis)adventures in Brazil would fill a book of their own but this chronicle focuses entirely on my experience of and perspective from traveling to and through South America. I chose the title because I think that more of us should travel in a way that forces us to quit our jobs and drop off the grid. There is no better way to have a more profound adventure than by learning the language and leaving the beaten gringo path. The experience you have when you converse with the locals, befriend people, and take lovers is always going to beat that of the tourist who is at port for a day in the middle of cruise. I didn't just travel. I got to know the cycles of the countries I visited and lived in. I also have friends in pretty much all of the capital cities that I visited. It was an experience that has enriched my life and that I wouldn't trade for anything.

The title also has a double meaning for me as someone who identifies with the counter-culture. Though I am a U.S. citizen by birth and am actually descended from people who fought in the American Revolution, I don't identify with the American project, particularly that of imposing hegemony on the rest of the planet. I identify with world citizenship and-- I don't care how controversial this is—with the worldwide abolition of borders. If you don't like that then don't buy my book because you will be triggered. I won't shed a single tear.

Publishing this was not my original intention. I really just wanted to write a travelogue that my friends could read so they could share in my journey. However, it ended up being something that really resonated with people since most of us are stuck at our stultifyingly boring day jobs. At some time or another, all of us have wanted to just run away from it all and what I did comes pretty darn close to that.

As I write this, I am fantasizing about leaving the country for a long time again. There is much to cause discontent no matter what your political persuasion is. But I want to do something that is a little bit crazy and, frankly, kind of dangerous. I want to bike across Siberia in the winter or hitchhike through war zones. The farther away from civilization that I can go the better. My inspiration is the Quaker Benjamin Lay who was an abolitionist a century before it was cool. He eventually got so fed up with our shit that he went to live in a cave for the remainder of his life. We should all tune out, drop off the grid, and go native.

CONTENTS

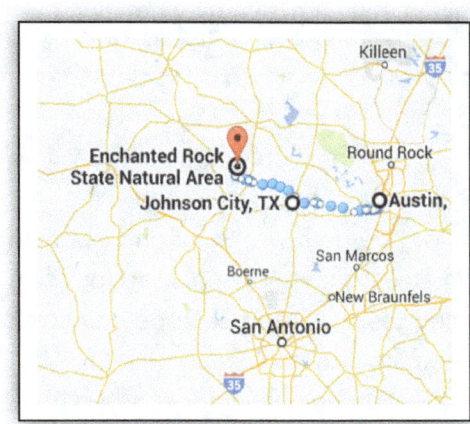

Introduction:
Preparing for My Adventure
& Saying Goodbye To Austin

Monday, 7/2/2007

In October, I am planning to ride my bicycle from my hometown, Austin Texas, to not quite the southern tip of Argentina, and afterwards to Rio de Janeiro. I will not pass through every country in Central and South America, but I will pass through many. I rode a shorter ride in the summer of 2001 down the west coast of the United States. In that trip, I spent $2,000, rode 2,900 miles, and took 2 months to do it. In this trip, I hope to spend no more than $10,000, I estimate that I will ride up to 20,000 miles, and that I will take up to a year doing it. When I arrive in Rio de Janeiro, I hope to find work teaching English. I taught English before in Mexico for a year. I would like to stay in Brazil long enough to effectively learn Portuguese. I do not have definite plans for my return. I have saved up a healthy chunk of cash from waiting tables and living a simple, car-free lifestyle, and I hopefully, do not have to worry about running out of cash.

Why am I doing this? I am doing this because life can be tedious and, dare I say, stultifying. I am young, I do not have people who depend on me, and I have managed to escape the impoverishing traps of massive student loans and car ownership. As far as the method of travel that I have chosen goes, I can't think of a way I would rather be going. I am 28 and proud of the fact that I have never driven a car.

The bicycle ride to work is almost always the most enjoyable part of my day. I love going on long bicycle rides, and zooming down hills. I even love riding up hills because I see every hill as a personal challenge to be conquered. Life gives you hills. When one spends a lot of time on a bicycle, bicycling becomes a metaphor for life. You discover a lot about yourself when you overcome adversity. I am looking forward to the adventure.

I am now at the moment where my departure is imminent. It is that point in time where I am realizing how crazy I am, but I have already committed to a plan by purchasing all of the gear I am going to need for my trip. I have spent around three thousand dollars on my bike, gear, and vaccinations. Traveling is not cheap, even by bicycle. I am prepared to spend ten thousand more, if I have to. My bicycle is a bike-commuter's wet dream. It is a road bike with larger wheels and racks for four saddlebags and a G.P.S. device onto my handlebars.

I'm pretty sure that I can get to where I want to be on this bike. The rest of my inventory includes: a bunch of socks, winter layers, rain gear that covers my entire body, a camera, tools and knives, my bike lock, bungee cords, a first aid kit, water purification tablets, a camel back, books to read, notebooks to write in, hiking boots, a tent, sleeping bag and pad, mosquito net, bicycle shorts, clothes, etc.. I am going to dedicate one of my front saddle bags to food and extra water.

I will probably carry a lot of energy dense foods that are mostly nonperishable like canned sardines and tuna, beef jerky, saltines, and peanut butter. This is more an emergency supply of food for when I am in less populated areas. Otherwise, food can be obtained cheaply all throughout Latin America.

I rode back-to-back hundred mile days with all of my gear, a couple of weeks ago, to get accustomed to riding with everything, and make sure that it was comfortable. I learned that I am capable of riding many miles consecutively but that I should probably ease into it. The Texas Hill Country is beautiful but brutal. There are a lot of long rolling hills with steep grades that can be pretty tortuous when you are exhausted.

I left my house at 6:00 a.m., rode 112 miles, and ascended 6,167 total feet to arrive at Enchanted Rock State Park right before sunset, which was at 7:30 p.m. I felt pretty exhausted and wondered if maybe I was pushing myself to hard. The next day, I was still feeling pretty tired and consequently left at 9:00 a.m.

I followed the highway instead of back roads and arrived in Austin at around 9:00 p.m. I had to be at work the next day so I had no choice but to will myself back to Austin. The total distance I traveled on Day 2 was slightly shorter in distance, and I ascended less to get back to Austin because Enchanted Rock is at a higher elevation.

Still, I rode 100 miles and encountered the scariest part of my training ride when I had to ride on U.S. 290 from outside Dripping Springs to Austin after the sun set. There is hardly any shoulder and there was a lot of traffic passing me by at highway speeds. I was feeling

pretty exhausted at work the next day, but not too exhausted to go a show. By the following day, I was fully recovered.

I feel like I am in shape to begin my journey. I have spent most of the last week just tying up loose ends, hanging out with friends, and enjoying live music around town. I worked my last shift at Hut's Hamburgers a couple of days ago. I will miss all of my coworkers. We were like a big happy family for many years together. Anyway, the departure date is but a few days away. I will soon embark on my personal odyssey. Just going to Big Bend will be very challenging, for it is in the most desolate part of Texas. There are roads where I will have to travel 50 miles between towns. It will test my wits and endurance just getting to the border. I like to think that I am young tribal warrior going off into to the wilderness to prove my manhood by surviving.

The First Ten Days

Day 1, 10-8-2007

Miles Traveled (mt): 62.8, Total Ascent (ta): 3053 ft, Campsite Location (g.p.s.): N 30°14.582' W 98°33.847'

I left the city at about 11 a.m. This was about two hours later than I planned. I felt like I was chasing rain storms all day for I kept catching peripheral showers. I camped somewhere between Johnson City and Fredericksburg. I don' feel like I am even remotely exhausted. Onward to Argentina and then to Brazil! I am going to dedicate one of my front saddle bags to food and extra water.

Day 2, 10-9-2007

mt: 75.6, ta: 2254 ft, gps: N30°56.101' W99°16.921'

When I left Austin, I expected to have to worry about dehydration and heat exhaustion. Instead, I have had to worry more about hypothermia and pneumonia.

For the first half of the day, it was raining. It was not wet or cold enough to justify wearing my rain gear. Whenever, I would stop somewhere the air conditioners would make me shiver.

I hate air conditioners with a passion, especially since nobody ever shuts them off when it is raining. I passed through old Comanche territory today. The town and the county of Mason are both named after Fort Mason which was a military base put there to protect settlers (read invaders) from Comanche and bandit raids. I slept hobo-style under a bridge. I prefer not to pay for a place to sleep if it is possible.

Day 3, 10-10-2007

mt: 97.6, ta: 2172, gps: N 31° 28.409' W 100°30.046'

I officially left the Hill Country today. I noticed the flattening of the terrain almost immediately today because I was zipping along at about 17 miles an hour after I left the town of Brady. I ran into a team of cyclist that was relaying from Alberta, Canada to Austin for the Lance Armstrong ride. I told them they should go eat at the restaurant I just quit, after working 7 years. I am sure that the folks at Hut's would be thrilled to wait on a bunch of cyclists that I sent their way.

The disadvantage of flat terrain is that there are less hiding spots along the road for me to put my tent. I bit the bullet and stayed at San Angelo State Park for $11. I took advantage of the facilities and had my first shower since I left Austin. I am a dirty, dirty boy. As far as I can tell, West Texas is suffering from a plague of crickets.

Day 4, 10-11-2007

mt: 70.4, ta: 2037 ft, gps: N 31°11.695' W 101° 29.068'

I got a late start because I had to do some routine bike maintenance. The spokes on my rear wheel were extremely loose. This is something that I think that I am going to have to pay closer attention to.

I saw something funny today. There was a young man flying a confederate flag from his Japanese pickup truck in the town of Mertzon. That just ain't right on so many levels. We were both looking at each other from across a parking lot, like the other one was crazy.

Here in West Texas, you can see for miles in all directions. It makes you feel tiny and insignificant. Trucks rule the road here. You would probably get laughed off the road if a Mini-Cooper or Toyota Prius were your car of choice. I am glad that I am a city boy, because there doesn't seem to be much to do here, other than huff gasoline and shoot shit. Convenience stores and fast-food chains seem to be the main meeting places here in the countryside. I am watching my mouth and avoiding certain topics of discussion altogether. Religion and politics are taboo subjects, as far as I am concerned. Liberal, rural Texas is not.

Texas seems to be the champion of ironic place names. I passed through a town called Big Lake, today, without a lake in sight. Eden doesn't seem to be much of an Eden unless you are a cricket.

Day 5, 10-12-2007

mt: 93.06, ta: 2432 ft, gps: N 30° 52.677' W 102° 53.331'

Today, when I left my campsite, I immediately noticed that the wind was coming very strong from the south. "No problem," I thought to myself, "I am going west." But, lo and behold, the wind shifted, not favorably. I had to charge into a strong headwind for 50 miles today.

This was, by far, my most grueling day yet. A good strong headwind can provide more resistance than the steepest hill. I was wondering if it is always windy at this spot. Sure enough, my question was answered, when I rode by about a thousand wind turbines. It seems like wind is supplanting oil as the number one energy source in West Texas. I rode by many dormant oil rigs, and even an oil rig graveyard. All of the turbines were operational.

I rode by the site of the first oil discovery in the Permian Basin, today. It was named Santa Rita #1 after the patroness saint of the impossble. They named it Santa Rita because they had to drill over 3,000 feet over a period of 4 years to strike oil. Nowcdays, oil companies routinely drill over 3,000 feet. I have even read that there are deep sea oil rigs that go down over 10,000 feet.

For those of you in Austin, the original oil rig for Santa Rita #1 is on the U.T. campus. It is that big talking monstrosity at the corner of San Jacinto and M.L.K. It is the reason why U.T. has one of the largest endowments of any university in the nation. I think they spent all of the money on the new stadium expansion and Mack Brown's salary. What a waste. I ended up camping in a pretty sketchy location, today. Hopefully, I won't get arrested or find any mesquite thorns in my tires tomorrow.

Day 6, 10-13-2007

mt: 59.1, ta: 3869 ft, gps: N 30° 12.392' W 103° 13.919'

I thought that the headwind was bad yesterday but it was much worse today. The numbers belie the difficulty of today's ride. The wind was so strong that it would stop me dead in my tracks while going downhill. As far as I am concerned, I would be perfectly happy riding my bike down Route 666 straight to Hell, if I had a nice strong tailwind. That's right; I would sell my soul just to avoid this

headwind. To make matters worse, I got my first flat of the trip. Believe me I was cursing God/the Gods. Fortunately, the flat was easily fixed.

I was excited when I saw tarantulas and prairie dogs today. I got a good picture of a tarantula but the prairie dogs would not let me get close enough to take a picture. There used to be billions of these critters but the ranch-

ing industry, with help from the U.S. government, made them an endangered species. I also saw a hawk that was probably hunting prairie dogs. Hawks almost never pose for the camera. The wind eventually abated for the last 20 miles of my journey, today, and I was able to make peace with God/ the gods. My arduous trek was rewarded with the most beautiful sunset that I have seen thus far on my journey.

Day 7, 10-14-2007

mt: 58.9, ta: 2188 ft, gps: N 30° 17.526' W 104° 01.441'

All the technology in the world could not have prevented my dumb ass from missing the turn off for Big Bend National Park, this morning. By the time that I had realized that I was on the wrong road, I had reached the point of no return. "Oh well" I figured, "I will get to visit Big Bend some other day." I was just going to pass through anyway. The road I accidentally took also fortuitously went the direction that I needed to go anyways.

The scenery was like scenery in a cowboy western movie. There were lots of desert mountains. It is a very beautiful place. I rolled along at a leisurely pace even stopping to take a nap when I found a nice reststop. I even managed to avoid a headwind for all but the last 10 miles of my trip. I got a flat for the second day in row, because my patch malfunctioned. I never trusted patch kits anyway. I just cut off the valve stem and made a double tire liner for my front tire. Hopefully, I won't have any problems with it for a while.

I am getting closer to the border and I am worried about the I.N.S. bugging me while I am camped under a bridge. My campsite is less than a quarter mile from the I.N.S. Marfa headquarters.

I am somewhat of a history buff, so I often take exception to the way history is reported. I learned today that Fort Davis was named after Jefferson Davis, and that it was erected to defend settlers from Indian attacks. These attacks came primarily from the Plains Indians i.e. the Apache, Kiowa, and Comanche Indians. The thing I took exception to, was the way that the Indians were portrayed as people who were hostile towards the settlers for no reason at all. If the white man encroached upon my lands, fenced off my hunting grounds, and decimated the game (i.e. bison) that I subsisted on, I would be pretty fucking hostile, too. The Plains Indians were already nomadic since they followed the buffalo herds, so they made very effective guerrilla warriors.

After the Civil War, the U.S. army turned their attention to the Indians and waged a campaign of annihilation and subjugation of these nomadic peoples. Palo Duro Canyon, in the Texas Panhandle, is the site of a large U.S. Army massacre of Comanche. To refer to the massacre, which took place at Wounded Knee in South Dakota, as a "battle" is an egregious misnomer. The members of the army regiments that were killed were killed by friendly fire, as the army had surrounded an encampment of Sioux. That is enough of my little rant for now. When I woke up today, it was very cold. This was due to the fact that I am at an elevation of 4,500 feet. I was happy to find out that Presidio is at a lower elevation for I prefer heat over cold. I crossed the border today. I immediately thought to myself that I am a crazy fool!

Day 8, 10-15-2007

Kilometers traveled (kt): 129, ta: 2579 ft, gps N 29° 33.978' W 104° 39.133

I passed through a customs checkpoint and a military checkpoint, today. I took advantage of both, and had them refill my water. The police did not want to search my things but the soldiers did. They did a pretty thorough search but they missed the pound of cocaine I was carrying in my rectum. I was very happy to reach the town of Coyame for I was able to eat real food, not just beef jerky. I was quite the rock star in Coyame, several locals followed me around and bombarded me with questions. I eventually had to extricate myself to move on.

Day 9, 10-16-2007

kt: 65.7, ta: 4014 ft, gps: N 29° 25.575' W 105° 07.877'

The desert on the Mexican side of the border seemed like a barren wasteland compared to the U.S. side. Fortunately, it is well populated, and there have been places to obtain water that weren't on my map or G.P.S. device. I have to ride about 120 miles to Chihuahua City. I don't think that I will make it in one day. Note to all. I am keeping track of the kilometers I travel now since all of Latin America follows the metric system. I didn't travel very far today for I did not want to overexert myself. Fatigue in the desert can be deadly. Not only was it hot, but I had to climb over multiple mountains. After climbing over the first mountain, I was rewarded with a spectacular view of Peguis Canyon. I had no idea that this canyon existed and when I saw it, I was awestruck. I wanted to stay there and look at the canyon all day but, alas, I had to move on.

Day 10, 10-17-2007

kt: 138, ta: 3471 ft, gps: N 28° 38.138' W 106° 04.671'

Today, I more than doubled the distance traveled yesterday, for I had passed all of the big mountains. I still had to travel through mountain roads, but the ascents were less challenging. It was still good and hot and, being in the desert, there was hardly any shade. Still, I made good time, and reached Chihuahua City before sunset. The drivers in the city are much meaner than in the countryside. When I am on country roads, the drivers will usually pass me with at least 6 feet to spare. In the city, I consider myself lucky if I have more than a foot to spare.

When I arrived in the city, I had an accident while avoiding a truck. I bent the part of my front fork where the right saddlebag attaches. I also bent the screw that held my saddlebag onto my fork. I was lucky, though. I was able to bend the part of the fork back in place and I was rescued by Sergio Richarte, the most heroic mechanic in the world. He helped re-thread my fork and obtained a new saddlebag screw. Without his help, I would probably have to cut my trip short. To top it all off, he refused compensation. For this, I'm eternally grateful.

Day 11, 10-18-2007

kt: 0, ta: 0 ft, gps: N 28° 38.138' W 106° 04.671'

And on the 11th day he rested. I am sitting in an Internet cafe planning my journey. I hope to find some more inner tubes, and other mundane tasks. I will enjoy the city and take some pictures today.

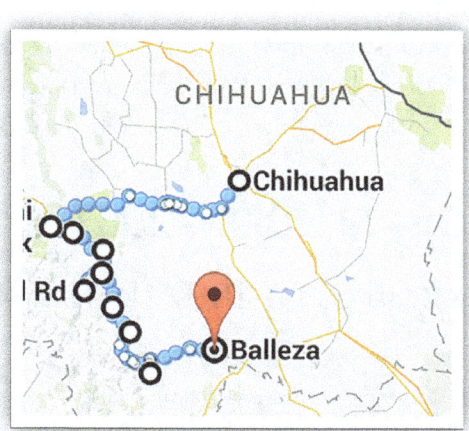

La Sierra Tarahumara

Day 12, 10-19-2007

kt: 77, ta: 2676 ft, gps N 28° 31.930' W 106° 30.422

When one decides to live the life of a nomad, they must always guard against growing too comfortable in any one area. I think I was already becoming too comfortable in Chihuahua City. Why leave when there is good, cheap food in every corner of the city, and I would have to expose myself to desert conditions, again. For these reasons, I took my time leaving the city this morning. I ate a nice large breakfast and surfed the Internet for about an hour. It is easy to become ensconced in the comforts of the city.

But I have to keep moving. There are too many beautiful places to see, to stay in one place for too long. I am very excited about visiting the Sierra Tarahumara. The whole mountain range abounds with beautiful places. There are waterfalls, canyons, hot springs, river gorges, etc.. The conditions are going to be very different than the desert. There is even a possibility that I might see snow. I am already at a higher elevation and expecting a cold morning. This will definitely make it harder for me to get out of my sleeping bag. The scenery and the climate should be changing soon. Hopefully, I have what it takes to survive the cold. It will all be good preparation for the Andes. I don't think that I have ever been at an elevation above 10,000 ft in my life. Onward!

Day 13, 10-20-2007

kt: 91.2, ta: 2890 ft, gps: N 28° 27.414' W 107° 20.232'

As I predicted, I started late because it was cold and I did not want to leave the warmth of my sleeping bag. The first twenty or so kilometers of my day were all uphill. The scenery and the ecosystem changed. I started to see a lot less desert plants and more pine trees. The higher elevation seemed to support apple orchards for I passed by several large, industrial-scale operations. I have no doubt that Mexico is self-sufficient in food production.

I passed through several areas of larger communities of Mexican Mennonites. They are easy to spot because they wear funny-looking hats and often have fair skin and blue eyes. I am pretty sure that it is a pretty closed community but they do, occasionally, venture into Babylon to buy supplies. The Mennonites I saw did not seem to be narco-mennonites, for they were driving a pretty beat up pick-up truck. Obviously, though, the dominant capitalist culture has begun to infiltrate their traditional culture. They have managed to stay closed-off to the rest of the world, to maintain their fair hair and fair skin.

I managed to call one of my friends in Mexico City today, and I was very excited to get a hold of him. I can't wait to visit all of my friends in el D.F. and see all of their various bands. It is going to be so much fun! My campsite tonight is kind of sketchy. It is just off the side of the road. My tent is on an incline because I wanted it to be hidden from the road. That means my sleeping bag will be sliding off of my sleeping pad all night. There is a dead, rotting goat close to my tent. I am just far enough away from it so that I don't notice the smell. The goat looks like it has been sucked dry by the chupacabra. I am going to sleep clutching my buck knife so that I can be prepared for any epic battles with the chupacabra.

Day 14, 10-21-2007

kt: 65.6, ta: 4097 ft, gps: N 28° 22.029' W 107° 51.894

The mountains are getting bigger, and I have definitely left the desert behind me for now. I had a pretty frustrating day because I kept having problems with equipment failure: first with my bike rack and later with my tent. When I was ascending a big hill I noticed that all of the gear on my back rack was wobbling. At first, I thought I had a flat but, I realized that the screw and bolt that had held my rack on had rattled off.

I tried to look for these pieces but, soon, gave up for it was like trying to find a needle in a haystack. I was worried that I was going to have to commit my cardinal sin and hitchhike. I don't want to use gas, if I don't have to on my trip. The problem was solved, temporarily by cannibalizing my bike rack and using a screw from one place and putting it in another. I later found out that this was a problem because the bolt on other side of the screw was getting in the way whenever I would try to shift into my highest gear. This deprived me of that extra gear for hauling-ass down mountains. The first thing that I did when I reached the town of Tomochic was seek out an auto mechanic to see if I could get a better screw. We had to grind the screw down with a pneumatic grinder to make it work.

I am always impressed with the ingenuity of mechanics here. Again, when I tried to offer compensation, it was refused. I don't know how the mechanics here feed themselves if they are always offering their time for free. I will always be indebted to Ezequial from Tomachi.

The tent comes with a bigger piece of pipe that can be fitted over a tent pole for emergency repairs. I also think that I can fix the problem with a little super glue. There is a loose fitting that can probably be glued back.

I have had a lot of time to think to myself, and I have worked myself into one of my frenzies. The governments of Mexico and of all the states of Mexico publish lots of propaganda, in just about every medium, patting themselves on the back for how much good work they have done. I think that they have taken way to much credit for any improvement there has been. It is probably more likely that the billions of dollars sent home by Mexicans working in the U.S. has more do to with any improvement. All I know is this. I passed through several small Indian villages, today, and these people are still dirt-poor. They live in dilapidated shacks with no electricity or running water. I saw churches in some of these villages but no schools. It is no wonder

that illiterate Indian villagers come to the big cities to beg. You can see them in any city in Mexico with their hands held out, not saying a word. It is sad, but they probably do better for themselves begging in the city than staying in their villages. The least the government could do is stop wasting their money on propaganda and actually build schools in these villages so that when people do, inevitably, leave their villages, they at least have skills so they can get jobs in the city. As of now, no one would hire an illiterate Indian who can't even count. What else are they going to do but beg?

Day 15, 10-22-2007

kt: 58, ta: 4285 ft, gps N 28° 10.160' W 108° 12.544'

It was cold last night despite the fact that I slept in my clothes in my sleeping bag. It seemed like it was freezing cold this morning when I woke up. The mountains here are beautiful, but I doubt that I could live here, for I would not want to wake up until it got warmer sometime in the early afternoon. Speaking of the afternoon, it was a beautiful day by then. I was starting to enjoy the mountain roads. All day long, I crawled up the steep grade of one side of the mountains and then hauled-ass down the other. Sometimes I would rest at the top of a long climb.

It was while resting at the top of a long, steep ascent I met a man who told me he was going to pick up several kilos of marijuana in the other direction. I asked him if he had any and he gave me a dime bag while jumping into the back of a pick-up truck. I hadn't smoked since Austin, so I was grateful. I even rode through a military check-point with the weed. The trick is not to act suspiciously.

My plans were to ride as far as possible today, but when I reached the lookout point over the waterfall in the mountains outside of Basaseachic... I had to stop. I rode my bike right up to the lookout point, for it is handicapped accessible, and therefore bicycle accessible.

Neither words, nor pictures, can fully capture the beauty of this place. The gods of the forest still live in the mountains here. There are parts of the forest here that have probably never been touched by man, because it is too difficult to access. I sit here, writing this, while watching the sun go down over the mountains. I am going to stay here tonight, watch the stars, pray to the gods of the forest, and then watch the sunrise over the mountains in the morning. Only then, and probably not even then, will I have had my fill of this place.

Day 16, 10-23-2007

kt: 43.6, ta: 3769 ft, ft. gps: N 28° 06.545' W 107° 57.494'

It was another cold day when I woke up this morning. I was smart this time, and slept under even more layers. Because it was not the busy season at the waterfall, I was able to sleep in an unused structure that had walls on all sides and a roof. I did not even set up my tent though I should have because some mouse or rat bit into my camel-back valve while I was sleeping (I was wondering what that was scurrying across my sleeping pad, last night?). The camel-back still works, though. It just has a slow leak out of the valve.

Today was the first day in which I had to ride on an unpaved road. This definitely adds another layer of difficulty onto my trip. Not only is it hard on the body and the bike, but it is very desolate, and I have had to go into my emergency provisions to eat.

I still have plenty of food and about 9 liters of water so I think that I have enough to make to San Juanito, which is another 57 kilometers away on this same dirt road. My bicycle shakes and rattles as it goes downhill. I have to always look ahead 50 to 100 feet for dips in the road while I descend. My hands are tired from braking. I did not even make it to the halfway point between the cascade and San Juanito, though I came close. I was happy that I made it up the never-ending, dirt-road hill of my worst bicycling nightmares. It topped out at 8,600 feet. My campsite is just on the other side of the mountain at about 8,500 feet. Tonight, it is going to be very cold so I built a campfire. I will build one in the morning, too.

My day has been very challenging but, also very rewarding. It is so beautiful here that if I died and my body was never found, I would be okay with that. My body would be absorbed into the earth in one of the most beautiful places I have ever been. There is so much unspoiled nature here, including creeks with crystal-clear water. I would be tempted to jump in, if I didn't know already that the water is freezing cold.

My body has adapted to the nomadic lifestyle. I am always ready to eat, yet I can ride for long distances without eating much. I've stopped at places after traveling, then devoured a half-chicken with tortillas & salsa, and dessert. Yesterday, I even accidentally ate raw chorizo sausage, without any ill effects.

Today, I ate a whole can of beans; then used the can to cook the rest of my chorizo into a chorizo chili, served with saltines. It was quite delicious, and I was very pleased with my ingenuity of cooking without cookware. This is especially true, since this was the first hot food I had eaten all day. I should have more than enough food to make it San Juanito.

Day 17, 10-24-2007

kt: 61.9, ta: 3869 ft, gps: N 27° 56.637' W 107° 35.581'

Last night, the wind was cold and howling but I was as snug-as-a-bug in my tent. I put on the rain fly so the wind didn't bother me. I slept in and made a fire in the morning. When I checked my bike out, there really wasn't anything wrong, other than it being dusty and low tire pressure. I pumped up the tires and applied the last coat of oil I had to all moving parts. My bicycle was happy.

The ride got progressively better, because the road was improving, slowly but surely. Civilization is coming to these parts. I saw all sorts of various earth-movers and dump-trucks. There is no plumbing or electricity but the people expect it soon, with the paving of the roads.

I despise the ubiquity of Coca-Cola, but I was very happy to see a Coca-Cola sign on the outside of a house on the side of the road. This meant that they would probably have water and something to eat. To my pleasant surprise, they even had pollo en mole, with tortillas and rice. This, and the fact that the roads were mostly paved, made the last 20

kilometers of my trip much more pleasant than the first 40. When I reached electrified civilization, I gorged on hamburgers, fries, juice, and ice cream. I then road to the outskirts of San Juanito, found a campsite, and made another fire. I am starting to grow fond of camping in the mountains.

There are two things I learned in Boy Scouts: always be prepared, and know how to make a one-match fire. It is simple: first you make a pile of tender, then you put kindling on top, and, afterwards, you put the wood on top of that. The nice thing about the mountains here is that there is more wood than you can shake a stick at. The pine needles make great tender, although that means that you have to be constantly vigilant to make sure your fire doesn't spread. I prefer to make a fire circle with a radius of at least two feet for two reasons: some of these igneous rocks explode if they are too close to the fire, and I can scrape some coals aside for cooking. It is always nice to have hot food on a cold night.

Day 18, 10-25-2007

kt: 89.3, ta: 5491 ft, gps: N 27° 31.992' W 107° 49.576'

There was frost on my tent this morning when I woke up. No problem, I just made another fire, and I was warm and toasty. Compared to the unpaved mountain roads of yesterday, the roads today were like heaven. It was like I

was floating on a cloud. I no longer had to hold onto my brakes for dear life, while descending the mountain hills. I made good time to both Bocoyna and Creel, so I figured that I would try to reach Copper Canyon today.

Upon arrival at my campsite, I realized that I had accidentally left my (bike lock) chain somewhere when I stopped. I frantically hurried back to the places I stopped looking for my chain but to no avail. I can get another chain, but it probably won't be as good as my trusty kryptonite chain. I will look for another chain in the next city. When I am in el D.F., I will look for another kryptonite chain.

Copper Canyon is so beautiful that when I was frantically searching for my chain, I couldn't help but take a moment to notice how beautiful the full moon was, rising over the canyons at sunset.

I am camped close the viewing area and I had another impressive campfire meal. This time, I had roasted marshmallows for dessert. I realized that I can cook rice in the sardine cans. With a little onions, jalapeños, and lime juice, I will have a nice little fish stew. I think I will have this for breakfast, tomorrow.

Day 19, 10-26-2007

kt: 50.5, ta: 3532 ft, gps: N 27° 42.908' W 107° 36.892'

I am sitting in an Internet cafe planning my journey. I hope to find more inner tubes, do laundry, and other mundane tasks. I got another late start because I decided to help an old lady, who was a food vendor, carry some heavy items in exchange for a few gorditas. The lady made an excellent salsa with a mixture of tomatoes and tomatillos and had the secret ingredient of oregano in it. I didn't leave Copper Canyon until almost 1:00 p.m. I only rode three hours and rested today.

The, normally grueling mountain roads were quite fun. I would move very slowly uphill sometimes for miles at a time and then fly down the other side. My top speed was 66.3 kph. I went so fast that my eyes would tear up. Most of the time, I was riding and holding my brakes, for there are some sharp curves on steep grades. After all of that exhilaration, I would sometimes rest at the bottom of a long, steep descent.

When I was coming back into Creel, I saw it! My chain was sitting in the same spot I had rested at earlier, only 50 kilometers away from where I noticed it was missing. I felt like such a lucky fool. I felt lucky that I didn't have to spend any extra money on a new chain, and I felt foolish because I rode for 50 kilometers without noticing that I wasn't carrying a 10-pound chain over my shoulder.

I celebrated by purchasing a comal at the ferretería in Creel. A comal is a pan that can be placed over wood or charcoal to cook food. It has been used here in Mexico traditionally for centuries or more. The ferretería is the store that sells all things metal. One can find screws, bolts, cooking utensils, and anything else that is metal. Ferro is the Spanish word for iron. I will enjoy the city and take some pictures today.

I am looking forward to using my comal. I can now make some more elaborate campfire meals. Anything that can be cooked in a frying pan can be cooked in my comal. One doesn't need a fancy camping stove to make all sorts of food. In fact, there are traditional Mexican foods like mixiote, cochinita pibil, and tamales that don't need to be cooked with any cooking utensils. They are all wrapped in a protective leaf pouch, so they can be put directly on top of the coals. The leaf is either corn, maguey, or banana.

I have been meditating a lot on fire as of late. The ability to harness fire is the skill which sets us apart from all other species, and has allowed us to adapt to all environments. Fire is what has made me come to enjoy camping in the cold, cold mountains. Recently, I have also been meditating on trash a lot. Even in the most desolate places, it seems like the vast majority of people don't respect the planet and throw their trash wherever.

Sometimes, I wonder, when an archaeologist finds some ancient artifact, if they are just finding the litter of some Paleolithic redneck. I follow the philosophy of packing out what I pack in and I wish other would, too. We would have a much nicer planet if everyone just took responsibility for their messes.

Day 20, 10-27-2007

kt: 54.5, ta: 2887 ft, gps: N 27° 22.487' W 107° 30.052'

This morning, there was frost on my tent again. The reflection of the sunlight on the frost covered grass in the distance was sublime. Today was like any other day in the mountains. Up hills, then down hills. The scenery was beautiful. All was good, until I crashed going downhill.

I am fine. Just a scrape on my elbow, and pretty scared, because wiping out on a mountain descent is never fun. I broke one of the hooks holding my front right saddlebag. I had to ghetto-rig my saddlebag onto my rack, using bungee cords and a rope I had found along the side of the road in Texas (I knew that rope would come in handy).

I would like a more permanent solution. Maybe I can buy a replacement hook, but it would be difficult to obtain one in Mexico. I am going to buy more bungee cords now. Its possible a replacement part can be made for me in a metal shop. The hook was plastic but metal is better.

When I reach civilization, I will see what I can do. For now, I'll ride more slowly when going downhill.

After my accident, I did not ride very far. I came across a beautiful river gorge with an abandoned house and decided that this would be a good place to set up camp and lick my wounds. I should reach a town of decent size tomorrow.

Day 21, 10-28-2007

kt: 51.7, ta: 5100 ft, gps: N 27° 07.089' W 107° 17.996'

Today was a better day than yesterday. There were no wrecks, my ghetto-rigged saddlebag remained secure, and it was noticeably warmer when I woke up due to the lower elevation at which I camped. Someone in Creel told me there was not a lot of ascent between Creel and Guachochi, but they have obviously never ridden a bike on the highway between the cities, for I have ascended almost 8,000 feet in the last two days with more to go. I ran into people from Oregon today, on two separate occasions. The first time, there was a whole pack of retirees on an adventure tour. They gave me water and I was grateful. The second time, I met a man on a motorcycle, who told me he had been traveling through Latin America off-and-on for the last twenty years. I learned some useful information from him. For example, I learned that Colon, Panama is a gnarly crime-infested city; and though the Andes are at a higher altitude than the Sierra Tarahumara, they are actually warmer due to their proximity to the equator. He and I talked for a while, and had a good conversation. I got his email and will add him to my contact list.

For those of you that don't know, the Sierra Tarahumara is named after the Tarahumara Indians. These people have lived in caves in the mountains, probably, for millennia. Some of them still live in caves. I don't know much about the Tarahumara, except that they have rituals involving psychedelic mushrooms, and they have runners among them who can run for many, many, miles; for it is a part of their culture. I saw that there is an ultra-marathon through the canyons here, and wondered if many Tarahumara compete in it?

These days, the women here wear very colorful clothing, almost as if for show, and sell baskets and jewelry in the tourist towns. The only way you can often identify the men is by their, obviously, Indian features and by the sandals they wear. I don't know how they wear sandals without socks in these freaking cold mountains. I did see a few older men dressed in more traditional garb.

I saw an eagle today. It was the second time I had seen one recently. The other time, I saw a flock of parrots chasing an eagle away from their nests on the unpaved road from Hell. I haven't seen much other interesting wildlife of note so far. The bears and rattlesnakes are hibernating and pumas instinctively avoid man. The fact that I have a campfire probably keeps the critters away too. Surprisingly, I haven't seen deer since I left Texas.

I am becoming more and more comfortable cooking with a campfire. It is real easy using a comal. Tonight, I made Mennonite cheese quesadillas. I know three things about the Mexican Mennonites: they wear funny-looking hats, shun society, and make some damn good cheese. I am even glad that the one restaurant in the town that I passed through was closed. The food I would have gotten there would probably not have been significantly better than the quesadillas I made. Anyway, I now sit by the dying embers of my fire feeling re-energized and ready for tomorrow. I am having a great time and I hope that this trip never ends!

Day 22, 10-29-2007

kt: 64.6, ta: 2621 ft, gps: N 26° 42.184' W 107° 04.660'

I wrote a poem about my favorite subject, as of recently. Here it is:

"My Little Fire"
My little fire which burns so bright,
You keep me warm throughout the night.
Without your warmth, I just might,
Die before the morning light.

Granted I am no Shakespeare, but it comes from the heart. I've grown accustomed to finding frost on my tent in the morning. This morning, my tent poles even froze together. It was cold enough, all day, that I never once changed my pants to shorts. I had a pretty relaxing ride today. Once I reached Guachochi, I found food and an Internet cafe. I even found out where I needed to go to find replacement parts for my saddlebags.

If you ever need to make new metal parts in Mexico, you need to find a taller de torno. Taller just means workshop and I am pretty sure that torno means lathe. None of the machine shops in Guachochi had a drill press, so I will ask around in a bigger city. I now know what to look for.

All is good because my ghetto rigged saddlebag seems to stay on better than the bags that aren't broken. I am going to buy more bungee cords.

If anyone ever asks, Novarra makes shitty saddlebags. I am pretty pissed-off that I spent $500 for saddlebags and they have plastic parts. The only good thing that I can say about them is that they are, indeed, waterproof. Novarra makes shitty bikes, too. When I find a machine shop, I am going to replace all of the plastic parts with metal ones.

Los Cumbre de Sinforosa are, indeed, very beautiful. The desert and mountain ecosystems intersect here for there are Maguay cactus and century old plants to go along with the pine trees. It only costs a dollar to get into the park, and the park attendants were very helpful. They left the bathroom open and showed me a good spot to collect fire-wood. The funny thing is the bathrooms don't have lights, toilet paper, or even toilet seats, but they have automatic, motion-activated soap dispensers.

Tomorrow I will have, sadly, left the Sierra Tarahumara, but I won't miss the coldness of the mountains.

In fact, I even look forward to riding in the hot desert, again. Someone recently asked me if I was scared of camping in Mexico. I feel safer camping here than in Texas. There's less fenced-off land here, and most of the folkds here are good people. I haven't had any problems.

Day 22, 10-29-2007

kt: 0, ta: 0 ft

I managed to get into some good fun trouble, this morning. When I was about to leave the national park, I met some guys that I guessed were drug dealers. They asked me if I smoked weed, and I said yes, so they took me to a nearby ranch and gave me an ounce of the nicest weed that I have ever seen in Mexico, up until that point. They offered some cocaine, too, but I didn't want any. The guy who was driving even had a 9 mm. I knew I could trust them because they let me shoot their gun.

We got high and drove around the ranch herding cows for a while. We then went into town and they gave me even more weed, that was even better than what they gave me before. I swear, I have about a quarter pound of weed on me now. I have to figure out where to hide it all, so I can get through military checkpoints. I love hanging out with generous drug dealers! Cheo, the driver, is now my best friend in Guachochi. He said if I have any problems with the law here, that I should tell them I am a friend of Cheo's. Olale!

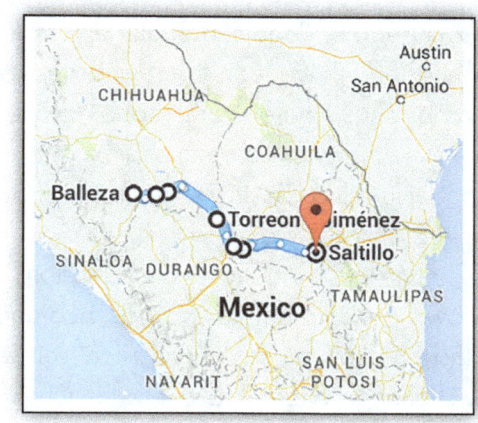

Hanging Out in Hidalgo de Parral & Crossing the Desert

Day 24 & 25, 10-31-2007 to 11-1-2007

kt: 94, ta: 3338, gps N 26° 55.355' W 106° 19.836'

Today was a fun day for riding for I mostly rode downhill, especially at the end of my journey when I descended over 3,000 feet. I swear, I rode downhill for the last 20 kilometers of my trip. The descents were more fun, too, because I could see farther ahead so, I wasn't afraid to just let go of the brakes and zoom downhill. The ecosystem has changed back into c desert ecosystem. There are no more pine trees or manzanillas.

They have been replaced by desert succulents and oak trees. The scenery is beautiful. I was going to stay at a motel tonight, but I did not have enough cash and there were no cash machines in Balleza. Oh well, I just have to camp, instead. I have to make it 97 kilometers to Hidalgo de Parral, with only 76 pesos, which is around $7. I can do it because I have lots of food and water.

Day 26, 11-2-2007

I stayed in Hidalgo de Parral

I wake up with the sun, therefore I wake up much earlier than most of the Parralenses, as the people from Hidalgo de Parral are called. I went to find the taller de torno, but it was not open yet. I got to eat the first tacos of the day, at the taco stand next to the workshop. They were quite delicious. I eventually found a machine shop that could make the part I needed. It will only cost $15 for all eight pieces. Try replacing any specialized part like that in the United States for that price.

Hidalgo de Parral seems to appear in the pages of Mexican history books disproportionately for a city its size, of about 120,000 inhabitants. It was founded in the seventeenth century as a small mining town. There was silver in the surrounding mountains, so the town became a major

city by the early nineteenth century. It was the capital of the republic, when Benito Jaurez brought the government of Mexico here while fleeing from French forces. When the American Punitive Expedition came here, under the command of General John Pershing, they were driven out of town by a riot of the townspeople. This is also the town in which Pancho Villa was killed. I went to the spot where he was assassinated. There is a museum dedicated to him.

Since it is the Day of the Dead, I thought I would buy some pan de los muertos, and share it with El General at his tomb in the pantheon or cemetery, outside of the city center (His bones were actually exhumed and put in one of the corners of the Monument to the Revolution, in Mexico City). The cemetery here is huge and was filled with people. People brought flowers and food for their ancestors. They cleaned up and de-weeded around the tombstones. There were groups of people singing and playing instruments at some of the gravesites. It was a very beautiful thing. I wish we celebrated the Day of the Dead in the United States.

Mexico is a land of contradictions. It is flooding right now in the southern states of Tabasco and Chiapas and yet I haven't seen a drop of rain since I left Austin. I am sure this will change once I make it to the jungle. The government, which at one point conspired to assassinate Pancho Villa, now celebrates him as one of Mexico's greatest folk heros. When I went to put a flower on Pancho Villa's tomb, it was closed off, and an arrangement of flowers had been left by the municipal government of Hidalgo de Parral. On the same day that the Mexican Navy found 23 tons of cocaine in a ship off the coast, I was rolling through a military checkpoint unimpeded. The soldiers were more curious about my trip than what was in my bags. I still remember how the soldiers in the first checkpoint I rode through, in Northwestern Chihuahua, were listening to narcocorridos while they were searching all of the cars and the trucks. The narcos that I met in Guachochi were some of the nicest and most generous people to me, even though they carried guns. I kind of like being in a land of such contradictions. It is always fun to make ironic observations.

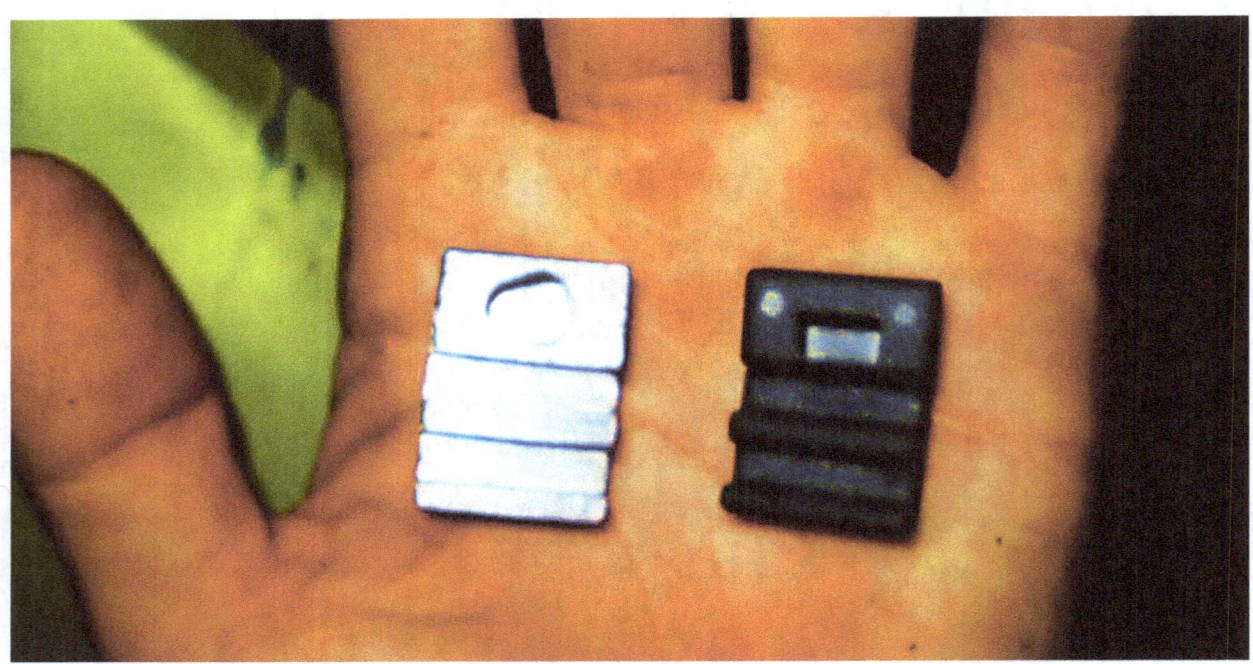

Day 27, 11-3-2007

kt: 38.6, ta: 973, gps: N 27° 00.347' W 105° 20.317'

I left the city with about four hours left until sunset. I spent some time at the internet cafe and later I went to pick up my parts at the taller de torno. After spending some time fixing my front saddlebag, it is now as good as new. Most of my riding today was flat, and I can tell that it is flat all the way to Jimenez, Chihuahua and I can tell that it is going to remain flat because the distance on my GPS and that on a sign, on the side of the street, matched when I was about 50 kilometers away.

Normally, in the desert, the number one hazard to my survival is dehydration. For this reason, I like to leave the city for the desert with no less than 10 liters of water. Water is always on my mind. I am intimately aware of the amount of water that I am carrying at any time.

The second most dangerous hazard to my survival is probably rattlesnakes. It is warm enough here that the snakes are not hibernating. For this reason I always step carefully when I am looking for a campsite. After selecting a campsite under a bridge today, I walked by a large snake hole but did not see any snakes. I would like to see a rattlesnake in the wild someday, though at a distance.

Desert scorpions and Black Widows are probably tied for third place. Both are potentially deadly and both could crawl into my sleeping bag unnoticed and bite me when I get in. Today right before sunset, when I was looking for a place to put my tent, I saw a black widow. It was underneath a bucket that I had flipped over. It was bigger than I expected, and I had to agitate it with a stick to see the red spot on its abdomen, to make sure it was what I thought it was. It indeed was. This was a picture perfect female specimen. It was quite beautiful. I took a picture of it and then left it in peace. I then promptly chose to put my tent about 100 feet away from it on the other side of the bridge. My tent was well zipped up, so no black widow could enter. I see no reason to kill a creature because it poses a threat to me.

Day 28, 11-4-2007

kt: 90.3, ta: 880, gps: N 26° 17.558' W 103° 52.862'

The land is flattening out and mornings are not as cold as in the mountains. This makes for easier, though less scenic, riding. Jimenez seems like one of those towns that grow in the middle of farm and ranch country; like a small version of San Angelo, Texas. It should be pretty flat all the way to Torreon. This means limited camping options. I'm sleeping under a bridge for the second night in a row. Hopefully, there won't be headwinds tomorrow.

Day 29, 11-5-2007

kt: 101, ta: 737, gps: N 26° 17.558' W 103° 52.562'

The land is still flat, but, I can see distant blue silhouettes of mountains. The desert is beautiful. Sometimes you just need to look more closely to find the beauty. Despite the scarcity of water, life abounds. There's large amounts of insects, birds, reptiles, and desert rodents. I don't always see them, but I hear them scurrying away in the brush as I ride by. I have seen many hawks the last couple of days, as they seem to be the top predator around here. I even had the privilege of seeing them hunt.

Today I discovered that they will indeed, let me ride on the toll roads for free. There are many posted signs that say that no bicyclists are allowed, but that doesn't seem to bother the gatekeepers who blithely allow me to continue on my journey. The toll roads have big shoulders, and seem to get less traffic, so I don't feel like I always have to watch over my shoulder when I ride. However, there seem to be fewer places to stop and stock up on food and water though.

Day 30, 11-6-2007

kt: 103, ta: 1163, gps: N 25° 34.409' W 103° 23.404'

Today, I wanted to ride straight through Torreon, Coahuila, but I saw the perfect urban campsite as I was leaving the city.. My campsite is in an urban wasteland type area, with lots of overgrown bushes obscuring my tent. I am pretty sure that not many people go here because I had to make my own trails through some horrible, thorny, dead bushes. I didn't notice until I was at my campsite, but I popped my first spoke of the trip. This is a problem that lightweights such as myself almost never have. With all my gear, though, my weight is a lot closer to the American average. This is about the only repair that I am not prepared to fix on the road. I can always keep rolling with this problem; I just may need to disconnect one of the brakes. Fortunately I am in the city, and shouldn't have too much of a problem finding a bike shop to replace my spoke. This is a large urban area, as Gomez Palacio, Durango and Torreon are twin cities of the desert. They aren't even 10 kilometers apart, and they are effectively one big city. There are probably more than a million people that live here.

Hopefully, after getting my bike serviced, I can be on my way after lunch. I am on Mexican time though, so my hopes aren't too high. That is what I get for waking up at least two hours before anyone else.

Day 31, 11-7-2007

kt: 42.8, ta: 411, gps: N 25° 29.889' W 103° 06.551'

There are a lot of bicyclists here in Torreon. It is definitely a common mode of transportation here. Since we cyclists are a lawless bunch, they had to pass a law in Torreon making it illegal for bicyclists to go the wrong way down the street. I still ride wherever I want, however I want. The first chunk of my day was spent fixing my bike, wondering around markets, and surfing the Internet. It only cost $3.50 and only took half an hour to fix my bike. The bike shop was right across the street from one of those huge, labyrinthine marketplaces. It is always fun to get lost in these marketplaces, observing the sights and smells of every hidden corner.

If you have a sweet tooth to indulge, Mexico is the place to be. This is where the flavors of chocolate and vanilla were discovered. You can't travel a few blocks without running into a dulcería or candy shop. This is not to be confused with a nevería / paletería, which sells ice cream and popsicles, a pastelería which sells cakes, nor a panadería which is a bakery that mostly sells sweet bread. All the dentists in this country must work overtime.

Anyway, being the lean. mean, fat-burning machine that I am, I indulge wherever I go I hardly ever have a meal in the city without also having dessert. I have even found a couple of useful survival foods in the dulcería. One is called a palenqueta de cacahuate which translates to peanut candy bar. It has lots of calories from fat, sugar, and protein and it keeps well without refrigeration. The other useful survival food is called até. For those of you in the United States, this is what we call fruit leather, except they don't sell até in thin strips like in the U.S. It is sold in kilogram blocks for about a dollar. A pack of 20 palenquetas de cacahuate cost me $2. I am now well stocked up for my journey into the desert. I found a nice little mesquite grove to camp out in today. There have not been any fences in the desert since I left Torreon. It is nice, because camping options are greater.

Day 32, 11-8-2007

kt: 31.3, ta: 333, gps: N 25° 36.528' W 102° 54.613'

I wanted to try to ride 100 miles through the desert, today, but my hopes, along with both of my tires were deflated when I rode through a brier patch. I have had pretty good luck with flats until recently but boy, did my luck run out. Those who have ever owned and ridden a mountain bike should know that fixing a flat caused by thorns can be one of the most hellish and Sisyphean tasks. I spent, at least three hours, underneath the hot desert sun, with ants crawling all over me, picking out thorns from my bicycle. At least the ants weren't fire ants, and I had the partial, moving shade of a six-foot-tall mesquite tree.

I wanted to make sure that I got all of the thorns out because they can become embedded in the tire and cause chronic flats. My eyesight has always been good and this served me well, for there were some tiny, little, pernicious fuckers stuck in both tires. I had to use the point of my small knife blade to dig out all of the thorns. By the time I finished fixing both flats, it was already the afternoon, and by the time I finished eating a late lunch, there were only two hours left until sunset. At the end of the day, I was happy that I didn't have to fix any more flats, because that would have ruined my next day. This trip, for me, has been more than just a long bike ride. It has been a spiritual journey as well. Religiously, I am what you might call a dirt-worshiping neo-pagan. I prefer not to label my spirituality though, because I don't expect anyone to think exactly like me. Anyways, I worship the sun, moon, winds, mountains, forests, etc. I feel like I prove my worth as a young warrior from the bicycle hippie tribe, by riding over mountains and confronting strong headwinds. Bicycling is a metaphor for life. Well, for me, bicycling is my life. Sometimes in life you have to overcome obstacles to continue on. Every hill, headwind, or flat tire is only a temporary obstacle on the way to reaching my goal. I am now stronger and wiser for having dealt with this adversity. Humanity thrives on adversity. It is what forced us to adapt to new environments. I am confident that I can conquer any obstacle in my path.

I have still not seen any fences for a long time. It would be gallons of gluttonous, gasoline-guzzling, gleeful fun to have dirt bike here. One could ride for many miles unimpeded. That being said, I have my tent set up in a wide-open space about a 100 yards from the highway. It is beautiful here. There are large patches of beige-colored sand, interrupted by a variety of desert succulents and bushes. The sunset over the mountains today was beautiful. It seemed almost like a reward for my patience in fixing my flats. I feel ready for tomorrow's challenges.

Day 33 & 34, 11-9-2007 to 11-10-2007

kt: 101, ta: 966, gps: N 25° 39.406' W 101° 57.508'

I covered a lot of ground, today, despite having two more flats. The first flat was probably caused by a stubborn thorn. I dug out two more of those sneaky, evil, little fuckers that had escaped my vigilance the day prior. The second flat was caused by a faulty patch. I am determined to make it to Salt llo using patches, instead of my last inner tube. There are two important things to remember when using patches to fix a flat: always rough the tube using sandpaper, and always deflate the tire completely, before putting on a new patch. Otherwise, the patch will probably fail shortly. I still don't have a lot of faith in patches, and I am resolved to leave Saltillo with no less than four inner tubes. There seems to be an even greater variety of succulents in this part of the desert.

Some deserts are just sand, but this desert is a thriving ecosystem. I could run out of food and water here and survive because I can identify several varieties of edible cactus that also have water stored inside. If worse comes to worse, I could always live off of grasshoppers and prickly pear, both of which are in abundance here. I could even have a survival party with 5 others and have rattlesnake cooked in maguay leaves. Mmmmmmmm, delicious! That being said, I will not run out of food or water here because there seems to be a prototypical dusty Mexican desert town every twenty kilometers or so.

This highway seems to be a major trucking corridor, so all the little towns have at least one tienda de abarrotes, or convenience store, where I can stock up on food and water. Many of the restaurants here have names like "El Caminero" or "The Trucker." If they don't have trucker related names, they have pictures of semis right next to La Virgen de Guadalupe. I have had some close encounters with the rigs on the highway, but, for the most part, this highway has more than enough spare capacity for a wee, little, bicyclist. There were mostly two lanes today, so I aggressively claimed one as my own. Most drivers defer to me, because they don't want to clean the mess off of their windshield or grill. Out of all the American corporations here in Mexico, there is none more ubiquitous than Coca-Cola. They have an amazingly efficient distribution system here. If I were an economics teacher, I would use them as a case study for how a corporation from the developed world could tap into developing markets. Coca-Cola is in places where there is no plumbing, electricity, or even paved roads. They have developed a number of products for the local market here, based on tropical fruit flavors. It seems like most people here prefer Coke to water, not unlike the U.S. I have a feeling that I could live in a rural village in communist North Korea and still find Coca-Cola. Communist dentists need jobs too, after all.

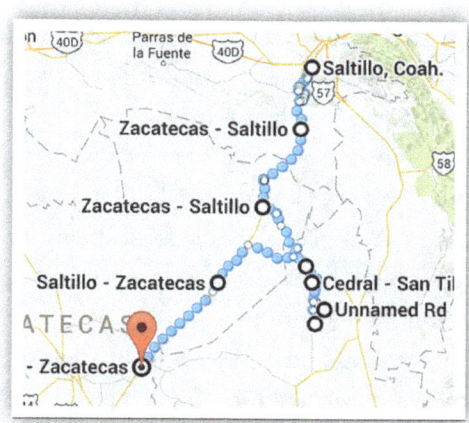

From Saltillo to Zacatecas

Day 35, 11-11-2007

I rested in Saltillo.

By "rested" I mean that I rode my bike all over the city without my gear.

Day 36, 11-12-2007

kt: 55.8, ta: 1853, gps: N 24° 59.181' W 101° 04.954'

When I woke up in Saltillo, I discovered that my rear tire had deflated again. Patches are temporary, only to be used to get you to the next city if you are touring. Since I was in the city, I used my last inner tube.

Waking up with the sun is great when you are on the road, but not so great when you are in the city. I found a bike shop, a laundromat, and an Internet cafè, all before anyone was there. I probably rode around in circles for about two hours, before any of these places were open. Anyways, I was able to take care of my errand, so I still had the rest of my day for fun.

The highlight of my day was when I went to the Museum of the Desert. I learned that 60% of Mexico can be classified as desert. The two large deserts in the north are the Sonoran and Chihuahuan deserts. They are separated by the Sierra Tarahumara. The large desert in the south of Mexico is mostly concentrated in the states of Puebla and Oaxaca and is therefore called the Poblano-Oaxacan desert. The Chihuahua desert used to be under water, and was a forest as late as 12,000 years ago. There is evidence of human habitation when it was still a forest, so I can't help but wonder if humans weren't at least partially responsible for the desertification of the area. It is nice to

be cut off from the outside world. I don't have a cellphone, television, radio, or consistent Internet access. Whenever I am in the city, I usually spend a lot of time online, either writing my blog or catching up on the news. I usually work myself into a frenzy reading about the incompetence of the world's most expensive military.

I can't believe the US military lost track of 190,000+ guns in Iraq. Why the fuck are we spending over half a trillion dollars a year, only to aid the insurgency it supposedly fights? Our military is great at destabilizing countries but not at re-stabilizing them. Unfortunately, with Iraq, we created the mess and we are obliged to clean it up. You break it you buy it. I've got a feeling that we're eventually going to abandon Iraq to anarchy. Another strongman dictator, like Saddam Hussein, will come along to re-stabilize Iraq. We'll financially and militarily support this dictator. So much for spreading democracy, we knew it was a fucking lie, anyways.

Speaking of democracy, how can we call this two-party, Tweedledum & Tweedledee, monopoly on power a democracy? We are not really given real choices. The Republocrats agree on the necessity of having a bloated military, maintaining the prison industrial complex, increasing the police powers of the state, keeping health care private, keeping immigrants out of the country, and continuing the drug war, etc.

These are issues with which I passionately disagree with the Republocrats on. I will not be in the country during the next election. I considered trying to send in an absentee ballot, but that might be difficult due to my lack of a permanent residence.

In order to send in an absentee ballot, you are required to contact the Secretary of State of the last state in which you resided and provide them with an address where they can send an absentee ballot. You then have to mail it back to them well before the election date. It would be a better system if Americans who were living abroad were able to vote in the embassies.

Even if I could vote in the embassies, I would probably vote for Mickey Mouse or Hulk Hogan as president since I am not really given a real choice. There are only two candidates that I have even a modicum of respect for: they are Ron Paul and Dennis Kucinich.

I only like Ron Paul because he is principled, to the point where he is the only congressman who voted against the Patriot Act. However, I disagree with his politics, and therefore, I would never vote for him.

I will not vote for Dennis Kucinich until he grows the cojones to abandon the Democratic Party. Until then, I will never trust him because I learned from the Bill Clinton experience that Democrats lie. The rest of the candidates could all be assassinated and our country would probably be better off for it. We all know that the next president of the United States is just going to maintain the status quo just like every president before them. The Democrats will never impeach Bush because they want to keep the power that he illegally usurped when they are in office.

I am on my way now to Real de Catorce, San Luis Potosi to go on a vision quest. Yes, that is right; I am hoping to find peyote. The peyote cactus is an endangered species, but this is only because the U.S. exports their insane drug war. If peyote were legal, which it should be, it could be legally cultivated, and hence, not in danger of extinction. There has never been a documented case of peyote overdose or addiction. It even has strong antibacterial qualities which makes it an effective substitute for penicillin. Why is it illegal? It is illegal for the same stupid reason that marijuana and psychedelic mushrooms are illegal: the prison industrial complex would collapse without the drug war.

When so many people from police to prison guards to D.E.A. agents depend on the drug war to provide them jobs, they will never vote for a politician who wants to end drug prohibition. The drug war is Frankenstein's monster run amok. It is a self-perpetuating war that will probably never end, until the system collapses in on itself. Peyote has been consumed for millennia by many Indian tribes: Apaches, Kiowas, Comanches, Tarahumara, and Huichols all have sacred peyote rites, to name a few. The Huichol Indians make a 400 kilometer trek to Real de Catorce, or "Wirikuta" as they like to call it, to consume massive quantities of peyote at el Cerro Quemado, or the Burnt Hill. They believe the gods of their ancestors reside in the hills of Real de Catorce. When they go searching for peyote, they say that they are "hunting deer." I

am a mixture of mostly European peoples, but I have a small amount of Indian in my blood. Despite the fact that I am obviously white, I have always felt more connected to the Indian part of me, than the European part. For this reason, I wish to fulfill my vision quest. I was so happy to be cut off from Bab-ylon. Why did I have to read the news? It almost seems like a form of self-flagellation. I am now back in the desert, away from all those news sources. The only thing that matters is that I survive, and I make it to Brazil. I am so much happier, now that life is so simple. You know what they say: ignorance is bliss.

Day 37, 11-13-2007

kt: 80.6, ta: 2038, gps: N 24° 25.682' W 101° 22.858'

I swear that the desert between Torreon, Coahuila; Saltillo, Coahuila; and Zacatecas, Zacatecas is like the Bermuda Triangle of flat tires. There was another flat in my front tire caused by thorns, this morning. The hole in my inner tube was very small, so I decided to give my patches another try. It has held well so far, but I wouldn't be surprised if it is flat again tomorrow. If there aren't too many thorns, I can fix a flat in less than fifteen minutes.

The desert was very un-desert-like this morning. There was a gray cloud covering the whole sky. I thought that it might even rain. I should not have doubted the powerful desert sun though, for soon enough, the clouds began to clear out, and it began to warm up. I am over 6,000 feet here so it is definitely cold at night. There seems to be a new variety of cactus appearing over each hill. I passed through "forests" of Desert Palms. Mexico is home to about 95% of the varieties of cactus in the world, so I am always finding something different. I love cactus and I think that it is one of the most beautiful plants, especially when it is flowering.

I am starting to chip away at those latitudinal lines on the globe. Within a week, I will have passed the Tropic of Cancer, as it is on the way to Zacatecas. I made a slight change of plans, and decided to ride to Michoacan to see the monarchs, before I go to el D.F. I see monarchs flying south every day now so I feel a sense of urgency to go see them. This way, I won't be in a hurry to leave el D.F. when I am visiting my friends.

I could have covered a larger distance, today, but I took too many breaks. It worked out in my favor though, because while I was resting at a convenience store, the owner gave me a whole bunch of dried beef. This is something that I always like to carry, so I was happy that I didn't have to spend a whole lot of money to stock up.

Since I have been fulminating on the subject of the drug war and the growth of the police state, I thought I would write a little bit about the police here in Mexico.

There are many different kinds of police here, and I will try to explain the differences between them and the jurisdictions they cover.

The policia municipal are only found in larger cities. They are usually the least well equipped of the various police forces here. They drive the older and smaller cars, if they even have cars, and they have the oldest and lowest quality guns. Sometimes they carry AK-47s but they usually just have an old revolver or two. I once saw a municipal cop in Mexico City with two revolvers and an AK-47. They can be on foot, on a horse, on a bike, motorcycle, or in a car. Some of them direct traffic, but most of them just hang out. The policia rural are found in the countryside where there might be a few towns that are close together. They drive 4X4 pickup trucks, and they mostly seem to hang out.

The policia estatal police the state highways, though barely. They all have cars, though their cars are not as nice as those of the federales. Again, I never see these guys doing much of anything.

The policia federal have the coolest toys out of all the police forces here, and have the largest jurisdictions. Some of them drive new Dodge Chargers and carry M-16s instead of AK-47s. They will set up roadblocks on the highway, and collect bribes from truckers who don't have proper documentation. They don't seem to be too interested in searching vehicles though, at least not so far.

A.F.I. or the Agencia Federal de Investigaciones is kind of like the D.E.A., A.T.F., and F.B.I. all rolled into one. They also have the coolest toys and can set up roadblocks wherever they want. I passed an A.F.I. roadblock today, where they were searching every car, but I used a Jedi mind trick and rolled through unimpeded. I even waved hello to a couple of A.F.I. agents carrying machine guns. I think that they have drug sniffing dogs too, but they are on the side of the highway that goes north because drugs go north, and guns go south.

The military should not be forgotten when discussing the police here since they run most of the check points in Mexico. They are essentially an auxiliary police force used to fight the drug war. At each post, there are several men who search cars and several sentries who carry G-3 machine guns. Sometimes, there will even be a mounted machine gun at the post. Those in charge of check points carry metal pointers and stick them in the hollows of cars looking for drug or weapon stashes. I rolled through two of these posts unimpeded today. One of them even had drug sniffing dogs, though they were upwind from me. I usually wave hello and roll on through. I am prepared to pretend that I don't understand Spanish well enough to understand the sign that says, "Punto de Revision."

One cannot discuss the police or soldiers here without discussing the system of bribery that enriches them. The police here do not earn a lot of money, especially when compared to police in the United States, who start out at about $40,000 a year in most cities.

They expect bribes the way a waiter in the U.S. expects a tip of at least 15%. The actual process of bribing a cop is more of a negotiation than anything else. When I lived in Mexico City, I saw a friend of mine bribe his way out of the back of a police car with a $10 watch that he told them was worth $20. If you're a skilled negotiator, you could probably spend less money bribing a cop than going through the bureaucratic judicial system. Considering that every time I've ever gotten a ticket, I go see a judge and pay a fine, I don't see that big of a difference between Mexican and American systems. The Mexican system just eliminates bureaucratic middlemen.

The police in the U.S. don't set up random search checkpoints, as this has been ruled as an unconstitutional unreasonable search. The police in the United States can't detain someone without a reasonable suspicion that they have committed a crime. It is only a matter of time before the Supreme Court overturns that and deems random searches to be constitutional. Our government happily exports the drug war abroad, but never constitutional principles constraining law enforcement officers in the U.S. The rest of the world suffers an increase in the police powers of the state, in the name of fighting the great American War on Drugs.

The drug war is doomed because there isn't a cop or a soldier who can't be bribed. American policy makers should go back to school to learn about supply and demand. You cannot eliminate the demand by eliminating the supply. As the supply decreases the prices will go up because the demand remains the same. When the prices increase, the drug dealers have more money to bribe police and soldiers. Also, no crack head is going to stop smoking crack because the prices increase. They will just rob two people instead of one to get their fix. I guess I can't complain about American tactics in the drug war, though, because the Communist Chinese government executed opium addicts in mass. The Chinese solution did effectively eliminate demand and hence opium addiction, but at what cost? That's the only effective military solution to fighting the drug war. Are we prepared to go that far?

Day 38, 11-14-2007

kt: 98.9, ta: 1271, gps: N 23° 35.350' W 100° 57.811'

Today was another peaceful day in the desert. After riding on a highway, that was well populated with truckers for the first 30 kilometers, I turned onto a "highway" that had very little traffic. I had the road all to myself most of the time.

Despite the lack of traffic, there are still little towns every 20 kilometers or so. I am well stocked up on everything but it is nice to know that there are places that I can get food and water. Goat herding seems to be the main form of economic activity here.

Speaking of goats, I ate cabrito for the first time today. It seemed like they must have slaughtered it out back because I was picking goat hairs out of my food. Despite the goat hairs, the cabrito was delicious. I am not going to cop out by saying that goat tastes like chicken. Goat meat has a unique flavor that tastes kind of like chicken but a little different. For about $13, the cabrito was the most expensive meal I've eaten in Mexico, so far.

Being the gastronomical adventurer that I am, I am always looking for new foods to try. Sometimes I discover new favorite foods. I am hoping to eat iguana when I am on the beach. I have eaten the intestines of cows, which is called tripa, but I have not worked up the courage to eat the eyes or tongue of the cows. I have even tried grasshopper, though squeamishly. If you think about it, dried grasshopper is not too different from dried shrimp, which I have also eaten. In Saltillo, I tried pan de pulque for the first time. Pulque is a creamy alcohol that is made from the mezcal cactus. It is used as the leavening agent in the bread. I can't wait to find out what new flavors I will discover as I continue south. I have not gotten sick yet as my body can metabolize raw meat.

Day 39, 11-15-2007

kt: 38.6, ta: 3018, gps: N 23° 41.513' W 100° 53.324'

I thought that the road between Basaseachic and San Juanito was bad. But the road, nay trail, that leads to Real de Catorce is far worse. The path is so rocky and steep that I had to get off of my bike for the first time and push it uphill. Believe it or not, this is actually more exhausting than riding uphill.

When I was taking a break, I asked Ja to provide me with the strength to push my bike up the remaining 30 degree inclines. Ja provided strength, in the form of a man who helped me push my bike up the hill. Even with help, pushing 80 pounds of bike and equipment uphill is neither easy nor fun. By the time that I reached Real de Catorce, I was exhausted and famished. I ate three hamburgers at once. I probably could have eaten more but that would have been gluttonous. Anyway, Real de

Catorce is beautiful, but I can't seem to find peyote here. The man who helped me push my bike uphill told me he could help me find some in the valley tomorrow morning.

Even if I don't find peyote here, I would consider this trip worth it for I met a hippie from Guanajuato who told me I could stay with him when I pass through.

Day 40, 11-16-2007
kt: 38.5, ta: 303, gps: N 23° 53.095' W 100° 59.133'

I came to Real de Catorce looking for peyote, but alas, I did not find it. It is not a secret anymore that peyote can be found in the vicinity. The sad truth is that too many people come to Real de Catorce looking for peyote and it is harder and harder to find. It is definitely endangered around here. This would not be a problem if the cultivation of peyote were legal as people could plant fields of it for consumption.

When I left town this afternoon, I was sad that I did not accomplish my goal of finding peyote, but I was nonetheless happy that I came. In the morning, I woke up to the symphony of the roosters crowing and walked around the cobblestone streets. When I returned to the place I was staying, I was thrilled to find a woman selling tamales and champurrado. Champurrado is one of the many reasons I love Mexico. It is a hot chocolate beverage that also has cinnamon and sometimes almonds in it. It is thickened with masa. Being that this is the first time that I have found champurrado after crossing the frontier, I drank four cups of it. That alone made my day.

To leave Real de Catorce, I followed the same path from whence I came. The descents along the path were so steep and rocky that I walked my bike along large portions of it, because my brakes would not stop my fully-loaded bike. It took me a lot longer than I would prefer to descend into the desert valley, but I am happy that I made it out of the mountains alive.

When I reached the junction in the highway where I needed to turn, some men told me that there was a hill outside of the city where a bunch of peyote grew. I figured what the hell, I can set up my tent in the open desert and go searching for peyote. I saw many cool varieties of cactus and many holes where it looked like something had been dug up, but alas, I did not find peyote. Maybe I will look again in the morning but I feel like I have to keep moving.

Day 41, 11-17-2007

kt: 24.2, ta: 400, gps: N 24° 00.196' W 101° 02.019'

Happy gps: N 23° 53.173' W 101° 02.019'

Today, I traveled a lot farther in the spiritual realm than in the physical realm. It was an unusual day in the desert. It rained last night when I was sleeping and there was a fog blanketing the desert when I woke up this morning. After breaking down my campsite, I figured that I would try one last time to hunt for peyote. With the fog and the many forks in the path, it was easy to get lost in the open desert, so I marked a way point in my G.P.S. device where I left my stuff. I then rode off on my bicycle about a kilometer and a half from my campsite and began my search. I did not have to search long before I found what I was looking for, in abundance. I then extracted a button that was about four inches in diameter and rode back to my campsite. The peyote was my breckfast this morning.

As far as I can tell, peyote does not like rocky or grassy areas but prefers sand. It mainly grows at the bases of desert bushes and barely pops up over the surface of the soil. If this is not enough information to help you with your hunt, I have provided the exact coordinates, above, for a nice peyote field. I could see at least three plants from these coordinates and was able to find many more by walking around this area.

To try to describe a peyote trip to someone who has never tried it is like trying to describe the color blue to a someone who has been blind their entire life. You just have to try it to know what it is like. It is not as bitter as I expected.

Both beer and coffee have more bitter flavors. I definitely felt different but cannot describe in words how I felt. There were no tracers or visual effects. Though I felt different, I cannot say that the peyote had a debilitating effect. I felt like I could work under the influence if my dilated pupils did not freak out my customers. Granted I only consumed one good-sized button, whereas, when it is taken ritually, it is taken in much greater quantities.

After I started coming down, I ventured into the town of Vanegas to find some food. I was ravenous because I hadn't eaten anything, except the peyote all day. I ate two plates of chicken in mole sauce. It was quite delicious. Though the effects of the peyote had worn off, the woman at the food stand knew exactly what I had been up to because my pupils were still as big as saucers. She just kind of chuckled as she asked me if I had eaten a cabezita or little head as peyote is often called. She did not care that it was a crime to extract peyote. She was just happy that I was patronizing her food stand.

I was able to get a little bit of riding in today, after my late lunch. It remained overcast all day but looked particularly gnarly ahead so I set up my camp about an hour early. I did not want to ride into the lightning, thunder, and heavy rain that lay ahead. The sunset was quite beautiful as they often are on these stormy days. I will go to sleep tonight with the satisfaction of knowing that I accomplished one of the goals of my journey.

Day 42, 11-18-2007

kt: 94.7, ta: 1553, gps: N 23° 52.629' W 101° 44.157'

My only goal today was to get back on the highway going in the direction of Zacatecas. I achieved that and added another 40 kilometers on top of that. Tomorrow, I should pass the Tropic of Cancer.

I ate in two restaurants today, and both of them were strange places to be. The first only had one picture on the wall, and that was of Elvis in a cowboy hat. There was a little retarded kid there, who was torturing a poor kitten. The second restaurant was right next to an electrical sub-station but had no electricity. It looked like it was going to rain so I asked the owner if I could set my tent up out back and he told me I could stay in the covered porch area which was even better. He even busted out a peyote button and started eating it when I told him I had just come from Real de Catorce. At the second restaurant, I even ran into a pair of Austinites asking for directions to Real de Catorce. What a strange coincidence, no?

Day 43, 11-19-2007

kt: 92, ta: 1391, gps: N 23° 15.975' W 102° 20.012'

My gear is breaking down but I continue moving. The extra 4 liter bag of water that I carried on my rear rack sprung a leak. I was carrying about 4 liters too much water anyway. It was extra weight. The plastic part on my G.P.S. device which clips onto my handlebars has some micro fractures in it and does not function optimally. I am going to try super-glue, and if that fails, I have been imagining several other solutions.

Today, I popped another spoke on my rear wheel. My rim seems to be fubar and I think that I am going to have to replace it. Even when I disconnected my rear brake the tire was rubbing against my bicycle frame which is problematic because this will rip holes in the sidewalls of my tire leading to chronic flats. I thought that I was going to have to hitch a ride because my bike would not roll. Luckily, I popped my spoke next to a work crew that was clearing overgrowth and trash from the road.

There was one point when the entire work crew stopped what they were doing for about half an hour to help me fix my bike so I could, at least, roll unimpeded by unnecessary friction. It took a while, but after loosening most of my spokes and clipping one more, we were able to make my wheel straight enough to ride. It is only a temporary solution though, and I am on my way to Zacatecas with only my front brake. I probably won't be able to get it fixed tomorrow, because it is a national holiday (more on that shortly). Unfortunately, I am going to have to shell out the big bucks for a new rim.

Tomorrow is el 20 de Noviembre. It doesn't really have a special name but there is a 20 de Noviembre street in just about every city in the Republic of Mexico. It was on November 20, 1910 when Francisco Madero issued his Plan de San Luis Potosi which was a call to arms against the dictatorship of the aging Porfirio Diaz.

He claimed that Porfirio Diaz had fraudulently stolen the elections. The next day, people in the north heeded this call, and shortly thereafter, Porfirio Diaz abdicated power and fled into exile. Francisco Madero was released from jail to assume the presidency. Thus began the saga of the Mexican Revolution.

It started out relatively bloodlessly, but after Fransisco Madero was later overthrown in a coup d'etat and executed, the powder-keg that was Mexico exploded. This period of the revolution pitted the Constitutionalists forces against the anti-Constitutionalists forces and did not end until the Constitutionalists forces consolidated power and drew up the Constitution of 1917. After the revolution was over, 1/15th of the Mexican population at the time, had died in warfare.

Climbing Mountains, & Hasta Chilangolandia

Day 44, 11-20-2007 to Day 46, 11-22-2007

Day 44: kt: 71.4, ta: 2132, gps: N 22°46.490' W 102°34.283'

Day 45: I stayed in Zacatecas

Day 46: kt: 52.1, ta: 732, gps: N 22° 32.941' W 102°15.093'

After crossing the Tropic of Cancer, I have noticed a slight change in the ecosystem. It is still very much like a desert prairie but there seems to be more moisture and more trees. When I woke up, I went to Zacatecas, and there was thick fog covering everything. It had not rained the night before but my tent was wet as if it had. The wind coming from the south had a very tropical humidity. It remained, more or less, overcast all day on the way to Zacatecas. Right when I arrived in the city, it began to rain and hail. Fortunately, I did not have to travel very far to get to the hostel in which I stayed.

Zacatecas is a cool, beautiful city. It was a silver mining city during the 18th and 19th century and its colonial wealth is evident in its architecture. There are many obviously old buildings here that were made by skilled artisans that were brought there by the silver barons of the time. The central city is covered with winding cobblestone streets which are clogged with traffic. This can make maneuvering through traffic quite difficult at times.

Today, it is still a thriving city. It receives a lot of tourism and it is a college town so there are lots of young, beautiful people and a night life here. One of the cooler things that happens here on a nightly basis is called a callejoneada. The name comes from the word callejon which means alley. The callejoneada is a wandering street party that comes complete with musicians and a donkey laden with mezcal. The party grows as it travels through the streets. I could definitely live in Zacatecas.

The place I stayed at is wonderful, and named Hostel Villa Colonial. It is smack dab in the middle of the city, and has one of the better views of the town's cathedral from its rooftop terrace. It is affordable, but nice, and travelers come there from all over the world. The owner speaks Spanish and English and does his best to make everyone feel welcome. While staying there, I even met two other cyclists who were biking to Argentina: Sjaak from the Netherlands is biking from Alaska to Argentina and Ryan from Canada is biking from his home in Winnipeg to Argentina, and possibly through Africa and Europe afterwards. I got contact information from both of them, and I am hoping that we cross paths again for they both seem like pretty cool fellows.

I managed to get my bike repaired but with some difficulties, as again, no one seems to have the same size rims, wheels, tires, spokes, or inner tubes as I have. Once I get to Mexico City, I am going to get my entire rear wheel replaced with new spokes. In retrospect, I should have probably purchased a mountain bike because it is much easier to find replacement parts. I usually have to go to several bike shops before I can find what I need.

It was hard leaving the city and my new friends today, but alas, that is the life of a nomad. I took my time leaving the city. When I finally left, I was happy to discover that it is mostly downhill or flat while leaving in the direction of Aguascalientes, Aguascalientes. When I chose a place to set up camp outside of the city of Ojocaliente, Zacatecas I decided to hop a fence due to the lack of good places to stay. When I was sitting by my campfire, a man on horseback rode up to where I was. He didn't seem to mind at all when I told him I would leave in the morning and put out the fire. He shook my hand and then rode off. It is always easier to ask for forgiveness instead of permission.

I have added cow brains and cow blood to the list of different foods that I have tried. They are called sesos and moronga, respectively. I was also happy to find a woman that sold tamales and atole in the morning. She not only had champurrado but also had atole de guayaba or guava. It is quite delicious. I have been feasting of Mexican food for Thanksgiving.

This is the time of year when I normally spend time with family and friends but I am sitting in my campsite alone, right now. I miss all of my family and friends, but I am not even remotely longing to go home. Every day is exciting and stimulating, and I have never felt happier or more secure with myself before. Even the aches and the pains I felt in my body whenever it got cold have left me. I am in as good a shape as I have ever been. I feel rejuvenated and don't want this trip to ever end.

Day 47, 11-23-2007

kt: 95.1, ta: 2336, gps: N 21°46.952' W 102°16.857'

As far as I can tell, I have entered the agricultural heartland of Mexico. Ever since I started approaching Zacatecas, I have seen nothing but farmland. The towns seem to be getting bigger too. The central part of Mexico is the most densely populated part of the country. Every town I pass through seems to have at least five thousand people living in it. This is nice for me because I have many more food options and I don't have to worry about running out of water.

I rode about 80 kilometers to Aguascalientes by 3:00 p.m. today, so I had plenty of time to surf the Internet and find food. Aguascalientes is a large city of over a million people. It seems to have a large industrial sector as I passed by a Nis-san factory and several other large plants today. It has malls, movie theaters, and everything that you would expect to find in an American city of the same size. This is not to say it is like an American city, because it is very much a Mexican city. For a city its size, I found riding my bicycle through it to be quite pleasant. There seems to be plenty of space for bicyclists and I saw everyone from kids to old men riding bikes.

I am camped out on the southern edge of the city as I was unable to make it out of the large urban area. I found an abandoned building, which Mexico seems to have an abundance of, and set up my camp. I am hidden so I shouldn't be bothered by anyone tonight.

Day 48, 11-24-2007

kt: 68.1, ta: 2634, gps: N 21°17.230' W 102° 00.182'

I lost some time today, when I had to fix a flat. That comes to 11 flats thus far on my journey. It is all right though, because every flat I fix is penance for when I would so gleefully break glass bottles on the street, when I was a kid. The flat terrain has been replaced by rolling hills, not unlike those of the Texas Hill Country. The wind was coming strong from the west. Some of the gusts of wind almost blew me into the highway. I am just happy that it wasn't a headwind because that would have made a hellish day.

I crossed into the state of Jalisco today and should cross into the state of Guanajuato tomorrow.

I ended up taking the cuota road between Aguascalientes and Leon. This saved me money because there were limited places to stop. I have only eaten tuna melts, palenquetas, and até today, for I have a ton of all of those items. I am just trying to lighten my load a little. About an hour before sunset, I saw the perfect campsite on the side of the road. By perfect, I mean that it is close to the road, well obscured so I could have a fire, and on the leeward side of a hill, meaning the wind would not bother me. After seeing this, I decided it was time to stop because I could not pass up such a nice spot. The extra time before sunset gave me time to start studying my Portuguese-English dictionary. It is never too early to start preparing for my eventual Portuguese immersion.

I feel like I have come to master the rhythm of fire. I have started fires, without lighter fluid or paper as tender, in a variety of ecosystems. The dying embers of the fire I built tonight are keeping me warm as I write this entry in my journal. There is fire in my belly from the warm food I prepared and I can now pick up hot coals with my fingers without burning myself. I have tamed the flame.

Day 49, 11-25-2007

kt: 54.6, ta: 1600, gps: N 21°04.102' W 101°35.660'

I have really come to understand the meaning of highway robbery a lot better while being on the road. Mexicans seem to really take it to heart. There are places on the highway that seem to mark up the prices at least 60% from what you would expect to pay in the city. Because of this, I make my best efforts to buy all of my food and water in the cities now.

My appetite continues to astound me. At my most ravenous, I can eat more than three pregnant women combined. I learned today that I can, indeed, eat a whole chicken by myself with tortillas and salsa in one sitting. I figure that is more calories in one meal than the daily recommended amount for the average person. I should have eaten a lighter meal though, because I became sluggish and tired. I even felt kind of feverish, but, I can't say this is because of the chicken. I decided I would quit riding early and rest up for tomorrow.

Day 50, 11-26-2007

kt: 92.6, ta: 1861, gps: N 20°28.875' W 101°12.825'

It turns out that my fever was nothing that 12 hours of sleep couldn't cure. I felt fine this morning, though I drank several liters of fresh squeezed orange juice as a precaution. The juice is getting cheaper as I ride south which pleases me a whole lot. When I lived in Mexico City, I probably drank 2 or 3 liters every day because it was so cheap.

I passed through Irapuato, Guanajuato, the self-proclaimed strawberry capital of Mexico today. Alongside the highways leading into the city from all directions, one will find hundreds of roadside stands selling fresas con crema. I did indeed, indulge. I even brought some dried strawberries covered in Chile for later. Mexicans and I would definitely agree that sweet stuff can be spicy. Those who have tried my habanero-chocolate covered strawberries can attest to that.

I decided to skip going to Guanajuato City today, even though I had a free place to stay. I spend money in cities like I have a week to live. I am more interested in natural places than historic places anyway. If I wanted to visit a historic place, I would have gone to Dolores Hidalgo, Guanajuato. This is the town where Father Miguel Hidalgo rang the church bell on September 16 , 1810 and issued a sermon to those who congregated known as the Grito de Dolores. This is essentially the Mexico Declaration of Independence from Spain.

Day 51, 11-27-2007

kt: 101, ta: 3945, N 19° 42.263' W 101°10.979'

This morning, I found some thorns embedded in my skin which I had not previously noticed. I then proceeded to dig them out with my knife. They could become infected and they cause a constant annoyance, so I would rather endure the temporary pain of stabbing myself to remove foreign objects than leaving them as they were. This is not the first time that I have had to remove foreign objects from my skin and I am sure this problem will only get worse when I get to the jungle.

I have not seen hills like the hills I climbed today, since I left the Sierra Tarahumara. It is different here, though. I am definitely no longer in the desert. There seem to be a lot more jungle plants than cactus.

This is not to say that I am in the jungle, because it is still pretty dry here. With that being said though, I can feel more humidity in the air and it is noticeably warmer in the night, even though I am at roughly the same altitude as before. I rewarded myself when I got to Morelia, Michoacan by renting a room and taking a shower. I should be well rested for tomorrow when I get to ride through an area they call Mil Cumbres. This translates to a thousand summits. Woo hoo! Fortunately, I think this refers to the general area and not the road itself.

I worry that every time I go traveling, I cause some cosmic shift in the universe that leads to friends of mine getting hurt. When I rode my bike down the west coast in 2001, a friend of mine lost his leg in a motorcycle accident. This time, some friends of mine got hit by a drunk driver, though they are relatively okay. Also one of my BMX heroes, a man named Jimmy Levan, had a skateboarding accident and was comatose for the last two weeks. He is now out of his coma and is recovering, but his insurance doesn't pay for everything. He still owes a lot of money in medical bills and I wish him a full recovery. I have had the privilege of meeting him and getting to hang out with him for a while and he is a very down-to- earth, likable guy. He hasn't let being a superstar get to his head. I hope that this is the last bad thing that happens to any of my friends.

Day 52, 11-28-2007

kt: 44.1, ta: 3004, gps: N 19° 40.816' W 100°53.644'

I have added Morelia, Michoacan to the growing list of cities here in Mexico where I could live very comfortably. It is another beautiful colonial city nestled in the mountains. It probably has the best preserved aqueduct that I have seen in Mexico, thus far. There are lots of young, beautiful people here as it seems to have its fair share of universities. I fall in love with another Aztec goddess every day. The difference between Morelia and the other colonial towns that I have visited is that it is on the edge of the jungle.

The markets in Morelia are amazing, though not necessarily more amazing than those in other cities. The farmer's markets in Austin are pretty pitiful compared to these markets. There are so many fruits and vegetables for sale here that you can only buy in Mexico. Mamey is probably my favorite fruit, that can only be found here. For breakfast, I had two licuados de mamey to go, with my two cups of cinnamon atole, and one cup of fresh-squeezed orange juice. I then finished that off with a quesadilla, made with fresh tortillas, mushrooms, and chili peppers. For brunch, I had a torta made with puerco adobado, which is a chili marinated pork; beans; avocado; and cheese. The lady who made the torta gave me some excellent fire-roasted tomato salsa to go with it.

The food of Mexico is alone, enough to make me consider never returning to the U.S. again. I would very happily live out the rest of my days exploring the markets with the Mexican abuelitas every morning and enjoying the flavors of Mexico.

Morelia is a wonderful city, but I have to keep moving. I really, really want to see the monarchs. With that being said, I moved on at a very leisurely pace today.

Though the mountains here are as high as the Sierra Tarahumara, it is a very different ecosystem. There are probably more jungle plants than pine trees at lower elevations, for these mountains receive a lot more precipitation. Once you reach an elevation above 8,000 feet it is mostly pine forest but the pine trees are much bigger than in the Sierra Tarahumara.

About an hour and a half before sunset, I heard thunderstorms approaching so I hastily set up camp. Right after I set everything up, I witnessed the fiercest hail storm I have ever seen in my life. I did not see any golf ball-sized hail, but it hailed enough to make the ground look like it was covered in snow.

I am camped out at over 8,300 feet so it will be cold tonight and tomorrow morning. There is a large fallen, rotting pine tree close by so, in the morning, I will dig out some dry wood with my buck knife and attempt to make a fire. Man's ability to survive in the wild largely depends on his ability to make a fire in any weather condition. I hope that I didn't just accidentally plagiarize my "Army Field Guide to Survival".

Day 53, 11-29-2007

kt: 70.1, ta: 3134, N 19°45.337' W 100°41.309'

It was surprisingly not freezing cold this morning. My tent was unusually dry as well. I have woken up on days when it did not rain at all, when my tent was wetter than it was this morning. With that being said, I still decided to test my incendiary skills out by building a fire to cook with. I found some dry tender and mostly dry wood covered in pine sap underneath the rotting tree. I then proceeded to coax fire out of the wood. It was not easy and I had to cheat by using toilet paper as tender, but I was able to

cook a warm breakfast with my little fire. If this were truly a survival situation, I would already have a cache of dry fire wood set aside and protected from the elements. So, I was pleased that I was able to make a fire at all.

I thought that I was close to the summit at 8,300 feet but I didn't top out until I reached 9,500 feet. The road wasn't in the greatest condition but it had a whole lot of race-track turns that lean to the side as you turn. I love these turns as it sometimes almost feels like you are riding horizontally on a wall. I however, had to keep myself on a short leash, when I saw a sign that said grava suelta or loose gravel. Loose gravel can be deadly for a bicyclist. It will cause you to lose traction with the road just as easily as ice. When you are going 40 mph down a mountain, the last thing you want to see around a blind turn is loose gravel. Eventually, the gravelly road gave way to the smooth asphalt, so I got to get a little bit more fun in before it started raining.

Boy, did it rain. While I was stopped at a store around 2:00 p.m. buying water, the sky just opened up. I tried to wait it out but I eventually realized that the rain was not going to relent. It was time to dig out my rain gear from my bags and put it on for the very first time of my trip. I usually don't like to wear it unless the rain is heavy or cold because I can get quite hot while fully suited up. This rain was both heavy and cold so the use of my rain gear was more than justified. There was even a little hail, though nothing like last night. I never gave thanks for Thanksgiving, so I just wanted to say that I am thankful for my waterproof boots, jacket, pants, jacket, gloves, and bags. I am thankful that I have a dry sleeping bag and dry socks so I can change out of my sweat-soaked socks at the end of the day. Mexicans are wonderful people but horrible drivers.

The number of crosses on the side of any Mexican highway will attest to that. I have ridden my bike on straight, one-mile stretches of road where you can see for miles in both directions and still, I've seen dozens of crosses. The problem with drivers here is that they are just too aggressive. Today when it was pouring, and the streets were beginning to flood, I saw many people trying to pass slower moving traffic in front of them. Being that this was an undivided, two-lane highway, this pretty much pissed me off.

I would usually hog the lane and angrily gesticulate that I wanted them to return to their lane before I inevitably relented and allowed them to pass in this manner. I would like to see one of the crosses on the side of the road read, "Loved by all except others on the road." because I know that a large number of these people likely died as a result of their own asinine driving.

I managed to make it to Los Azufres today which was nice because the hot springs were quite a treat after riding through the cold rain. You can see the steam rising from them as you approach on the road. I am camped out right next to a stream that is fed by these hot springs. I am hoping that this will make my campsite warmer as I am above 8,000 feet again.

Day 54, 11-30-2007

kt: 59.6, ta: 3110, gps: N 19°37.229' W 100°16.807'

I made it to Angangueo by 2:30 p.m. After seeing the steep, rocky hill leading up to the butterfly sanctuary, I decided that it would be less trouble to leave my bike at the bottom and hike to the top.

There were some curious onlookers watching me as I locked up my bike so I asked them if I could leave my stuff at their house and away I went. As usual, the sanctuary was a lot further than people told me. Instead of five km away, it was closer to ten. I managed to shorten my trip to the top by hitching two rides. Hitchhiking is easy here as most people with trucks are happy to offer a ride.

I made it to the butterfly sanctuary with just enough time to hike the last two kilometers to see the monarchs. I am in exceptional condition and I just about killed the old man who was my guide/babysitter hiking. Fortunately, he seemed a bit sprier when we descended the trail.

The best time to go to the sanctuary is noon and in the late afternoon. At this time, clouds come in and it gets colder so the butterflies cluster together to stay warm.

There were a few butterflies flying around but the vast majority weighed down branches of the trees in clusters. I was not able to use the flash in my camera or cross the barriers so I was, unfortunately, unable to take any good pictures of the butterflies. By the time I left the sanctuary, there was only about half an hour of sunlight left.

I tried to get a ride down to Angangueo, but I scoffed at the $30 the man wanted to take me down the ten kilometers into town. For $30 I can buy a lot of food. I was not as lucky hitching a ride to the bottom as no one was going down to Angangueo at night. I had to walk all the way to the bottom by myself. It was well past dark when I arrived at the place where I left my bike. The family that lived at the house, where I left my bike, was very nice and helpful. They invited me inside for dinner and showed me where I could find an affordable hotel. I was very grateful as I was very hungry and worried about where I would sleep because it looked like a thunderstorm was approaching.

Day 55, 12-1-2007

kt: 41.5, ta: 2788, gps: N 19°27.030' W 100°14.220'

I am not one that buys the religion that others are selling, but if I were buying I would buy the religion with more tradition and better architecture. I have not seen a single church in the United States that comes close to equaling the ornate architecture that every single church in central Mexico seems to have. Just about every town in this part of the country has a church that is at least 200 years old and was constructed by skilled artisans. If you want to sleep in, tough sh t, because all of the churches here ring their bells early in the morning. This is a tradition that hearkens back to the colonial times when they would ring their bells calling all of the Indians to morning mass. The friars would whip those who were tardy. Now that is effective proselytization.

As usual, whenever I rent a room, I don't leave town until the early afternoon. Going from Angangueo to San Felipe, there is a large downhill stretch. I played leap-frog with a big rig until I reached this stretch of highway. I would pass it at all of the speed bumps and it would pass

me going uphill until I finally obliterated my competition on the long, steep descent. When I waved hello to the driver at the bottom of the hill where there was an intersection, the driver gave me a loud honk of approval.

The rest of my day was all uphill and I decided to quit riding about 2 hours before sunset, to rest my weary calves. They were aching from the 20 kilometers of mountain hiking I did the day before. I can ride my bike all day long, but I used different muscles for all of my hiking.

I saw something today that would make a vegan cringe. Hell, it would probably make a lot of meat-eaters cringe. While I was resting at a convenience store next to someone's house, I saw a butcher come and slaughter a sheep right there, about three feet away from me. He drove up in his truck, chatted and joked around with the family for a while, and then killed the sheep. He perfunctorily grabbed the sheep and turned it over on its back, stabbed in the throat with a small knife, and then stabbed in in the brain through the same hole with a larger knife.

It seemed like he had done this a thousand times before because the whole process lasted only a few seconds. The sheep even had a death twitch as it kept kicking the sides of the truck while the butcher paid the family. I think I could kill an animal for food, though I would do it a lot more squeamishly than the butcher did.

Day 56, 12-2-2007

kt: 82.8, ta: 3909, gps: N 19°17.163' W 99°36.134'

From Zitácuaro, Michoacan to the border of el Estado de Mexico, it is about 30 kilometers of pure ascent. I was ecstatic when I finally got to go downhill some. I am in Toluca, Estado de Mexico right now, and I should be able to make to my friend's house well before sunset tomorrow. I'm so excited that I get to see my friends.

I saw something that I found quite amusing today. There was a little girl, not much older than eight years old, who brought an empty forty ounce malt liquor bottle to a convenience store for a deposit and then, promptly, bought a new one. She was probably buying this for someone who was older, but that shit wouldn't fly in Texas.

There are some unexpected hazards of the roadway here in Mexico. Today, I had to dodge a loose spare tire, and I have had to avoid the shrapnel from an exploding semi tire. Hopefully, there will be no more unexpected obstacles in my journey.

Day 57, 12-3-2007

kt: 74.5, ta: 2766, gps: N 19°14.702' W 99°07.637

When I woke up in Toluca, there was a frost covering everything: my tent, my bags, the grass, etc. It was only after the fact that I found out that Toluca is the highest city in the republic. There are small towns that are at a higher altitude but not any large cities. The field where I was camped out at was at an altitude of 8,500 feet. It's funny but it did not seem that cold to me. Maybe, I have grown accustomed to these higher altitudes. I was even wearing my shorts by 9:00 a.m. This was a mistake for, by the time I had reached the top of the mountain range between Toluca and Mexico City, I had reached an altitude of 10,200 feet. I had flirted with 10,000 feet several times in the Sierra Tarahumara and Mil Cumbres mountain ranges but this was the first time that I reached the official 10,000 foot mark.

The cold mountain wind was blowing hard. This inspired me to put on my sweater, gloves, ninja mask, and wool cap for the long descent into Mexico City. Needless to say, the ride down the mountain was very fast and took a lot less time than the ride up the mountain.

Day 58-62, 12-4-2007 to 12-8-2007

I stayed in Mexico City

I knew I had reached Mexico City because I started passing the traffic, rather than the other way around. It is pretty much gridlocked from about 15 kilometers out of the official city limits all the way through the city. I have compiled some rules for navigating the city for those who have not undergone the baptism by fire:

1. A red light is only a suggestion. Most people do not think that it implies a mandatory stop.
2. If you are in the far right or far left lane and you want to continue straight ahead, watch out. I have seen people cut across five lanes of traffic to make a turn.
3. Give the taxi and bus drivers as much space as possible. They are fucking crazy! They regularly execute maneuvers that would make a Nascar driver shit his pants. If someone in front of you is flagging them down, watch out! They won't hesitate to cut you off with inches to spare.
4. Do not let yourself become aggravated. This will only make the situation worse. Chilangos, as

Mexico City residents are called, are notoriously impatient. They completely overuse their horns. It is not uncommon to hear someone use their horns for 2 or 3 minutes straight. You have to somehow block out the horns and develop a Zen-like acceptance that you are only going to move at a snail's pace.

5. Pay attention!!! The moment you blink, you could lose your life. Drivers here will run you over without stopping.

Trying to fix my bike here in Mexico can be beyond frustrating. I rode all over the city, traveling to many bike shops looking for spokes. I probably went to about ten different shops asking if they had the right sized spokes only to be turned away. One shop in the central city even sold me the wrong sized spokes. I am determined to get my bike fixed. Si se puede. Yesterday, I was happy to see that the same naked protesters that were here, when I lived here before, are still here. Now, they play drums and dance while wearing Vicente Fox and Carlos Salinas masks. The protests seem to be largely ignored, but at least they are entertaining. I am so happy that I ride a bicycle and not a car. Between the protests and the random road blocks there seems to always be a long detour for the drivers. I swear, sometimes the police here set up roadblocks for their shear amusement. I blithely ignore all of the roadblocks and go wherever I want. The police let bicyclists do whatever they want to do.

I Love Mexico City! & Into the Heat

Day 60-71, 12-6-2007 through 12-17-2007

I stayed in Mexico City

People might wonder, with all the crime, traffic, and pollution, why I love Mexico City as much as I do? The answer is simple. This city is filled with so many wonderful, amazing, talented, and beautiful people. It is overflowing with culture. I would even go so far as to say that it is the cultural capital of Mexico. All the musical acts throughout the country have to come here and perform if they even want to have a modicum of success in the rest of the country. Mexico City, has been the home of many famous artists including Diego Rivera, Frida Kahlo, David Alfaro Siqueiros, and José Clemente Orozco to name a few. There is huge amount of art and amazing architecture in every corner of the city. One only has to go la Ciudad Universitaría (C.U.), as the U.N.A.M. campus is called, to see some of the most impressive murals in the world. The library there is even covered in murals on all sides made entirely from rocks that were collected from all parts of Mexico. One of my favorite places in C.U. is the Espacio Escultorico. It is a natural park area with massive sculptures, which you can climb and walk all over. Though there are many impressive works of art and architecture in C.U., you would have to spend many days exploring the city to see all the notable artistic, architectural monuments abounding in the city.

I had the privilege of seeing some very good music when I was in the city these last two weeks. One group was from Xalapa, Veracruz. Their name is Sonex and they play Son Jarocho fusion mixed with elements of hip-hop

and flamenco. Another group named Paté de Fua had an Argentinian front man with all Mexican musicians. They play a mixture of tango and jazz blended with various other Latin elements. My friend Edgar plays in a band called Los Malditos Hippies. They play a mixture of ska, reggae, and cumbia. Edgar also plays in a Mexican hardcore band called Cannabis Cerdos. All of the above bands can be found on MySpace if you would like to listen to any of them. There are many talented musicians that call Mexico City their home.

There are so many incredible museums here that you could spend months exploring all of them. Among some of the more notable museums are the National Anthropology Museum, the National Museum of Art, and the National History Museum. I have been to all of those museums before, so I decided to visit one of the more obscure museums when I was here. Last Thursday, Edgar and I rode our bikes to the Museum of Torture. This museum houses some truly horrifying instruments of torture with notes in both English and Spanish about their uses. One of the more interesting things that are at the museum is the shackles and chain in which Christopher Columbus was brought back to Spain after his third voyage to the New World. Among some of the more interesting things I learned was that it would often take days for someone who had been impaled to die, for though the spear would go through the anus all the way to the mouth, it would miss most of the vital organs.

Often, the spear would even have a rounded point so it would take longer to pierce through the body. I left the museum impressed with the ingenuity that people have, when it comes to conceiving new forms of cruelty to perpetrate against their fellow brothers and sisters. I think that most of humanity is good, but that there are some really evil motherfuckers out there. The problem we have is that, throughout history and today, many of these evil motherfuckers happen to be in positions of power.

I stayed with La Familía Medina during my stay here in Mexico. They have been the most wonderful and gracious hosts. They have fed me and let me stay here rent-free for two weeks. Whenever I would wash dishes to help out they would always insist that I leave them in the sink. Both parents are retired. Their son Edgar, who I have already mentioned, is a very talented guitarist as well as musician in general. Their daughter Idania, designs costumes and acts in a theater group which I also had the privilege of seeing perform. Luis Fernando, the nephew who lives with them is eight-years-old and enjoys swimming and playing the trumpet. Bidel, the daughter of Idania is the newest addition to the family. She is cute as the dickens, and is the princess of the house. La Familía Medina shares their house with five cats, and three dogs so, as one might imagine, it is quite a zoo.

I spent most of my time here hanging out with Edgar going to parties, museums, lucha libre, etc. It seems like Edgar knows everyone in the city because wherever we went, we would run into friends of his. Now is the time of the posadas or Christmas parties and one can find parties in the streets of Mexico, where everyone is dancing to salsas and cumbias, and where there are free food and drinks. Techno is still pretty popular at parties thrown by college aged people here. Though I don't like techno quite as much as I like cumbias and salsa, I still had a good time at the parties because I met many beautiful women. I swear, it seems like every woman here between the ages of 15 and 35 is absolutely drop-dead gorgeous.

After leaving one of these parties I witnessed further proof that the cab drivers here are insane. The cab driver who gave us a ride home pulled a Dr. Jekyll and Mr. Hyde routine. When my friends and I got in the cab, he was calm and polite. He drove patiently and chatted with us about various subjects. As soon as someone cut him off though, he was a different person. He rolled down his window, cursed the driver out, and then proceeded to drive a lot more aggressively: he started driving a lot faster and flew over speed bumps to the point where we had to hold on tight or risk injury. I guess Mexico City drivers would have that effect on anyone, because I definitely found myself cursing people out when they didn't give me enough respect on the road.

The lucha libre matches here are a cultural phenomenon that are worth witnessing. The luchadores are much

like American wrestlers except even more over-the-top. They still have the staged battles between the good and bad guys or the technicos and rudos as they are called respectively, only the moves are more acrobatic. It is not uncommon to see the luchadores flying over the ropes, out of the ring, and hurling into their opponents below. If someone removes the mask of a masked luchador they will lay face-down on the ground motionless as if their source of power has been stolen from them. My favorite match was between three dwarfs and three normal-sized people. Though the matches are obviously staged, I couldn't help but be impressed with the athleticism of the luchadores. You have to know how to fall and roll to be a successful luchador.

I have done quite a bit of shopping here in Mexico. While electronic equipment is more expensive here, just about everything else here is less expensive. You can buy pirated C.D.s, D.V.D.s, software, clothing, etc. Most of the pirated goods are sold by ambulantes as the street vendors are called. The ambulantes are a feisty bunch who often block roads and steal electricity from the city's power grid. They are known to have pitched battles with the police whenever they try to crack down on piracy. There is an advertising campaign by a conglomerate of companies that says that pirated goods are of lower quality than the originals but the sad truth is that the originals are not that much better. I have several pairs of pirated Adidas socks which I bought here over three years ago, which still do not have any holes in them. I bought two pairs of full length bicycle tights for about $20 each. They would cost $100 in the United States. Tepito is the center of ambulante culture. It is also known as one of the more dangerous parts of the city. In Tepito, you can buy D.V.D.s for 80 cents. You can buy drugs and guns. You can find hookers and contract hit-men for $1000. I have even seen tattoo stands on the street, which I am sure are dirt cheap. Needless to say, I went to Tepito to do some shopping. I bought some $5 "Oakleys" and some C.D.s. The reality is that, during the day, your chances of getting shot are lower than they are in a mall in Nebraska. During the night though, a white

boy would stick out like a flaming queen at an N.R.A. rally. I would never go to Tepito at night.

I did not go to Tepito to get my new tattoo. Instead, I went to a shop that Edgar took me to, that was close to C.U. I still got a good deal. I now have a tattoo that covers my chest from nipple to nipple. It only cost me $200. The same tattoo would cost, at least, $1000 in the U.S. The artist, who goes by the name of Russo, took great care making sure that the conditions were sanitary. Don't ever let anyone tell you that tattoos don't hurt. Even after nine hours under the needle, the pain was barely tolerable. I had to bite down on tongue depressors and I would trem-

ble in pain whenever Russo filled in the areas around my nipples or sternum. The pain was worth it, though. I now have a tattoo that is a mixture of Greek philosophy with the peyote inspired art of the Huichol Indians. My tattoo is an artistic rendition of the reunion of the four elements of earth, wind, water, and fire, into the fifth or quintessential element, which is life itself.

Those who know me well know that I am a lover of the funny expressions that exist in language. I learned some funny ways to refer to sex during my stay here. If you want to say that you are about to have sex, you can say, "vamos a matar el oso" (we are going to kill the bear) or "vamos a ponerle Jorge al niño" (we are going to put the

Jorge on the child). Cops are commonly referred to as tira, chota, puercos, or cochinos. Coca-Cola is sometimes referred to as agua negra de los Yankee imperialistas. I even saw a bumper sticker that said Coca-Colonización. At a party, when I was having a conversation with Edgar, I told him that in my religion, I dance as a form of worship. He then asked me what my religion was named. I was just joking around but, together, we invented the words Ganjobiciclatolico and Ganjobiciclatolicismo to name my religion. They are formed from the words ganja, bicicleta, and catolico which I don't think that I need to translate.

I am going to miss all of my friends in Mexico City but, alas, it is time to move on. I will soon head to the Pacific coast of Mexico and then to Guatemala.

Day 72, 12-18-2007

kt: 19.5, ta: 859, gps: N 19° 13.387' W 99°08.535'

I ended up staying in Mexico City one more day because I didn't want to hurry to do my errands: I needed to buy new gloves, burn my photos to a C.D., and mail my photos and Christmas presents for my mom to Austin. Moreover, I wanted to party with Edgar one last time before I left the city. I even drank a little alcohol, though, not quite as much as Edgar, who fell off his bike twice, while we rode back to his house from the party. I woke up late and didn't leave Edgar's house until 2:30 p.m.

Leaving Mexico City is, thus far, the hardest thing that I have had to do. My actual departure was a very poignant moment. The whole Medina family gathered in front of their house so we could all take pictures to-

gether. I tried to hold back tears but ended up crying under my sunglasses. I am really going to miss all of my friends and the Medina family. I am very seriously considering moving back to Mexico City when my journey is over. At the very least, I am going to have to find more time to visit.

I barely made it out of the city because I had to make a few stops. Upon looking at my rear rim, I noticed that there are cracks where the spokes and spoke nipples connect. As the right-sized rims are impossible to find in el D.F. (Believe me, I tried), I had to use another ghetto-rig solution: I used metal epoxy paste to seal the cracks. Right now, my rim is straight and the cracks seem to be well sealed so I am hoping to make it, at least far enough to

replace my rim. I am just going to have to ask around in every city that I ride through. I honestly think that the epoxy paste will hold for a while, though I am prepared to ride on my rear rim until my wheel explodes.

My campsite is in the mountains between Mexico City and Cuernavaca, Morelos. I am going to have to get myself back into my nomadic lifestyle. Hopefully, having a warm bed and shower hasn't made me fat and weak.

Day 73, 12-19-2007

kt: 80.8, ta: 2198, gps: N 18° 45.849' W 99°14.342'

My first twenty kilometers of the day was all spent climbing. The rest was all descent. Whee!!! I descended over 6,000 feet, passing through Cuernavaca on the way towards a town called Iguala, where I will turn off towards Zihuatenejo, Guerrero. Morelos is the state that Emiliano Zapata is from and where he started his rebellion against the Mexican government. I have set up my campsite on a hill overlooking a prison and a Mexican suburb. If you think that American suburbs are monotonous, you should see a Mexican suburb.

I have not gone on one of my political rants in a while, but I have seen some things in the news that have caught my eye. The countdown is ticking until January 1st when a new Arizona law making it illegal for employers to knowingly hire illegal immigrants goes into effect. Upon being caught the first time, the employer loses their business license for a year. The second time, their business license is revoked permanently. I think that this is a completely asinine law, but instead of dwelling on why it is stupid and racist, I would like to make some predictions:

1. The cost of construction will rise significantly. New roads and buildings will definetively be delayed and go way over budget.

2. Retail sales and, hence, sales tax receipts will see a sharp decline across the board, as illegal immigrants contribute significantly to the economy. The difference will be so stark that the coming national recession won't be enough to explain the decline. Some businesses such as fast food restaurants and used car lots will see even greater declines. Anyone who frequents any of these businesses in Texas can see that illegal immigrants are one of the main demographics which support these establishments.

3. Finally most of the illegal immigrants who live in Arizona will move not back to Mexico but instead, they will move to to bordering states.

I am sure that I have only scratched the surface in predicting the economic fallout from this law. I have based my predictions not on conjecture but on what have actually happened to small towns that passed similar draconian laws against immigrants. Believe me when I say that Mexicans notice these laws, as I have had several conversations with random strangers where they brought up the racism of Americans. Those racist bastards in Arizona deserve everything that is coming to them.

Another thing that has caught my eye in the news is the proposal of several of the leading Democratic candidates calling for health insurance mandates as the panacea for our ailing health care system. This is a bad idea. We would only be rewarding those who are primarily culpable for the mess we have today. I have read way too many articles about people with health insurance having to declare bankruptcy after an extended stay in the hospital, to trust the insurance industry to fix our health care system. Any functional solution we come up with will have to cut out the insurance middleman. It would also have to focus on preventative health-care, rather than reactionary health-care, where we wait for people to get sick before we treat them. Early diagnosis of cancer, among other illnesses, increases the likelihood of survival and decreases the cost of treatment.

I also noticed that Congress recently passed a new energy bill that called for a huge increase in ethanol production. While part of the bill calls for an increase in research into producing ethanol from bio-waste, which is laudable, the vast majority of the increase will come from ethanol produced from corn. This amounts to another massive government handout to corporations such as A.D.M. This will lead to an increase in food prices across the board as farmers will plant corn instead of other crops while trying to meet this artificially created demand.

It should be noted that arable land is scarce because we keep on paving over more of it while creating car-dependent suburbia. I am tired of reading about these pie-in-the-sky, technological solutions to our petroleum addiction and global warming. The only way to fix these problems is to reduce our demand: we should heavily tax gasoline and use the proceeds to build better public transportation systems. While we are at it, we should develop bicycle friendly transportation infrastructure as the bicycle is the only true zero-emission vehicle we will ever have, besides our own two feet. If more people rode bikes, we would also see the added benefit of reducing obesity and cardiovascular related illnesses, which significantly tax our health care system. I am in excellent cardiovascular shape and I have a single digit body fat percentage. I have several friends who have lost over a hundred pounds from regularly riding their bikes. Come on everyone, join the bicycle revolution!

Day 74, 12-20-2007

kt: 81.5, ta: 3093, gps: N 18° 20.825' W 99° 32.086'

The state of Morelos is not very large as I entered it yesterday, and left it today. It is noticeably hotter as well as more humid in the lower altitudes where I am. The gnats and mosquitoes love the heat as it no longer gets cold enough at night to drive them away. This is not to say that there aren't any mountains here. There are, they are just smaller. I haven't had to climb mountains in such heat since I left the northern part of the Chihuahuan desert.

I picked up some tourist pamphlets for the state of Guerrero, today. They only reinforced my decision to quickly pass through Zihuatenejo and Acapulco and enjoy the rest of the beaches of Guerrero. There are apparently a variety of virgin beaches where you can camp right along the beaches. I have no interest in staying in one of the four-star hotels in either Zihuatenejo or Acapulco. I however, look forward to seeing nesting turtles and ancient stone carvings. The beaches of Guerrero also offer a variety of regional dishes which I can't wait to try. My mouth is watering already.

Day 75-79, 12-21-2007 to 12-25-2007

kt: 20.5, ta: 1291, gps: N 18° 21.946' W 99° 39.917'

I spent the last four days in the town of Iguala, Guerrero with an attack of diarrhea. I really only had full-fledged diarrhea for one day but I stayed longer because my kidneys hurt, and I wanted to make a full recovery before I hit the mountains. Diarrhea is very seriously here: It can be indicative of a more serious illness and can kill by itself because it causes dehydration. I have had much worse cases of diarrhea in Mexico before.

During the Day of the Dead in 2004 (also known as Election Day in the U.S.) I had an attack of food poisoning that caused me to purge food out of both ends, lasting for three days. To combat diarrhea, one must drink a lot of water and find food you can stomach. The very thought of eating meat or dairy will make your stomach turn. I find that dry foods such as saltines and amaranth bars are the best things to eat. You generally have to force yourself to eat because you probably won't have an appetite. If the symptoms last for more than three days, check yourself into a hospital because you probably have something more serious than a mere case of food poisoning.

The town of Iguala is not a very interesting place for a tourist. It has about 300,000 residents, according to a local, but about all of the businesses shut down after 6:00 p.m. as if it only had 3,000. I have read, but not confirmed that the Mexican flag flying on the edge of the city is the largest flag in all of Latin America. It is pretty big and you can see it from far away on all sides of the city. I didn't do much when I was in Iguala other than stay in my hotel room and watch movies. I ventured out occasionally to surf the Internet or buy food and water. The hotel where I stayed at had a very basic cable package, so I had a lot of movies to choose from: both in English, with Spanish subtitles, and dubbed in Spanish. Some translations in the subtitles are laughable. My favorite was when pussy cat was translated to be vagina. Vagina is "vagina" in Spanish. It was one of those jokes with a double meaning. that was completely lost in translation. This same movie had a scene where the main character goes to Belize, and the soldiers there are speaking Spanish. In case y'all didn't know, Belize was a British colony until 1973 and English is the official language there. This just reinforced my opinion that Americans are culturally ignorant.

I took my time leaving the city today, for I did not want to overexert myself, while coming off of a sickness, by riding into the heat. The mountains are not as high as other parts of the country but the climbs are much more challenging because it is about 30 degrees hotter. I drank and sweated out more water while climbing 10 km, today, than I often do while riding 50 km. I expect more of the same while going towards the coast as most of Guerrero is covered in mountains. Hell, I expect more of the same all the way to Colombia.

Day 80, 12-26-2007

kt: 42.2, ta: 3946, gps: N 18° 21.393' W 99° 50.891'

I spent another day climbing hills all day in the somniloquent heat. Just about every time I found a shady spot, I took a nap. I like naps and they keep me from overheating.

The heat definitely slows me down. I am going to be moving slowly all the way towards the coast as the place is called "Tierra Caliente" or "Hot Land".

Day 81, 12-27-2007

kt: 75, ta: 2413, gps: N 18° 19.300' W 100° 17.912'

What goes up must come down, or so they say. I got to enjoy a long stretch of descent today after some initial climbing. This was definitely nice because it was hot and steamy. Suffice to say, I believe I have officially left the part of the country where it is ever cold. I had a scare today when a bus passed me with about two feet to spare, when I was descending a mountain. I was moving at 50 kph and two feet is nothing at that speed. I had almost no margin of error and I was almost forced off the road. If I was forced off the road at that speed, I would almost definitely die, with or without a helmet. At least the driver honked before bullying his way past

me. This is not the first near-death encounter I have had on the road, and it probably won't be the last.

I could have traveled farther today, but I am a sociable person, and probably spent at least an hour talking with people who were curious about my journey. I spent another hour and a half in an Internet cafe in Arcelia, Guerrero and found myself racing the sunset to find a decent campsite. I was lucky to find a flat, well-obscured campsite just off the side of the road. At just over 1,100 feet, I am pretty sure that this is the lowest point I have been at in all of Mexico. I expect to sweat in my sleep tonight.

Day 82, 12-28-2007

kt: 54.3, ta: 1061, gps: N 18° 20.011' W 100° 41.330'

I enjoyed another happily lazy day, today. Finding shade is more than enough of an excuse to rest. Someone told me, today, that this is actually the hottest part of the country. I am inclined to believe this.

If this isn't the hottest part of the country it is, at the very least, the most uncomfortable part of the country when you combine the heat, humidity, and swarming insects. Gnats and mosquitoes aren't a problem in the dry desert. The mosquitoes aren't as bad as the gnats, which swarm you as you come to a rest anywhere. To call the gnats evil or even to use the superlative "most evil" is an understatement. You really don't do them justice unless you describe them as, "the most evil motherfucking bastards the universe

has ever spawned." This is not hyperbole. Tomorrow, I'll wear my full-length bicycle tights despite the heat, because gnats are that bad.

Today, while approaching the town of Tlapehuala, Guerrero, I saw what could very well be the largest carved head in the world. It dwarfs any of the Olmec heads or the giant heads of Easter Island. It is a giant head about 60 or 70 feet tall, sculpted in the guise of Lazaro Cardenas upon his death in 1977. Lazaro Cardenas is the former president responsible for nationalizing Mexico's oil industry and is revered by all. To put this reverence in context, I don't think that there are any statues of Jesus or La Virgin de Guadalupe that come even close to the size of this head.

Day 83, 12-29-2007

kt: 50.9, ta: 3413, gps: N 18° 08.914' W 100° 56.451'

There is a discrepancy between what my GPS and map tells me is the distance to Zihuatenejo and what the signs in Ciudad Altamirano said. It is a difference of 100

kilometers. Unfortunately, I think there are still 200 instead of 100 kilometers. While I was riding through a small village that is not on my map or GPS, looking for food, I

happened upon a party with band, food, and everything. Being that I was ravished, I endured the stares of just about everyone so I could eat something. I was definitely an oddity being the only guerro and definitely the only person who rode my bike there. I am used to people staring at me, anyways. It turns out that the party was for a little girl that just got baptized today, though you wouldn't know it from all the debauchery that was going on. As is the case with most religious holidays here, it is really just an excuse to get fucked up. Almost all the men were piss drunk and everybody was dancing to Musica Durranguense which is essentially just Norteño music, as Durango is a state in the northern part of Mexico. The men eventually got me to dance with a girl even though I don't like dancing to Norteño with strangers, because of the proximity involved. I even drank a little beer. It was literally a little bottle of Corona that even said "Coronita" on the label. ¡Que lindo!

Day 84, 12-30-2007

kt: 33.9, ta: 3139, gps: N 18° 01.422' W 101° 06.795'

By the time that I wake up, it will be a new year. While many people in the U.S. will be partying, I will be sleeping. I guess my resolution this year is to be a little bit braver about flirting with beautiful women.

I saw some pretty exotic birds today but, as birds are pretty elusive creatures, I did not get any pictures. One was blue and yellow but was not a parrot and the other was brown and had a long tail.

Day 85, 12-31-2007

kt: 60.6, ta: 3576, gps: N 17° 51.697' W 101° 22.704'

I don't think that I have mentioned it, but Guerrero is one of the drug trafficking hot spots of Mexico. Last year, narcotraficantes threw a couple of decapitated heads of police officers into the police headquarters in Acapulco.

I met someone, today, who I would consider a victim of the drug war, but who the government considers to be a criminal menace. He served 16 years in prison for transporting 700 kilograms of cocaine. Granted, this is a whole truckload of cocaine, but the heavies transport boatloads of cocaine. He was not the boss, just the person who transported the merchandise. All one had to do was look around to see that he wasn't lying about this. I counted at least 9 people in the extended family who shared a two-room shack constructed from discarded wood and metal roof shingles. Moreover, two of the women were noticeably pregnant. There is no plumbing or electricity in this stretch of highway. The family was sharing a meager breakfast of tortillas and the Mexican equivalent of Parmesan cheese. Despite their poverty, they shared their breakfast with me and I accepted, as I consider it rude to decline people's generosity. As far as I can tell, the only ways to make money in these parts are by selling sodas and chips to those passing by on their way to Zihuatenejo, and through drug trafficking. It is no wonder that many people choose drug trafficking because these people are lucky to make $5 after subtracting the cost of the products they sell, as very few people pass by these parts.

The man, who will remain anonymous in respect to him and his family, told me that there are many people who get busted with truckloads of cocaine without ever knowing the true contents of their cargo. The transaction usually goes something like this: the owner of a "transportation" company approaches said person and tells them that their driver is sick and ask them to transport their cargo, which is usually disguised as something legitimate. The narcotraficantes can pay them less than someone who knew what the cargo was. Moreover, if the driver gets busted with the drugs, he is usually too afraid of reprisal to point the authorities towards the man who contracted them. The man who contracts the driver is usually a lieutenant and not a heavy, anyway. Many innocent men have fallen victim to this scheme.

The man was resentful of the 16 years he had to serve in prison, when there are those close to power who he termed "intocable" or untouchable. He mentioned, the brother of former president Carlos Salinas, who was strangled to death in his car 3 and half years ago, and the sons-in-law of former president Vicente Fox. These are not entirely baseless accusations, as I have read the same in the Mexican press. When Carlos Salinas's brother was killed, there was a blown up picture of the strangled corpse on the front page of the news the very next day. The article did mention that the murder was probably drug related, but I doubt the government ever did a follow up investigation.

I had to move on, though I wanted to listen to this man some more, as he spoke from a perspective that I can only imagine. Further down the road, I came upon the aftermath of a cockfight. I was attracted by the commotion, as I usually don't see such a large group of people gathered in one place in the countryside. There, on the ground, lay two dead roosters. I did not get to see the champion as the owner had already left with his rooster and his winnings. Personally, I consider cockfighting to be cruel, but I was not about to lecture twenty grown men, some of whom had been drinking, about the evils of animal cruelty. Anyway, it is not like they just throw the roosters away. They cook them and eat them. The owner of the house offered me cocaine, but I graciously refused explaining that my father was a drug addict and that it was probable that I have a genetic predilection towards cocaine addiction.

Moreover, I have never tried cocaine, and did not want to overdose many miles from any kind of medical facility. I told the owner that I was hungry and asked if I could have some food. He was happy to have something to offer me. After I had stuffed myself and tried to offer remuneration, the owner's wife refused payment. I thanked them profusely and went on my way.

The owner of the house, where they had the cockfight, asked me a question which I have heard many times before: Why don't Americans want Mexicans in the United States? I grow weary of apologizing for my countrymen. The answer is complicated but I have decided to simplify it. My response: most Americans are racist and jealously guard their wealth. I think that these people understand that not all of us are like that as I am a white American who has gone through the trouble of learning Spanish. I guess that I am an ambassador of good will for my country. There are, however, few people like me, and lots of Americans who fear and hate Mexicans.

I finally topped the mountains and got to descend for about 40 kilometers. There were several times when donkeys got in the way, when I was hauling ass. I almost killed myself laughing when one almost fell down while running from me. I should make it to the coast tomorrow.

Nuevos Amigos y Nuevos Paices

Days 86-87, 1-1-2008 to 1-2-2008

kt: 52, ta: 2147, gps: N 17° 39.335' W 101° 33.393'

I stayed in Zihuatenejo

When I finally made it to the beach, I was famished because I was sick of my palenquetas and cans of tuna. I didn't care that Zihuatenejo is a tourist trap. I ate at the first restaurant that I could find. I even ended up renting a room for $20, which is way too much for what I got. As I always do when I rent a room, I took a shower, or rather attempted to take a shower. There was no water pressure from the shower head, so what I took was actually somewhere between a whorebath and a shower. I could lather up with soap, but I had to use the sink to wash off all of the soap. At least there were toilet seats at the hotel. Hell, there was full cable, so I ended up watching a lot of CNN to get my news fix. Those who know me well know that I am a total news junkie.

The next day, while sitting at an Internet cafe, I saw: not one, not two, or three, but four cyclists touring the coast of Mexico. They are Collin from Vancouver Island, Canada; Scott and Casey from Portland, Oregon; and Mu Son from Denver, Colorado. I decided it would be fun to hang out with these guys for a while. We ended up staying in Zihuatenejo. I helped with translation at the bike shops as Casey is the only one with strong Spanish skills. We all ended up playing a game of three-on-three basketball with one of the locals. A rather sizable crowd gathered to watch us. We then went out to eat and split one of those monster platters that the restaurants make for large groups of people. When we went to camp on the beach, we were shooed away by naval officers, because we were in a military zone. We then grudgingly rode to the other side of the bay where we slept under the stars.

Day 88, 1-3-2008

kt: 89.4, ta: 2609, gps: N 17° 18.418' W 101° 03.343'

The first full day of riding with the group was a fun one. We are all in good riding shape and we were able to come to a pretty comfortcble consensus about most things: we all agreed it would be nice to lunch by the water, and we all agreed it would be nice to camp on the beach. I definitely feel safe camping on the beach with four others. I made a huge campfire, since there was an abundance of driftwood just lying around. Mother Earth is usually good enough company, but it is always nice to have conversations with others around the campfire.

We had an experience this morning with some horrible service at a restaurant in Zihuatenejo. The waiter literally fucked up every order except mine. He didn't even seem to be trying. I think it should be mentioned that the Mexican concept of food service is very different from American standards of what constitutes acceptable food service. Here, if you complain about your food, you will still have to pay for it, and you will probably be laughed at. The best system of food service is probably somewhere between the American and Mexican standards. I think that the American customer is completely spoiled with restaurants that will happily recook their food and take it off the bill when people don't like it. They best way to get what you want here is to keep your order very simple.

Day 89, 1-4-2008

kt: 129, ta: 1978, gps: N 17° 00.568' W 100° 05.923'

We made good time today because we all resolved to hammer it all day long. We all seem to follow the same rhythm: we were all up at dawn and all wanted to eat and rest at the same time. We should all make it to Acapulco tomorrow, around 11:00 a.m., so we can all run errands and hopefully be out of the city by 2:00 p.m. None of us really want to stay there.

When we were riding along the highway today, we came across a huge traffic jam. We pushed our way past all of the traffic only to find police blocking traffic from both directions. As cyclists are all natural anarchists, we didn't pay any heed to the roadblocks and rode right through. The source of the traffic jam was a gasoline tanker that had one of its tires explode, forcing it to skid out of control and pierce its tank, causing quite a conflagration. By the time we rode by, the tanker was completely burnt out and I am sure that it tied up traffic for many hours. I am sure glad to be on my bike.

Day 90, 1-5-2008

kt: 37.9, ta: 647, gps: N 16° 50.828' W 99° 54.505'

In the past, I have compared Acapulco to rectal cancer. I think I was probably a little harsh. It is more like bad indigestion. This was once a beautiful place but, has since been ruined by the explosion of tourists. There are high-rise hotels all over, but never fear intrepid explorer, there's actually affordable places to stay and to eat. The place we stayed at only cost about $9 per day. There are no toilet seats, but there is ample water pressure. Considering that I have grown used to having no toilets or running water, this seems quite luxurious to me.

We arrived in the city early and originally planned to pass through, but Casey had a serious run of bad luck with his rear wheel. His luck is worse than mine. By the time we reached the city, he had popped nine spokes and had to push his bike, while lifting the back wheel, to the nearest bike shop. Being that it is Domingo and a holiday nonetheless, we were unable to find any bike shops or laundromats that were open. Hopefully, we can all take care of our chores tomorrow morning and leave in the early afternoon.

I guess that I should mention the name of the holiday today: it is el Dia de los Tres Reyes Magos. Who are the tres reyes magos? They are the three wise men who brought gifts to baby Jesus. On this day, Mexicans eat Pan de la Rosca and give each other gifts in honor of the three wise men. If you find a little doll that has been baked into the bread, you are obliged to make or buy tamales and atole for all of your friends and family on February 2nd or el Dia del Calendario. I saw something hilarious today: after a presentation of Blancanieve y los Siete Enanos, there was a dance competition between little boys and girls for toys as prizes. Latin rhythms are already kind of sexualized but a little girl stole the show when she started pole dancing with the microphone stand. I couldn't stop laughing.

After I returned to the hotel, I hung out watching American movies dubbed in Spanish, while waiting for my friends. When I returned to my room, I discovered, to my horror, that ants had found my food. They completely covered my bed sheets and most of the food in my bag. At least they weren't fire ants. I didn't have much food left, anyway. When I told the doorman, he gave me new bed sheets and sprayed the room with industrial insecticide. Now that is what I call room service.

Days 91-92, 1-6-2008 to 1-7-2008

I stayed in Acapulco

kt: 109, ta: 3157, gps: N 16° 46.531' W 99° 11.975'

We ended up staying in Acapulco one more day to take care of all of our errands. It was fun. There is pretty good food for cheap all around town and I was able to get my Internet fix. Four of us went to see El Amor en el Tiempo de Colera. I appreciated the irony of seeing a movie in English with Spanish subtitles that was translated from Spanish to begin with. We, being four burly, un-shaven men, weren't the typical demographic who would want to see what was marketed as a chick-flick.

Leaving Acapulco was not easy because there was a large hill with lots of traffic, right outside of the city. After we left Acapulco, the land was flatter and there was less traffic. We all make pretty good time together. It sounds like we are probably going to part ways in Puerto Escondido. Maybe, I'll stay an extra day and try to surf.

Day 93, 1-8-2008

kt: 87.6, ta: 2358, gps: N 16° 38.578' W 98° 31.803'

Sometimes there is so much livestock roaming free through the towns that us city boys have some amusing encounters with the creatures. We were all awoken last night by some copulating horses outside of our tents. They definitely make some funny noises. In the morning we were awoken by a symphony, or cacophony if you prefer, of roosters. Anyone who has ever been around roosters should know that they crow well before dawn. It is like the roosters get together and say, "Okay everyone, it is 4:30 a.m. It is time for y'all to wake the fuck up!"

We were on a pretty good pace today until we made it to the town of Juchitan, Guerrero. It was there that we stopped at a store to rest and buy some supplies. There was a man in front of the store shoeing a horse while listening to an excellent band practice in the open lot next to the store. We ended up hanging out at the store and listening to the band for a while. I even got the band to play a couple of cumbias so my friends could hear one of my favorite genres of music. Before we knew it, there was only an hour left before sunset, and we had to leave and find a campsite. I am glad that we stopped and listened to Los Juchitecos, as they called themselves.

I finally got to try iguana for the first time. I am not joking when I say that it tastes like chicken. The texture of the meat and skin is definitely different but if I closed my eyes I could swear I was eating at KFC. I loved the red sauce that they served it with.

Day 94, 1-9-2008

kt: 87.7, ta: 2540, gps: N 16° 19.963' W 98° 00.901'

Today, we passed through the part of the Guerrero coast that has a heavy African influence. There is even a museum dedicated to the African influence in Mexico, in the city of Cuajinicuilapa, Guerrero. I can't say that I learned anything that I didn't already know, but I did have fun playing with all of the African instruments they had in the museum. I even found Chilate in the city. It's tasty but not much different from chocolate soy milk.

We finally left Guerrero for the state of Oaxaca today. I swear it almost seemed like it got another 5 or 10 degrees hotter once we crossed the border. We climbed some long ascents in the heat. It is the kind of climbing that would make you have a heat stroke if you aren't careful. We are all hoping that we don't have to do as much climbing tomorrow but we are ready if we have to.

The spot we camped at was next to a lovely waterfall. It is too bad that the city of aren't careful. We are all Pinotepa, Oaxaca dumps all of their sewage into the creek that the waterfall flows from, or so we were told. The campsite doesn't smell bad or anything, but we were told not to swim near the base of the waterfall. I still thought the sewer cascade was quite beautiful as many different kinds of birds flocked to it to bathe.

Days 95-97, 1-10-2008 to 1-12-2008

kt: 137, ta: 3574, gps: N 15° 51.687' W 97° 07.911'

I stayed in Puerto Escondido

kt: 116, ta: 4565, gps: N 15° 45.640' W 96° 07.352'

On the morning that we left for Puerto Escondido, Oaxaca, we were all pretty determined to make it to the city before sunset. We took very few breaks and had actually already ridden 80 kilometers by noon, so we actually rode into town several hours before sunset.

Puerto Escondido is quite touristy now but there are ample economically priced hotels. The place that we stayed at was called the Hotel Mayflower, but it was more like a hostel. For about $11 a night, we got a room with TV, free Internet, and billiards. The place was full of Europeans, though there were quite a few Americans and Canadians. Everybody seemed to be in a festive mood, so a good time was had by all. My only complaint was a club close to the hotel which played obnoxiously loud techno until 5 a.m. The church that was almost contiguous to the hotel would then ring their bells at about 6 a.m.

I went surfing, or rather, attempted to go surfing with one of the Oregonians. We both stood up so we got to feel pretty triumphant. Apparently, the big waves don't come to Puerto Escondido for another month and a half so we didn't get completely thrashed by the waves.

Today, we rode a shorter distance than when we rode into Puerto Escondido, but it was significantly more grueling. We had to deal with rolling hills all day long and were all pretty exhausted after riding a hundred kilometers. Our campsite is in the city of Santa Cruz Huatulco, Oaxaca. It is one of those cities that the government built just for tourists, but we can still camp on the beach. This may be the last night that we get to camp on the beach in Mexico, as the coastal road is going to start curving inland soon.

Day 98, 1-13-2008

kt: 114, ta: 4884, gps: N 16° 04.411' W 95° 24.109'

We all got a staggered start this morning. The Oregonians started riding about 40 minutes before the rest of us. I was really not in the mood to play catch-up, so I decided it was time to become an autonomous decision making unit again. Despite all of this, I still ended up putting in a pretty grueling day. The rolling hills along the coast of Oaxaca really add up. Combine this with the heat and I feel quite exhausted and famished at the end of the day.

Another piece of my gear broke today: my sleeping pad, which I have had for at least seven years, finally bit the bullet. It still seems to hold a little bit of air but there is a serious leak through the valve and some of the internal air chambers have busted, so there is now a large bubble in it whenever I inflate it. I am still going to keep my sleeping pad because, even though it no longer provides a good cushion, it still provides a layer of insulation for those cold days that lie ahead. I expect to see more frigidly cold days in both the Andes and in Patagonia. Someone told me that there is an REI in Buenos Aires. Maybe I will try to replace it there.

Day 99, 1-14-2008

kt: 67.1, ta: 1716, gps: N 16° 24.603' W 95° 05.020'

I was determined to make this day a lazy day. I succeeded in grand fashion. I slept in until the sun rose rather than wake up before and I took a two-and-a-half hour Internet break in Salina Cruz, Oaxaca, to go with the two lunches which sandwiched my Internet break. It looks like it is going to be flat tomorrow so I think that I will try to get another good day in.

If anybody ever asks, there are definitely virgin beaches in Oaxaca. They are unspoiled because they are still relatively inaccessible. I am sure that there are developers out there that want to build high-rise hotels along the entire coastline of Mexico.

I keep telling myself that I am not going to shave or cut my hair until I reach Buenos Aires, so I can have some extra warmth in the cold places I plan to travel through. That being said, I am starting to look thoroughly homeless. My beard and mustache are as long as they have ever been and really bother me anytime I eat anything like a sandwich or a taco. I don't know if I have the willpower not to shave it before Argentina.

Day 100, 1-15-2008

kt: 101, ta: 1573, gps: N 16° 28.314' W 94° 19.324'

Despite many breaks and even a nap, I was able to make some good distance today. If I can keep up the good pace, I should be in Guatemala in less than a week.

I saw a wind farm today. It is the first place in Mexico where I've seen one but, in all fairness, there don't seem to be many parts of Mexico with wind strong and consistent enough to power a wind turbine. I've seen a few isolated rural houses with solar cells, though there could be many more here, as Mexico has an abundance of sunlight. It seems that solar power is viable in about 80% of Mexico. When I think about it, there is a large stretch of Africa where solar power would also be a viable energy source. I would completely support an initiative to install solar cells in rural villages all around the developing world. The thought of these countries developing to use more fossil fuels for power frightens me very much. If we keep consuming energy in the same rate, the human race should be extinct in 100 years. Nuclear energy is not a viable option to clean up the mess we have created. If it was, it would be no big deal that Iran wants to build nuclear reactors. As far as I know, there is still not a viable manner to deal with nuclear waste. Whenever the government tries to bury its nuclear waste anywhere, people rightfully freak out.

Day 101, 1-16-2008

kt: 106, ta: 1330, gps: N 16° 00.204' W 93° 39.756'

I had some trouble sleeping in the mango orchard last night. The road I was at seems to be a major trucking corridor, as semis roared by all night long.

There were mountains to my left threatening my path, but the road stayed in the coastal plain. I'm getting a break until Guatemala, where I will have to charge right into them. I'm told that I am going to rise from sea level to over 8,000 feet. I had some good long, hilly days along the Oaxacan coast, so I think I'm up for the challenge. It should be remembered that all of these mountains are mere speed bumps compared to the Andes.

The countryside is beautiful here. Many of the mountain peaks look like they are each composed of different minerals, so they have a cool, multi-colored look. Some of the mountains along the Oaxaca-Chiapas border are speckled with trees that bloom with yellow and magenta flowers. I am deep in Chiapas territory now and the scenery should be more of the same tomorrow.

The plants are a little different here, but the one thing that really lets me know that I am not in Texas any more are the birds. Today, I saw a kingfisher, a flamingo, and two birds which I cannot name, but which I can describe: the first appeared to be a hawk with a red beak and blue mask; the second bird, seems like a large jay bird, with extra-long tail feathers, and a funny looking head crest. Birds are extremely elusive when you want to take their pictures, so I still haven't gotten any good pictures of them. I'm tempted to spend a whole day stalking birds with my camera. If I do this, I think it will be further south as the earth's biodiversity increases.

I rode until right before sunset and did something I don't usually do: I asked a family if I could camp on their property. They said yes and even brought me a whole bunch of water. The moral of this story is that the next time that a Mexican shows up at your doorstep asking for assistance you should show them some good old-fashioned American hospitality. I am not being sarcastic. Anyway, I am grateful to Bartolo and his family for being such gracious hosts.

Day 102, 1-17-2008

kt: 80.3, ta: 1668, gps: N 15° 03.917' W 92° 24.606'

I got a fair amount of slacking off into my day today. I keep reading the news on-line wherever I find an Internet cafe. Nothing new seems to be happening. I keep secretly hoping that one (or all) of the U.S. presidential candidates is assassinated so I will have something interesting to read about.

Day 103, 1-18-2008

kt: 98.4, ta: 1668, gps: N 15° 03.917' W 92° 24.606'

Even after two hours of Internet surfing, two long food stops, many 420 breaks, and a bath in one of the many clean tributaries that Chiapas has to offer, I still got a good amount of riding in today.

Provided that my dealings with both the Mexican and Guatemalan bureaucracies go smoothly, I should be in Guatemala by midday tomorrow. I guess that I am going to have to bid my beloved Mexico adieu. Until we meet again, my love.

I have been giving all of my gear the ultimate road test. My tires are almost bald though I plan to ride on them until I have chronic problems with flats. Both pairs of my pants/shorts have holes where I sit on my bike seat and neither one of them has effective back pockets anymore. My sleeping pad is kaput, though I have figured out how to make it more comfortable by under-inflating it. My GPS works great for logging my trip distance and total ascent, but the map is wildly inaccurate outside of the United States. I am usually several kilometers off of the highway, according to my GPS, even though I am right on the highway. I have seen important cities omitted from my GPS map, and more recently, they seem to be switched around as they are sometimes 30 kilometers off mark. The topographical data, though not entirely accurate due to the inaccuracy of my map, is still useful. All in all, I am glad I purchased my GPS device. I just wish I hadn't wasted that extra hundred on the World Map software.

Day 104, 1-19-2008
kt: 75.8, ta: 1832, gps: N 14° 46.407' W 92° 06.181'

I was awoken by a flock of chickens roaming free this morning. It was fun watching them interact. There were several roosters among them. They didn't fight to the death but they definitely did fight. They usually only fight when there is a woman involved. Pretty much all of the roosters would do their mating dance where they walk tall in circles around the hens only to be rebuffed or chased away by the bigger roosters. I started thinking about cockfighting, animal cruelty, and the relativity of different cultures. Cockfighting doesn't seem to be all that cruel when one begins to ponder the lives that most American chickens live. A chicken in the U.S. will live its entire life confined to a cage. I don't know how much training goes into a champion rooster, but I kind of get the feeling that they just naturally fight anyways.

What is more cruel: allowing a rooster to live mostly free life, then putting it up against a stronger rooster in a cockfight, or keeping a rooster caged up its entire life only to meet an efficient, mechanized death? I am not condoning cockfighting, I am condemning factory farming. Cultural relativity is crazy like that. It is kind of like how we say Muslim women are so oppressed because they have to wear a burka, but our own standards are so oppressive that the average American woman hates her body, because it doesn't hold up to our rigid standard of beauty. I wonder how many Muslim anorexic women there are. If there are any, they are probably in Dubai, U.A.E. which seems to perfectly meld the Muslim aesthetic with western profligacy.

I crossed the border today with some annoyances, but here I am in Guatemala. Talisman, Chiapas is like any other border town: its filled with beggars and hucksters. The hucksters swarm you like flies. I think that I even got hucked by a huckster today when changing my money. Oh well, I should have enough to reach Guatemala City. Next time I'm in a border city, I will shoo them away just like flies. No necesito ayuda ni tengo dinero. Larganse.

I will have the exchange rates written down and I will only use the moneychangers on the streets if there are no banks. I won't respond to any comment made in English and I will pretend I don't even speak it. If the people speak English to you at the borders, they probably want your money. If they offer help, they probably want your money. If anybody offers help, I will shoo them away. I had one guy following me around saying he would show me the immigration building. I did not need his help, since I can read.

He of course, wanted money for his "help". I told him I didn't have any. He was disappointed, but he left me alone after that. The next time I pass through a border town, I won't smile; remove my sunglasses (I learned that trick from the cops); or speak to anyone who doesn't work in immigration, customs, or sell food. I don't like to put up walls like that, but it is a defense mechanism. I smuggled the remaining weed I had, in my bicycle handlebars. My pipe was in my seat post. I didn't even need to go through that trouble since no one stopped to search me when I entered Guatemala.

Both Mexico and Guatemala are self-sufficient in marijuana production, so I don't think either country is too concerned about it crossing the border. It should be mentioned that Mexico has immigration checkpoints starting in Oaxaca and increasing in frequency in Chiapas. I do find it hypocritical of Mexico to so strongly enforce its own border to the south when it cries foul at U.S. immigration policy. I say this as someone who supports the removal of all barriers to immigration everywhere. In a perfect world, I could cross the border of any country while smoking a joint, and without asking any other government for permission to do so.

The average Guatemalan is definitely poorer than the average Mexican. You can see the increased poverty in everything. The police here don't drive brand new Dodge Chargers, but beat-up old Nissan's. The colectivos, as the trucks or vans that transport people are called, are weighed down with more people and there are usually even people hanging off the edges. This happens infrequently in Mexico but seems to be a regular occurrence here. Some of the people here can't even afford to build houses out of refuse scrap metal and instead, use plastic tarps to make makeshift tents. I even seem to see more women and children doing heavy labor. They do the labor that I usually see donkeys doing in Mexico. I still haven't seen a donkey, strangely enough. I saw several old ladies carrying large loads of firewood on their backs and I swear, I saw a five-year-old carrying a 50 pound sack of something on his back. Well, maybe he was older than five but he was pretty fucking small. These things are things that I would not often see in Mexico, but they seem to be a common occurrence here. Tomorrow, my joyride on flat land should be replaced with grueling mountain climbing. I am barely above 100 feet right now and I should have to pass over 8,000 feet on the way to Guatemala City. Woo hoo!

Day 105, 1-20-2008

kt: 44.8, ta: 2421, gps: N14° 42.036' W 91° 47.336'

I was still in a foul mood from yesterday's border crossing when I woke up this morning. A little riding took care of that. I soon found out that there are, indeed, cash machines between the border and Guatemala City. I have now re-upped on cash, and no longer have to worry about running out before I reach the city. Before my plans were to haul ass directly to the big city, where I could restock on supplies, but now I plan to take a more circuitous/grueling route to the capital. I am going to go through the mountains, through what is called, "Tierra Fria," to get to Guatemala City. I'll pass through el Lago de Atitlan, Antigua, and Chimaltenango, where there is a cool organization called Maya-Pedal.

I spent a lot of time farting around in Coatepeque, Guatemala reading internet news and looking up exchange rates for all of the currencies of the countries I plan to pass through. I had previously made the mistake of not writing these down but will not make this same mistake again. I try to learn from bad experiences. I wondered around the city looking for typical Guatemalan food rather than the Mexican standards, which are still ubiquitous. I found an old lady selling a deep fried vegetable called pacaya, along with another vegetable she called hierba mora. Both were delicious and cheap.

After eating my lunch, Guatemalans started giving me gifts of soda and vitamins. These are two things that I did not particularly want but I think it was the gods way of telling me that I could let down my guard and trust people again. I went ahead and took this as divine commentary and immediately let down my walls.

I am camped out on top of a hill that is under construction, probably to be another monotonous suburb. I have an excellent view, as I have climbed to almost 3,000 feet again. My campsite is in an old abandoned house that still has a roof. This is good because it looks like it could rain tonight. The jungle has quite suddenly engulfed me. When I was traveling along the coast of Chiapas, it seemed like most of the area was either ranch-land or under some kind of cultivation. Here, it seems like the jungle pervades everything.

Before I set up my tent, I saw a huge flock of hundreds of parrots. I tried to get closer for a good picture but to no avail. I find myself wishing I had a camera with a 30X optical zoom. With that I could have a lot more good pictures of birds. I am still looking for monkeys and I am sure that I will encounter them at some point in my journey.

A lot of people have written me telling me how cold and miserable Austin is right now. I say to them that the grass is always greener on the other side. It is very hot here, and I have a heat rash chafing my inner thighs. I can't wait to reach la Tierra Fria. When it is summertime in Austin and everyone is writing me about how hot it is in Austin I will probably be freezing my ass off in Patagonia. I knew that I was going to experience extreme weather conditions when I started this trip. I am well equipped for all weather conditions and look forward to the challenge.

Day 106, 1-21-2008

kt: 38.9, ta: 5893, gps: N 14° 52.190' W 91° 37.289'

I don't think I am going to see flat terrain again for a while. I ascended high enough today that low-lying clouds fogged up the road. The road was very steep to make my day very challenging. Normally, I can climb hills without getting off of my seat most of the time, but I was out of the saddle for most of the day today. When I got to the city of San Juan, Guatemala, which is right outside of Quetzaltenango, I was at such a high elevation that I had to dig out some of my cold weather gear. I expect more of the same all the way to Guatemala City.

Guatemala definitely has a more indigenous feel to it than Mexico does. Though I heard people speaking indigenous dialects in Southern Mexico, it seems like half the people I run into here speak some Mayan dialect. I even saw a teenage boy speaking Mayan on his cell phone. Many, of the women wear traditional dresses and carry babies on their backs and loads on their heads.

Most of the people I met, that have been to both Mexico and Guatemala, scared me into thinking that the food of Guatemala is horrible. Thankfully, this is not so. I have enjoyed Guatemalan tamales, called chuchos, and a really good masa empanada called a doblada that was filled with a mixture of cooked carrots and chicken. I look forward to discovering more flavors.

Day 107, 1-22-2008

kt: 35.2, ta: 1980, gps: N 14° 53.497' W 91° 25.429'

I woke up this morning to the sound of loud trucks passing by the hotel where I stayed at. This is not the first time that I have been awoken by loud noise. If it is not loud trucks, it is roosters. If it is not roosters, it will be monkeys. At least I am not awoken by the screeching of an alarm clock. That is the most loathsome sound. I tried to stock up on peanut butter, granola bars, and water in San Juan but to no avail. I couldn't find the former two anywhere, and the latter could only be found in half liters and five gallon jugs with nothing in between. Fortunately, Quetzaltenan-go was only 10 kilometers away and I was able to find all of those things there. I have a feeling that I will be having supply issues all throughout Guatemala.

It is going to be cold again for a while and this definitely makes me slack off a little more. I spent a whole lot of time just sitting in marketplaces soaking in the sights and sounds. I have a feeling that I will be doing a whole lot of this as there are many interesting sights and sounds here in Guatemala. Maybe I will even take some pictures.

Day 108, 1-23-2008

kt: 64.2, ta: 3659, gps: N 14° 46.297' W 91° 10.996'

When I woke up this morning, I was lazy as expected and did not want to leave my warm sleeping bag. Who would have thought it would be cold above 8,000 feet? Most of Guatemala is quite mountainous so it is surprisingly cold in many parts of the country.

The portion of the Pan-American highway which I traveled on today is mostly under construction. The government is expanding the two lanes to four lanes and they stop traffic in both directions for large periods of time. They of course let me pass, and I had the road to myself quite often. There are also disadvantages to the road being under construction: I had to go over some rocky stretches; I discovered a new road hazard in the form of falling rocks loosened by construction equipment; and when they

inevitably let drivers through, they are pretty pissed off. All that being said, I did make it to el Lago de Atitlan.

Now I am in the town of Solola, Guatemala which is on the northern border of the lake. The place where I am staying at only cost 20 Quetzales per night. This somewhere between $2 and $3. I could literally stay here for years without working with the money I have saved up. Granted my room is pretty spartan, but I like that. If I keep finding rooms this cheap, I might not camp in the rest of Guatemala.

One of the things that sets Guatemala apart from the rest of Spanish speaking Latin America, is that there are more evangelicals here than Catholics. I see very few old Catholic churches, and lots of new Evangelical ones in the countryside. I am going to have to look into the history of Evangelicalism in Guatemala. I have a feeling that Evangelical dominance probably has something to do Catholic neglect, and all of those Christian Childrens' Fund commercials I saw when I was a kid in the 1980s.

I kind of miss the Catholics, as the Evangelicals more aggressively proselytize, as they see it as their duty to save all of us sinners. I want to scream, "I don't buy the religions that others sell!" but I always end up being more polite, as I am an ambassador of good will.

Evangelism and the Guatemalan Civil War, Riding in Circles

Day 110, 1-25-2008

kt: 19.7, ta: 1925, gps: N14°43.150' W 91°07.262'

I spent an extra day in Solola doing a bunch of nothing. It was great! I wondered around the marketplace, close to where I stayed, watching people interact and finding out the names of fruits and herbs that I did not recognize. The town is very small and walkable, so I didn't even touch my bicycle. I walked around for a little bit longer and then spent most of my day in an Internet cafe. I had neglected transcribing my blog, and ended up typing until my fingers hurt. There was still a lot of work to do when the man who ran the Internet cafe kicked me out so he could close up shop.

Guatemalans do indeed drink atole in the mountains. This pleases me to no end even though my only two options are arroz con leche and arroz con leche con chocolate. I do love atole. El Lago de Atitlan is a place of celestial beauty. It was created when a volcano blew its top. It is a natural lake that is high in the mountains and flanked by several dormant volcanoes. The clouds here seem so close to the ground that you can almost reach up and touch them. They fly by at very high speeds, as this is a very windy place. I have no doubt that the ancient Mayans considered this a very sacred place. I took many pictures in many different lights. I am even camping in the mountains close to an overlook, so I can savor the beauty of this place for one last time in the morning.

I have done a little research into the prevalence of Evangelism in Guatamala. The Christian Children's' Fund (CCF) is indeed, one of the players in the history of the growth of Evangelism, but it is not the only one. To understand the growth of Evangelism in this country, one has to learn a little about the civil war that began in the 1980s and didn't officially end until peace accords of 1996 were signed. I have seen estimates that some 200,000 people were killed during the fighting. An independent inquiry declared that 93% of the atrocities were committed by government troops. Some might argue that the civil war is not quite over as many of those who played an active role in the slaughter of mostly Mayan campesinos are still in positions of power, and have not been brought to justice.

There were Evangelical and Protestant missionaries in Guatemala as early as the nineteenth century, but they didn't rise to prominence until a century later during the civil war. The watershed event that led to an explosion in Evangelism here is the earthquake of 1976 that killed some 20,000 people. Christian aid organizations began flooding into the country and aggressively proselytizing while helping with the rebuilding effort. They ended up staying and helping rebuild the country during and after the civil war.

During the civil war the Guatemalan troops, with the help of paramilitaries, razed about 400 villages. They killed the livestock and burned the crops. This was total war. Those who weren't killed were relocated to concentration camps where they were often forcibly conscripted into the army or paramilitary troops. I remember how I was surprised that I did not see any centuries-old Catholic churches, or colonial architecture, when I entered the country as almost every town in Mexico abounds with these old churches. They are absent because they were burned to the ground along with the rest of these villages. They have all been replaced by recently built Evangelical churches.

In the early 1980s an Evangelical minister by the name of Efrain Rios Montt rose to power after a coup d'etat, which was supported by Ronald Reagan and the Moral Majority. Pat Robertson, delighted that Latin America had its first "Christian" leader, and even flew in to interview Rios Montt five days after the coup. Robertson's television network C.B.N. even had a telethon for the same Guatemalan military that was responsible for most of the atrocities during the civil war. Rios Montt, like almost all outwardly religious leaders, turned out to be a bloody hypocrite. He presided over one of the bloodiest periods of the civil war.

It should be mentioned that this was the time in which liberation theology was in vogue with many of the Catholic parish priests of Latin America. Liberation theology is the idea that priests should not just help the poor get into heaven, but actually help them improve their lives. This is the same time period in which priests were being executed by the Salvadoran military just to the south in El Salvador.

Anyone who has ever been to an Evangelical church knows that Catholics are viewed with suspicion and are sometimes even regarded as a cult among Evangelicals. Combine this with the fact that so many Catholic priests were practicing liberation theology in the time of the Cold War, and it can be seen how an Evangelicals such as Rios Montt, would view these priests as communist sympathizers while the government was at war with a communist insurgency. Being a "good" Evangelical, Rios Montt allowed many Evangelical aid organizations to come in and feed, clothe, shelter, and "educate" those who were displaced by the war. Many previously Catholic Mayan campesinos converted to Evangelism at the time, because they didn't want to be viewed as communist sympathizers, when the Evangelical dominated government was waging a brutal war against communists. It was an act of self-preservation, like when Jews converted to Catholicism in the Spanish Inquisition.

Here we are today. The conversion of Guatemala continues. Many aid organizations only aid those who are Christian (read Evangelical and not Catholic). Rios Montt not only has not been brought to justice, but is a Guatemalan congressman and heads a political party known as La Frente Republicana de Guatemala or FRG. A huge American-style church has been built in Guatemala City. Remember that wide-eyed little girl who the bald guy from the CCF commercials of the 1980s would always trot out when asking for your money? I am willing to bet that she probably has about five children by now, and is probably as poor as ever. She probably takes all of her children to an Evangelical church too. It sometimes

seems like every woman between the ages of 18 and 35 is carrying a baby in the rural parts of Guatemala. We all know that Evangelicals have their heads up their asses when it comes to the effect that overpopulation has on the impoverishment of the developing world. I can't excuse Catholics for their intransigence on this issue either.

Day 111, 1-26-2008

kt: 49.1, ta: 3381, gps: N 14°39.678' W 90° 49.743'

The wind was raging outside of my tent all night long and this morning when I woke up. I have no way of ascertaining this but it seemed like the wind was gusting at about thirty miles per hour. Needless to say, I did not want to leave the warm confines of my sleeping bag this morning. I eventually managed to force myself to get up.

I was fortunately shielded from this wind by the mountains for most of the day. There were moments however, when fierce headwinds almost redirected me. The first part of my day was filled with challenging ascents and terrifying descents. The roads are extremely steep and not in the greatest condition. I was braking for dear life around a lot of the turns, as I felt like I was just a little bit more speed away from losing control of my bike, which weighs more than half my body weight with gear. This being said, I am glad that I didn't have to challenge the wind, as this would have been even more exhausting.

When I arrived in Chimaltenango, there was still plenty of time left in the day and I could have ridden further, but I was so close to Guatemala City, that I didn't feel like

rushing. My friend won't be back in the city until Monday night and we probably won't be able to meet up until Tuesday, so there is no reason to rush. I asked some firemen if they knew where Maya-pedal was and they said it was probably closed since it was a Sunday. I then asked them if they knew a cheap place where I could stay, and they told me that I could stay at the fire station for free. I had my own room with a television and everything. How cool is that!

The television in the fire station only picked up one station: the Evangelical station broadcast from Guatemala City. I watched a little bit of a cheaply made movie about a teenage girl who gets pregnant when she has sex with her boyfriend. She originally wants to get an abortion but changes her mind when she finds out what it entails. The movie ends with the girl having the baby with support from her middle class parents, so she can still attend school and even the university. Her boyfriend starts a personal relationship with Jesus and asks her to marry him at the end of the movie. Bullshit propaganda! I want to make a movie about a Mayan girl when she has sex with her boyfriend only to be dumped when he finds out that she is pregnant. She then ends up begging on the streets with her baby as her Evangelical family shuns her for having the baby out of wedlock. As is usual, her pleas for help will be ignored by the vast majority of those who walk by. The movie will end with her freezing to death while clutching her malnourished baby.

This all makes me want to research the availability of condoms in Guatamala. Mexico is majority Catholic but they have comercials for condoms where the pharmacist always sells a pack of condoms, "Con gusto." I have also seen posters, paid for by the government, advising victims of rape of their right to an abortion. They also sell pornography on street corners in Mexico. I have even seen little girls selling porn. My point is that Catholics seem a lot less hung up about sex than Evangelicals.

Days 112 to 1114, 1-27-2008 to 1-29-2008

kt: 70, ta: 3298, gps: N 14° 37.783' W 90° 31.143'

I stayed in Guatemala City

When I left Chimaltenango, I was kind of in a hurry so I could meet my friend in Guatemala City, and go pick up my new wheel. My old rear wheel has definitely seen better days. I took a slight detour through Antigua. I can't say that I was particularly impressed. It seemed like another tourist trap to me. The rocky roads only reminded me of how fucked up my wheel was and the prices seemed high throughout the city. I basically just stayed for lunch and a little internet surfing and then I was on my way to the big city. I had to climb up one side of a little mountain, ride on the top for a while and then zoom down the other side. I didn't realize it at the time, but I

topped out at 77 kilometers per hour. This was probably when I was passing cars in the left lane of the highway. With a fully loaded bike, that is not just staring-death-in-the-face fast; that is French-kissing-death-while-copping-a-feel fast. I live for that shit!

I spent most of my time in Guatemala City doing a bunch of nothing, but I did end up being productive by trying out new things. My bicycle is very happy now, it has a new wheel. I washed my dirty, stinky clothes and found some new flavors to try. I tried atole de platano and atole blanco which is an unsweetened atole soup.

Guatemala City has a reputation as an ugly city. I think that this is an unfair reputation. If you were to hang out in the Central Plaza, you might think that you were in a European city, if it wasn't for the man selling fresh goat's milk, squeezed from the goat's nipples right in front of you. The city however, is a dangerous city. I read a news article about how there was an average of thirteen murders a day during the first thirteen days of the presidency here. That is 4,745 murders a year if it continues at that rate. There's news reports every day about members of the Mara Salvatrucha killing bus drivers or pregnant ladies. At night, the city shuts down. Since I am not much of a drinker, I stayed at the hotel hanging out with the others who were traveling through.

The Mara Salvatrucha is a gang that was originally started in Los Angeles by Salvadoran immigrants. As the gang grew, they eventually started to allow immigrants from other Central American countries to join. They participate in drug dealing, human trafficking, and various other criminal enterprises. During the mid-1980s the U.S. government officials decided to deal with the problem of the Maras by deporting them back to the countries of their origins, where they only multiplied since these countries had no law enforcement resources to deal with gangs. El Salvador is still the epicenter of Mara activity but they have become quite prevalent in Guatemala and Honduras too. They are notoriously violent and I have read that they represent 60% of all Salvadoran prisoners. Their most infamous attack occurred when they boarded a bus in Honduras and killed every single person on board with machine guns. They are a problem which I am going to have to look out for.

I am happy to report, after a cursory investigation, that contraceptives and condoms are indeed available here. The Evangelicals haven't fucked everything up, yet. It doesn't seem to me that many people use them but, at least they are available.

I saw a strange natural occurrence today; a mother hen leading a flock of adopted ducklings. It was cute. I'm convinced that if a hen can adopt a bunch of ducklings, we can eventually live in a world without borders.

Day 115, 1-30-2008

kt: 64, ta: 2420, gps: N 14° 49.378' W 90° 08.947'

Today, there was a long descent leaving the city followed by rolling hills. I've descended enough that its not going to be quite so cold tonight. Hopefully, I won't have to deal with the mosquitoes or gnats just yet. I have already grown used to not dealing with them in the cold mornings. I look forward to riding through a flatter part of Guatemala soon.

Day 116, 1-31-2008

kt: 72.4, ta: 5145, gps: N 15° 02.634' W 90° 12.301'

I fooled myself into thinking I was mostly going to travel on flat land today. I could not have been more wrong. The terrain was challenging but the scenery was beautiful as is typical in the mountains. There were fewer semis and more space and this made me very happy. Hopefully, tomorrow I won't have to do as much climbing.

Day 117, 2-1-2008

kt: 80.2, ta: 3510, gps: N 15° 29.054' W 90° 22.846'

The countryside here is beautiful. I feel like I have said that so many times, but there are so many beautiful places in the world. It is a transitional ecosystem that has pine trees mixed with jungle plants. The banana trees looked out of place next to the pine trees, but there they were. The crisp, cool air made riding my bike quite pleasant. There were dozens of varieties of wildflowers and I took many pictures.

I could have ridden much farther than I did, but my Internet addiction was calling me. I just had to read the news. Hopefully, I will ride through a large stretch of land where there is no Internet. Today, I read an article on the ESPN web site about a black man who is doing the same thing as me albeit in a different continent. He claims to be the first African-American to do something like this. He is the first that I know of. When I think about it, I don't know that many black bike commuters. Lifestyle activism still seems like a very white middle-class thing to do.

The campsite where I am at is at the base of a hill covered in sunflowers. Pictures just don't do this place justice. I was discovered by the family that lives at the top of the hill. As most people are naturally curious, they came down to check me out. We talked for a while and they brought me some delicious tamales. They even offered to let me stay at their house but I was already set up, so I graciously declined. I know that I have been talking a lot of shit about Evangelicals here in Guatemala, so I figured that I would balance that out with some nice things to say. With the obvious exception of Rios Montt, most Evangelicals live truly Christian lifestyles. They are honest, hardworking, and more than happy to offer hospitality to strangers. These people are not hypocrites. Hypocrisy is probably the one thing that offends me the most about Christians in the United States. They support the death penalty but worship a martyr put to death by the Roman government. They decry homosexuality but have secret affairs with gay prostitutes. They only seem to remember the teachings of Jesus when it suits their interests. I think that poverty has a way of purifying religious beliefs and practices. In the United States, people really worship the almighty dollar and power, not Jesus.

Day 118, 2-2-2008

kt: 85.8, ta: 5103, gps: N 15° 53.566' W 90° 13.504'

When I woke up this morning, my tent was completely wet with dew. It was cold too. This problem was solved by descending 3,000 feet into the jungle. The first part of my day consisted of me zooming down mountains. I was just about the fastest thing around. Some of the hills here are so steep and have such sharp turns that I had some very scary moments. There is no room for error when you are rounding a curve at 60+ kilometers per hour with a fully loaded bike.

The second part of my day consisted of me going up and down hills in the heat. The hills gradually got smaller and mostly flattened out near the end of the day. This was exhausting and I worked up quite an appetite. I took an internet/lunch break in the town of Chisec during the hottest part of the day. I didn't get a whole lot more riding in during the rest of the day because I was still hungry and stopped to eat again.

The jungle here is very beautiful. It looks like something that you might see in the movies. All the plants are overgrown and the soil seems very fertile. I look forward to the next hot and steamy week.

Day 119, 2-3-2008

kt: 104, ta: 3395, gps: N 16° 31.902' W 90° 11.431'

There is a crack in my tent poles that is in the very worst possible place. It is in the one place that I can't cover with the repair tube. I have covered it with electrical tape and am hoping that it will hold. I have decided that electrical tape is the second greatest invention of mankind right after the bicycle and ahead of birth control. Electrical

tape is useful for patching the sidewalls of my tires when they wear out and for lashing my GPS device onto my handlebars now that the mount doesn't function properly. I am sure that I will find other uses for it as well. If I sold a universal fix-it kit, it would have electrical tape, super-glue, and epoxy putty.

I made good time today but I would have made even better time if it wasn't for the three flats that I had on the road. The Mexican state of Guerrero is the last place where I had a flat so I had a pretty good run of luck until today. I used patches until the third time when my tire exploded while I was looking for a hole so I could patch it. There was an old man at the store who told me he could use my old inner tube. I was happy to be able to recycle it rather than just throw it away.

Today was hot and frustrating to the point where I almost shooed away the children who had gathered to watch me fix my flat. I restrained myself because I realized that they were only curious.

I made it to the town of Sayaxche and found a $2.50 hotel room. I left to go find food and water, only to discover my fourth flat when I returned. I have checked my tire for stubborn thorns and did everything that someone who is fixing flat should do. Fuck you God!

Someone tried to charge me gringo prices today. He tried to sell me a cold hamburger for 8 Quetzals. I wasn't interested in the hamburger anyway, but I overheard him selling the same hamburgers to passengers passing by in the buses for 5 Quetzals. I may be a dumb gringo but I'm a dumb gringo who speaks Spanish. Moreover, I am willing to bet that at least 95% of those who read my blog can count to ten in Spanish. I was tempted to say something to him, but I decided to let sleeping dogs lie.

There are definitely some Mexican and Guatemalan differences in the words they use, and how they use them. Mexicans use the word tope for speed bump while Guatemalans use the word tumulo. Mexicans use estacionamiento for parking lot while Guatemalans use parqueo. Gringo is used as a derogatory word in Mexico, while it is purely descriptive here in Guatemala. In Mexico, they use güero to describe a light-skinned person. I still don't like being called gringo though. I ignore the dozens of children who cry out, "Gringo." as I ride by. I completely understand how my Korean-American friend

feels when people call him chino. The last thing that I have noticed is that Guatemalans always seem to say adios to those who pass by. In Mexico it is always buenos dias, buenos tardes, or buenos noches depending on the time of the day. Sometimes people say goodbye to me instead of adios. That and mister seem to be a few of the English words that everyone learns in school. I almost want to stop and explain that we never say goodbye without first saying hello and that we only say mister followed by a surname.

Day 120, 2-4-2008

kt: 81.8, ta: 2059, gps: N 16° 53.981' W 89° 48.980'

It still hasn't thawed out in North America, Europe, and Asia, but it is hotter and steamier than the devil's scrotum in the northern part of Guatemala called the Petèn. I got a late start, which was too bad, because it was already hot by 9:00 a.m. It was mostly flat today, though there was a headwind. I am going to wake up early tomorrow and hopefully, I'll get to Tikal by midday.

Today is Fat Tuesday or Super Tuesday depending on whether you are religious or political respectively. I don't trust Barack Obama one iota but I would enjoy seeing him beat out Hillary Clinton. Even though she is female, she represents just about everything that is wrong with the Democratic Party to me.

She is the kind of person who wouldn't make a decision without first conducting a poll, running it by focus groups, and discussing it with her campaign donors. We need presidents that would make decisions based on the courage of their convictions without worrying whether it is the popular choice. Hillary's Iraq vote is the perfect example of her cowardice. She is a smart woman and I know she knew better.

I am not a huge fan of football but I follow it enough to know that the New England Patriots were undefeated heading into the Super Bowl. I appreciate the irony that a team called the Giants got to be the giant slayer. Though I am not a fan of either team, I will never root for a team called the Patriots. To me, patriot is just a synonym for retarded, jingoistic frat boy. I like how I didn't know the outcome of the game until two days afterwards. That would be impossible in the U.S.

I read in the New York Times that more people tuned into the game to watch the commercials than the game itself. When did we all become such corporate whores? Commercials are supposed to be annoying. I close all ads on the Internet before they even load. Until advertising agencies embark on a quest to improve the world by teaching us how to prevent disease epidemics, fighting global warming, etc. I will always despise advertising. We don't need to buy more disposable shit. I don't care if the entire world economy depends on us consuming more and more. We need to find a better, more sustainable way of living if we don't want to become extinct in a hundred years.

Day 121, 2-5-2008

kt: 55, ta: 2065, gps: N 17° 13.486' W 89° 36.625'

I made it to Tikal by midday as I had hoped, but by then things had taken a frustrating turn. My tent pole officially broke, though I was able to make things function with electrical tape and a repair tube. I might try another epoxy solution when I find another ferreterìa. To make things worse, my jungle heat rash has returned. I am sure that this will make my bike ride pretty hellish tomorrow. I decided it was best to just leave all of those problems behind and enjoy the jungle trek through the ruins.

I ended up making most of the trek with Vicki and Aleph, a single mother and her son from Great Britain. They are living in Central America and Mexico for a year. I am sure that it is going to be a wonderful educational experience for Aleph and I hope he comes away with an appreciation of the diversity of the earth's cultures from this experience. I enjoyed discussing the trials and tribulations as well as the joys of traveling through Central America with Vicki. She gave me a heads up on places to visit and has me rethinking my decision to bypass El Salvador. She is planning to write a book during her sojourn here and I wish her the greatest of luck.

My feelings about Tikal are ambivalent. On the one hand, it is definitely a tourist trap. It cost about $20 just to enter the park if you are a foreigner plus all of the food is expensive. I even ended up paying $5 an hour

for a slow Internet connection with no headphones so I couldn't rock out to cumbias on You Tube. On the other hand, there are pretty impressive ruins here, and the flora and fauna are spectacular. I saw monkeys, parrots, and various birds which I don't know the name of. There are even some spiders that come out at night that have crazy iridescent eyes that reflected the light of my flashlight.

Day 122, 2-6-2008

kt: 69.2, ta: 2033, gps: N 16° 46.711' W 89° 48.519'

The low-pitched, throaty growl of the howler monkeys is what woke me up this morning. I would take that any day over roosters, loud trucks, or copulating horses. I spent some time looking at birds and then I was off. It was time to leave the tourist trap that is Tikal.

It was overcast until the early afternoon which was totally welcome because it made for the best riding weather. I took off my shirt, hat, and sunglasses and enjoyed it. It even seemed liked the animals stayed out a little bit longer. I even saw a toucan as it was flying away. If it had rained, I would not even have put on my rain gear. I have seen a lot less rain than I prepared for at the beginning of my trip, but it is better safe than sorry.

The area that I have been riding through strives to be a jungle but it seems like most of it has been cleared to make way for cattle ranching and mono-culture. The jungle is always encroaching. It makes me wonder if humans could ever truly destroy the planet before the planet destroyed them. A hundred thousand years from now, will the planet be a vast, barren wasteland ruled by super-intelligent cockroaches with opposable thumbs, who wonder and speculate about humanity the same way we do about the dinosaurs who ruled the planet before us, or will humanity survive, albeit in smaller numbers and humbled by the fierce backlash that nature will have against its destructive practices? Time will only tell. It is hard to tell if humanity is struggling against the encroachment of nature or if it's the other way around.

Everyone seems to be carrying a gun in this part of the country. It is legal for Guatemalan citizens without criminal records to own and possess weapons unlike in Mexico. Today, I even saw a man drinking a bottle of rum with his gun tucked into his pants ready to blow his dick off. I restrained myself from commenting to him about this, because it is a good rule not to antagonize those who are drinking and packing heat. Maybe this means my life-long dream of owning a one-stop gun and liquor store could be a reality someday.

I spent a larger chunk of my day than I would like trying to use epoxy putty to make a more permanent repair to my tent pole. This was all done in vain and, as night fell, I had to do the unenviable task of filing off the epoxy putty while being swarmed by insects so I could fit the repair tube over the pole. Tomorrow, I think I might try to

use the repair tube and epoxy putty in conjunction for a more permanent solution. The one thing that I learned from this is that if I ever see cracks in my tent pole that I should immediately epoxy the cracks shut before they become a bigger problem. I saw the cracks about three or four days ago and I decided to take the wait-and-see approach.

Boy was that a mistake. Anyhow, I managed to construct my tent tonight so things aren't that bad. I am going to check the details of the lifetime warranty for my tent though I have camped more on this trip than many people camp in their whole lifetimes. I seriously doubt they will send me a new pole outside of the U.S.

Days 124-126, 2-8-2008 to 2-10-2008

kt: 103, ta: 3385, gps: N 15° 39.375' W 88° 59.876'

I stayed in Rio Dulce

kt: 56.4, ta: 1598, gps: N 15° 23.160' W 89° 01.053'

I am back in the southern part of Guatemala. It is still hot and steamy but it seems to rain a lot more. I stayed in Rio Dulce for an extra day because the rains would not let up. I left the place where I was staying because there was a break in the rain. It didn't matter though because I got completely soaked in the afternoon. On the road, I met yet another bicyclist. His name is Christian from Switzerland. He is also going to southern Argentina. When we met, it had just finished raining, and he told me about a place not too far down the road from where we were called Finca Ixobel. Since I was wet, I rode with him there and stayed the night in a dorm rather than my tent. Finca Ixobel seems to be a tourist destination in itself rather than just a place to stay. You can go on jungle tours and horseback rides all within the property. There seems to be a fair number of people that stay there for extended periods of time. You can volunteer there for six-week periods of time for free room and board. Since I was in social mood, I hung out at the bar. The next morning, I was on my way south again. Christian and I parted ways, though not before exchanging emails.

When I made it to Rio Dulce, I met a man named George who is kayaking all of Guatemala's river systems. He has made several first descents down some class 5 rapids and says that

Guatemala is mostly undiscovered as a kayaking destination. He is making me think that I want to take up kayaking. When he is working, he is a National Park Ranger. As much fun as I am having, I couldn't help but be a little envious of him.

I read in the news that producing ethanol from corn actually releases more carbon dioxide than burning gasoline. This is because the increased corn production displaces other crops in parts of the world where they still use slash-and-burn agriculture, which dumps massive amounts of CO_2 into the atmosphere. Those of us in the developed world have to know that we can't have our cake and eat it too. Sooner or later, the technological solutions to our energy crisis will run out and we will have to use conservation as our primary strategy to combat global warming. Very few people here in Guatemala have air conditioners and they seem to do just fine. They also don't light every single street at night. There are so many small changes we could make in our lifestyle that would have a very real effect on our energy consumption.

I am trying to escape from the wet part of the country. Hopefully, I will have done so by tomorrow. I will, however, be in the cold part of the country, again.

Day 127, 2-11-2008

kt: 65.2, ta: 2443, gps: N 15° 05.622' W 89° 26.245'

Having a flat tire and finding an Internet cafe pretty much ruined my chances of riding 100 kilometers today. When I saw a lovely babbling brook along the road about an hour and a half before sunset, I decided to call it quits for the day since I found such a perfect campsite. I even took a bath, meaning I jumped into the creek naked.

They sure do like their guns in rural Guatemala. I saw man today who was carrying a 9 mm with four extra ammunition clips. You would never need this much ammunition unless you got in a shootout with other people. I wondered if the guy thinks he is a bad-ass, or if he is that scared of being in a shootout.

Day 128, 2-12-2008

kt: 57.9, ta: 1930, gps: N 14° 55.125' W 89° 54.572'

I have got to break free from my slacker ways. I could travel a lot faster if I wasn't such an internet addict. At least I am well informed. I know, for example, that Barack Obama has recently been sweeping the primaries and caucuses and has been taking in more campaign contributions than Hillary Clinton. As I have said before, I don't particularly like Obama but I strongly dislike Hillary Clinton on account of being a Clinton. Bill Clinton singlehandedly drove me from the Democratic Party. I unapologetically voted for Nader in 2000 and didn't vote for president in 2004. I have lost faith in the American democratic system and now focus my efforts on paying as little taxes as possible. Eventually, I will probably move out of the U.S. altogether so I am not financing the government.

My rear brakes are acting weird. I think that I am going to have to replace the cable housing when I get to Guatemala City. Right now, its just a minor nuisance.

I am camping right now in what is probably the driest part of Guatemala. A row of cacti separates me from the highway. I was just interrupted from writing my diary by the police who saw my headlamp. At first I turned off my headlamp to hide, but when I saw that they had their guns drawn, I decided that it was best to announce my presence. Once they realized that I was just some crazy foreigner, they were more at ease and re-holstered their guns. They told me it was dangerous where I was and I told them that I felt safe. They, of course, didn't say anything about me camping on public or private land. I am behind a fence but they didn't seem to care. There are too many laws in the United States. I know for a fact that what I am doing right now would be considered illegal for a variety of reasons in the U.S. I probably would be arrested or, at least, ticketed in Texas.

Day 129, 2-13-2008

kt: 100, ta: 6948, gps: N 14° 37.783' W 90° 31.103'

Since I have been slacking off so much, I decided it was time for a punishing day. I had to ascend from a valley to about 5,000 feet to get back into Guatemala City. The stretch of highway that I rode on is the worst in Guatemala as far as I know. There are long sections of highway with no shoulder and it is a major east-west trucking corridor. Needless to say, I don't find tight roping the edge of the road and zooming down hills, while being passed by ten semis at a time with inches to spare, to be a whole lot of fun. I am an adrenaline junkie but I still prefer to be in a little bit more control over my life.

HAPPY CORPORATE-GUILT-TRIP-YOU-INTO-BUYING-SOMETHING-FOR-THE-ONE-YOU-LOVE-OR-THINK-YOU-LOVE DAY. I HOPE Y'ALL DON'T HAVE TO DECLARE BANKRUPTCY AFTER TODAY!

New Countries, Hobbies, Mud Roads, & Maintaining Momentum

Days 131 to 135, 2-14-2008 to 2-18-2008

I stayed in Guatemala City

kt: 37.7, ta: 2193, gps: N 14° 33.533' W 90° 46.448'

I stayed in Antigua

kt: 68.2, ta: 2138, gps: N 14° 15.520' W 90° 46.448'

I have spent the last week and a half sitting around and waiting for a new tent part. The vast majority of my time was spent being a lazy little fart. I surfed the internet a lot and watched a lot of movies, since the place I was staying at had free Internet and free movies.

On my most active day in Antigua, I took a tour to the active volcano named Pacaya. We hiked to the top, where there is a large crater of mostly dry lava. Small streams of hot lava flow out of many cracks. While in the crater, it began to rain. Most of the rain vaporized before hitting the hot lava bed. That was pretty cool.

I did a little routine bike maintenance. My rear brake felt like there was no recoil, so I replaced the cable housing. This worked like a charm. The sidewalls of my tires are starting to burst, so I taped the insides up with electrical tape, hoping to extend their life a little bit. I want to try to squeeze another 1,000 kilometers into them. I find it unexpected that my brake pads are probably going to outlast my tires.

My ride out of Antigua was quite lovely. First, I had to climb about 2,000 feet over ten kilometers, and then I rode downhill for the last 58 kilometers. I descended almost 6,000 feet in this long downhill stretch. The temperatures where I am camping are noticeably warmer and I am going to have to contend with the insects again.

There was another unexpected road hazard today: vomit. While dodging puddles of puke, I saw the source leaning out of a bus and projectile vomiting. I made sure to let her know when I passed. Though not deadly like other road hazards, I did not want to be covered in someone's partially digested lunch.

Day 136, 2-19-2008

kt: 91.7, ta: 1546, gps: N 14° 03.780' W 90° 27.907'

There was a point in the road where there was no bridge and a bunch of boats. The boat operator quoted a price of 50 Quetzals and then doubled it when I was already on the boat. What could I do? I was probably the guy's only fare for the day, as the road I was on was infrequently traveled.

I suffered a mild case of dehydration today. Fortunately, I was only a mile from a town when it happened. Though I have heard many times before that it is bad to drink cold water, 90+ degree water does nothing to quench your thirst on a hot day. I started feeling fatigued at the 85 kilometer mark and was peeing a solid stream of concentrated yellow. I just took extra breaks and tried to satisfy my thirst with the hot water that I had, knowing that the next town was close.

Alvaro Colom, the president of Guatemala, has earned my respect by offering to declassify all of the military records from the Guatemalan civil war. This is a step in the right direction for the government to come to terms with the role its military played in the civil war. Of course, the military and right-wing opposition party has condemned this move.

I personally am of the opinion that a democratic government cannot have secrets. Usually, they are secrets of an unsavory, antidemocratic nature, that would enrage the population. The Freedom of Information Act (F.O.I.A.) of the United States was written with these thoughts in mind but is very limited in its power to shine the light on government activities. The U.S. government can use national security as an excuse to keep documents permanently classified. Unfortunately, the government's darkest and most unsavory secrets are classified thusly. I tried playing devil's advocate to think of a scenario where information should be classified. At first, I thought of keeping the information about invasion forces secret but then I realized that the government has no business invading anyone. Then I thought about keeping the president's security detail secret but I realized that the president shouldn't make anyone so mad that they would go through the trouble of hiring the small army necessary to assassinate him/her.

If I were in power, one of my first moves would be to eliminate the C.I.A. and N.S.C. They are not democratic institutions. A quick look at the history of C.I.A. supported coup d'états and counterrevolutions should sufficiently prove this. I don't think that C.I.A. agents who die in the line of duty are heroes. They die because they are meddling in affairs that they shouldn't be meddling in.

Since Ralph Nader has entered the election, I might actually vote. He comes the closest to approximating my views. I might end up frustrated with the absentee ballot process though, and give up. I am, and will always be, unrepentant about voting for Nader in 2000. There was not a large difference between the Bush / Cheney ticket and the Gore "I decry global warming yet live in an opulent mansion that has a larger carbon footprint than a small city" / Lieberman "I'm a war hawk that is endorsing the Republican candidate in 2008" ticket.

Day 137, 2-20-2008
kt: 77.1, ta: 2206, gps: N 13° 43.651' W 89° 59.014'

It is very hot where I am today and I drank a lot of water because I did not want to repeat yesterday's flirtation with dehydration. I can't wait to climb back into the mountains. Crossing into El Salvador was, to my pleasant surprise, painless and easy. The money changers didn't try to rip me off and, as it turns out, the stamp in my passport is good for Guatemala, El Salvador, Honduras, and Nicaragua. The downside to this is that I only have less than two months to enjoy the rest of Central America as I burned a whole month in Guatemala. I haven't noticed a whole lot of differences here, though Chicano Chic seems to be in fashion among the youth here.

Day 138, 2-21-2008
kt: 63.1, ta: 4175, gps: N 13° 51.664' W 89° 47.474'

So far, El Salvador is not half bad. The travel guide, which I inherited from an Aussie flying to Canada, makes it sound relatively expensive. Granted, I've only camped but I was able to stuff myself at a pupuseria for $1.15. For those of you who don't know, a pupusa is a gordita by another name. The presentation is slightly different, though. A pupusa is sealed and served with a vinegar cole slaw while a gordita is open and served by itself.

I underestimated how long it would take to get to Apaneca, El Salvador today. I'm camped pretty close to it, in a coffee plantation. My campsite is well elevated, so I should be snug and cozy in my sleeping bag tonight. Hopefully, tomorrow I will be able to see la Laguna Verde before I go to el Cerro Verde National Park.

There was an article recently in the New York Times about how the United States imprisons 1 in 99 adults. It imprisons 1 in 35 Hispanic men and 1 in 15 African-American men. I just wanted to make a couple of points about these statistics. First of all, our government should not imprison nonviolent offenders. The powers that be can come up with better, more creative solutions for drug offenders, thieves, and the like. Second of all, I do not believe that blacks and hispanics commit crimes at a higher rate than white people. I believe that their higher rate of imprisonment rather reflects systemic racial profiling by police and their lack of quality legal representation, due to their higher rates of poverty. In fact, I am willing to bet that if you did this same study using family income as an indicator, you would probably discover that poor people are imprisoned at a rate similar to blacks and Hispanics. Ask any homeless person in the U.S. and I am sure that he will tell you that being poor in the United States is indeed a crime. Why imprison so many people anyway? So we can have higher crime rates than Europe and most of Asia? I am tired of seeing the government resort to the same old facile, "tough on crime" solutions to the problems associated with crime. Maybe we should attack poverty through expanded educational opportunities instead.

Days 139 to 142, 2-22-2008 to 2-25-2008

kt: 48.8, ta: 2446, gps: N 13° 42.924' W 89° 43.277'

kt: 68.1, ta: 3242, gps: N 13° 42.595' W 89° 12.708'

I stayed in San Salvador

When I rode into San Salvador, I thought it would be nice to stay for a couple of days. I didn't do too much other than watch T.V., surf the net, and talk with fellow travelers. I figure that I earned the right to some serious downtime, since I exert myself so much on the road.

San Salvador didn't seem much worse than any other large city in Latin America. Contrary to its reputation, there are not large groups of Maras lurking around every corner. In fact, the city has many large American-style shopping malls filled with U.S. based chains. San Salvador is more prosperous than one might expect. The area around the central market seemed a little sketchy, but I had a good time getting myself lost in the labyrinthine hallways.

Day 143, 2-26-2008

kt: 58.1, ta: 1371, gps: N 14° 07.654' W 89° 08.923'

As usual, things don't always go as planned, or rather, plans changed. I wanted to go to Cerro Verde National Park, but I got sidetracked. I did manage to see la Laguna Verde but I wasn't overly impressed.

On the way to Cerro Verde, I stopped in a town called Juayùa where I found out that there is a weekend gastronomic fair. I of course had to stay, because I figured that I might discover some new foods. There was one food that was new to me. It was called a rigua and consists of fresh corn pressed of all of its liquids, cooked inside a banana leaf, and then grilled. It was good but didn't change my life.

I didn't make it out of Juayùa until early afternoon but it was still enough time to make it to the National Park. The only problem was that the entrance was not well marked. I missed it when I was zooming down a long hill.

It seems like the relationship between Colombia and Ecuador and Venezuela deteriorated after Colombia crossed into Ecuadoran territory to kill a senior F.A.R.C. commander. Both Ecuador and Colombia have mobilized troops on the border but I don't think that it is any more than chest-beating and posturing. This may not be front page news in the U.S. but it dominates headlines in Latin America. I don't think that this will affect my travel plans but I will, nonetheless, be monitoring the situation closely.

Day 144 to 145, 2-27-2008 to 2-28-2008

kt: 48.1, ta: 4198, gps: N 14° 26.224' W 89° 10.997'

kt: 42.1, ta: 4076, gps: N 14° 31.276' W 88° 56.936'

Crossing into Honduras was quite easy. I have developed a system for dealing with money changers: I make them quote how much money they will give me and I don't show them the money until   agree to their terms. I am always ready to walk away. I think that I will start gathering a group of them and let them compete for my money. The only surprise for me was that I had to pay the Honduran entry tax in a Salvadoran government building.

I stayed the night at a hotel since the lodging is cheap. They had a television with cable and the other patrons and I ended up watching a bunch of American movies dubbed in Spanish. Good fun was had by all. I got a late start because I was working on trying to solve the problem of my rapidly deteriorating tires. My solution has been to contact as many bike shops and hotels as possible that are south of my present location until I can find someone who can receive my tires for me. Hopefully, I will solve this problem by the time I make it to Colombia. The area I rode through today is a legitimate cloud forest. After ascending to 5,000 feet, I could barely see more than 100 feet ahead as I was right in the middle of the clouds. Of course, jackass drivers still pass in the opposing lane, even though they have no visibility whatsoever. When I finally got to the top of Honduras's highest paved road, I was rewarded with the strongest headwind I have ever experienced. Judging by the movement of the clouds, I was in the midst of a wind that was moving by at least 20 miles per hour. I couldn't rest my bike on its kickstand it was so strong. Fortunately, the wind was only at the very top. I rather enjoyed my descent. I rode past lots of wildflowers. Many villagers had planted extensive orchid gardens as this is the ideal climate for them. They were quite lovely. I am looking forward to going through more cloud forests in Honduras.

Day 146, 2-29-2008

kt: 51.3, ta: 4138, gps: N 14° 47.562' W 88° 46.781'

I have been slacking. In all fairness to myself, I have done 4,000 feet of ascent, the last three days in a row. Maybe I subconsciously want to enjoy the mountains for what they are worth. I take frequent breaks just to stare reverently at the stunning scenery.

I should probably make it more of a point to eat prepared meals whenever possible in more rural areas. I ended up ascending a mountain for another 20 kilometers today, after I had the opportunity to eat earlier on. By the time I reached the top, I was running on fumes.

Day 147, 3-1-2008

kt: 82, ta: 2812, gps: N 15° 17.347' W 88° 29.884'

I had several flats today, caused by faulty rim tape. It kept sliding over and exposing the inner tube to the spokes. The first time I just replaced a section of the rim tape. This only made the problem worse and caused a second flat. The second time, I replaced all of the rim tape with a double layer of electrical tape. It is holding now and hopefully, I will be able to make it to San Pedro Sula, Honduras by tomorrow.

It is a large city, so I should be able to remedy the problem there. I also discovered that two of the inner tunes that I was carrying were nonfunctional trash. They were labeled "German type" valves and looked like prestivalve tubes from the drawing on the box, but I should have examined them further when I purchased them. Oh well, they were cheap. I am now down to one inner tube and a hundred patches.

It seems like the standoff between Colombia, Venezuela, and Ecuador has cooled off somewhat. Moreover Colombia killed another senior F.A.R.C. commander, or rather a defector, brought in the severed hand of said leader to prove his death. I am somewhat worried that we might soon see a F.A.R.C. counter offensive of shelling of major cities, or worse for me, an increase in kidnappings. I continue to monitor the situation. I hope that the Colombian government doesn't think that it can successfully defeat the F.A.R.C. by killing off all of its senior commanders. Instead, this will only accelerate its transition from Marxist insurgency to drug cartel. This transition has already been occurring since before the fall of the Medellin Cartel. The F.A.R.C. would also probably lose its Colombian identity, and become a destabilizing force in all of the Andean nations. They will go wherever the enforcement is laxest or most easily bribed. The F.A.R.C. will only disappear when the insatiable demand for cocaine from the United States decreases. That will never happen because that would require an intelligent drug policy that attacks demand instead of supply. Our current strategy is the complete opposite of that, and feeds many a drug baron.

Day 148 to 149, 3-2-2008 to 3-3-2008

kt: 78, ta: 2729, gps: N 15° 29.921' W 88° 00.624'

kt: 63.4, ta: 1568, gps: N 15° 34.604' W 87° 36.903'

Getting to San Pedro Sula was simple enough. The road to the city was mostly flat and it wasn't ridiculously hot and humid, like the guidebook promised. The highlight of my day was when a young boy, who belonged to the owners of a restaurant where I ate, exclaimed, "Hombre feo!" or ugly man, and hit me in the back of the head. I shot him a very dirty look and he didn't bother me again. In all fairness to the little boy, I am starting to look a little grungy. My beard now measures over 3 inches, and my mustache is sun-bleached. I am starting to enjoy my vagabond experience. It still isn't enough to keep the beggars and con-men away though. They only see my pale skin. My goal is to be so grungy looking that beggars give me money. When I arrived in San Pedro Sula, I immediately made new friends. When I was on the side of the road, looking at a map of the city, I met Nora and Luis Fernando; an elementary school teacher and her grandson respectively. Nora helped me find a bike shop and offered a place to stay for the night. I got lost looking for her place. All of

the streets are numbered, but it turns out there was more than one intersection of 7th Street and 14 Avenue in the quadrant of the city that I was in.

I eventually was able to find her house by asking directions along the way. I almost ended up in one of those tragicomic situations, like Clark Griswold in American Vacation where he takes a wrong turn and asks directions in a bad neighborhood, only to have all of his hubcaps stolen. To limit the possibility of this happening, I only asked from people who were on the job: a security guard, a taxi driver, and a group of policemen. The latter group bought me some sugar cane juice and told me I was in a dangerous neighborhood, which was pretty obvious from all of the thuggish looking kids walking around. I ended up with a machine gun escort to Nora's house, so I felt pretty safe.

I found out after the fact that San Pedro Sula is where the most infamous Mara Salvatrucha massacre took place, where a group of men machine-gunned 27 bus riders to there to death for no apparent reason other than to gain notoriety. What I did not know is that this massacre occurred two days before Christmas. Most of the victims were returning from Christmas shopping for their families. That is fucked up. This massacre was recently in the news again, because a court just convicted the two men charged with orchestrating the massacre.

I left San Pedro Sula pretty late today after surfing the Internet and eating brunch. The scenery was flat and uninteresting until I crossed through a crossroads at the town of El Progreso. Afterwards, the flat terrain was replaced by jungle mountains, with crystal clear streams of water flowing down the slopes every kilometer or so. I am camped next to one of these lovely streams right now, staying out of the rain. The rain is not super heavy but it hasn't relented for the last hour or so. Hopefully, it will stop raining by the morning.

Days 150 to 159, 3-4-2008 to 3-13-2008

kt: 138, ta: 2111, gps: N 15° 47.179' W 86° 47.581'

kt: 6.8, ta: 53, gps: N 16° 05.547' W 86° 53.502'

I stayed in Utila (Bay Islands)

I wanted to get to Utila as fast as possible, so I could find a dorm before the rush of Semana Santa vacationers arrived. I knew that all of the beach towns were going to fill up and that all of the banks were going to close. Being that this was a potentially disastrous situation, I decided it was better to hunker down in one place for a while.

I was interested in scuba diving but the cheapskate in me was saying that maybe I would just snorkel, since it was cheaper. As soon as I put my face in the pristine water though, I knew that I was about to spend a lot of money on my scuba certification. I even took the advanced course so I can dive deeper and at night.

The coral reef here is an extension of the Belizian reef which is the second largest in the world after the Great Barrier Reef of Australia. When you first peer into the clear blue Caribbean waters, an explosion of shapes and colors overwhelms the senses. Fish of every color swim through coral formations of every shape and size. I saw parrot fish, angel fish, damsel fish, stingrays, starfish, barracudas, sea cucumbers, porcupine fish, groupers, and many, many, more fish covering the entire spectrum of the rainbow. After spending a lot of time underwater. I am officially hooked. I now want to dive in the Philippines, Indonesia, and many other places.

Utila is an interesting place that attracts an interesting assortment of people. The islanders mostly speak English with a Caribbean accent, but many speak Spanish as well. Scuba diving attracts people of all sorts. I roomed with party animals and Mormons. A couple of doors down, there was a small contingent of U.S. Army soldiers stationed in Honduras. Throw in a bunch of Europeans, some Canadians, and Latin Americans, and we were all one big happy family. One of the soldiers told me I was the craziest man that he ever met, which surprised me because I figured that he would probably know some marine who base jumps into war zones or something like that. He gave me the number for the U.S. Army base in Honduras in case I need to be evacuated in an emergency. Hopefully, that won't be necessary.

Day 160, 3-14-2008
kt: 54, ta: 1243, gps: N 15° 41.545' W 86°30.265'

I am now back on the road. It seems like the rainy season is fast approaching as it started sprinkling and then pouring in the afternoon. I decided to wait the rain out instead of using my rain gear. If it starts to rain every day, which I think it might, I will probably start carrying my rain gear at the ready and ride in the rain. I am warm and dry right now and grateful for being so.

When I was setting up camp today, a woman came and told me I was in a dangerous place to stay. To emphasize her point, she told me that the authorities had found a dead body in the same general area. I wasn't too scared, since I figured that the body was dumped there rather than murdered on site. To allay her fears though, I moved my still empty tent behind some bushes where it was better hidden. She even checked in on me later. I have a guardian angel.

Days 161 to 162, 3-15-2008 to 3-16-2008
kt: 59.2, ta: 1274, gps: N 15° 26.668' W 86° 22.571'
kt: 38.6, ta: 2684, gps: N 15° 17.357' W 86° 30.320'

Some days are smooth sailing with lots of flat ground and beautiful weather. Today was not one of those days. It rained most of the day and when it wasn't raining it was infernally hot and steamy, causing me to peel off all of my rain-gear. To call the road that I rode on a "dirt road" would be too generous of a description. It was more of a mud road. When I asked a policeman which road to take to La Union he pointed at this road and my heart just sank. I saw buses riding down it though, and I figured I could make it if they could make it. I am sure glad that my new tires were knobbies and not slicks. My traction was pretty good on most of the road but there were parts where I was sloshing around in mud pits. My favorite part of the day was when I came to a fork in the road that had no clearly labeled signs pointing to the right direction to La Union. I took a guess, chose one direction, and asked the first people that I saw if I was following the right direction. They told me I was, so I didn't have to turn around. I am now sitting in my tent and wearing dry clothes and hoping that it doesn't rain anymore tonight.

Day 163, 3-17-2008
kt: 30.3, ta: 2168, gps: N 15° 06.263' W 86° 34.087'

I woke up this morning to yet more rain. After several long ascents, I had sweated so much that my rain gear was practically useless. When I finally found a place to eat, I stayed for awhile so I could dry off and

ate four portions of food, since I had been subsisting off of cookies and almonds since the morning before. After I finally made myself leave, I managed to reach the leeward side of the mountain where it obviously hadn't rained in the last couple of days because the cars still kicked up dust. I'm hoping there's no more rain on the 100 kilometers or so of dirt road that remains. I was pretty miserable when I was cold, wet, and hungry. However, I'm a firm believer that what doesn't kill you only makes you stronger.

Day 164, 3-18-2008

kt: 48.2, ta: 2441, gps: N 14° 52.240' W 86° 39.531'

It rained a little bit at night but, other than that, it was dry all day. Thank the lord, Hallelujah! I rejoiced in not having to wear my rain gear. Once you sweat inside your clothes in the cold mountains, your rain-gear is useless. The towns are getting bigger which means there are more places to eat but there is still no pavement. In most of the villages here, they never see white people. When I roll up on my bicycle, it is like I am a rock star and a circus, all rolled up into one. I am usually swarmed by locals asking about my trip. My belly was happily full, or I might have bristled at all of the attention.

I am camped right now on the top of a hill on the side of the road, underneath a moss covered pine tree. Tomorrow, I am determined to reach pavement again. I hope to celebrate my birthday in civilization.

Day 165, 3-19-2008

kt: 69.8, ta: 3404, gps: N 14°32.543' W 86° 43.109'

I reached pavement today. Yay!! I think I now know how a sailor, who has been lost at sea, feels like the first time he sees land. All told, the road was about 143 kilometers of bone-rattling, tick-infested, desolate, and muddy hellishness. If my useless travel guide or GPS had given me better warning, I might have avoided the road altogether but I am stronger for having survived it. I will say though, that it sure did feel good to go down a hill with no brakes again after I finally left the dirt.

Some of the Internet cafes in the countryside might as well be filled with typewriters. They are that useless. It would often take 10 minutes for a page to load, if it loaded at all. When I get to Tegucigalpa, I am going to find a true high-speed Internet connection so I can watch Youtube videos to my heart's content.

It seems to me that people everywhere are so irrationally afraid. Their eyes bug out in shock when I tell them that I am camping in the countryside. They always tell me

that they have found dead bodies in these parts. Usually, not even a car passes by in the night. The people who are murdered are usually murdered for a reason. I am just passing through without stepping on anyone's toes. Nevertheless, the locals always seem to believe that the countryside is populated by roving bands of narco-satanists, who roam the countryside looking for foreigners to torture, kill, and skullfuck. I haven't been skullfucked yet, knock on wood... I blame the media for putting the fear in these people's hearts.

Day 166, 3-20-2008
kt: 111, ta: 5209, gps: N 14° 06.410' W 87° 12.166'

I passed through two different ecosystems today on the way to Tegucigalpa. The first was pine forests and the second, just to the north of the city, looked like it could be somewhere in Texas. It was very much a desert area. I passed through a large shantytown outside of the city and I was eager to get out. I saw what looked like a couple of glue addicts having an argument, only for one of them to pick up a huge rock, and threaten the other one with it. Fortunately nothing happened. I saw this all from the other side of the street, as I had the foresight to cross the road when I saw these two.

When I arrived in the city, the sun was setting and I, of course, arrived in the part of the city that my tourist book referred to as the dangerous part. I soon found out that the whole city is sketchy. This is definitely the sketchiest seeming city in Latin America that I have visited thus far.

I was starving so I stopped at a place that sells baleadas (Honduran bean tacos) and gorged on them. A old homeless man came up to the lady and wanted to buy a baleada, but he didn't have the 35 cents necessary to buy one. He was too proud to beg and began to walk away. The lady sold him one for 25 cents instead. I bought him a baleada too, as I was feeling kind of guilty after eating 9 and watching him go hungry. The sad thing is that he probably goes hungry every day. I know there is poverty in the United States, but we have so much food that we throw away perfectly good food. You have to make an effort to starve in the U.S.

I found out that the itching on my head is indeed lice. I probably picked them up on that dirt road along with a few ticks and dozens of ant and mosquito bites. I bought some shampoo but if I have to, I will go to the nuclear option, and shave my head. I will keep the beard and mustache though, so I can go from a vagabond look to a satanic look. It is nice to stay in a place and not get eaten alive by bugs, so I am enjoying a stay of a couple of days here in the capital.

....

Hitchhiking and Knife-Fighting, & To South America Part I

Day 166 to 171, 3-21-2008 to 179 3-26-2008

I stayed in Tegucigalpa

kt: 22.1, ta: 2009, gps: N 14° 02.636' W 87° 06.017'

I ended up staying in Tegucigalpa out of laziness rather than because I loved it so much. As much as I love the mountains and the beaches, I am a city boy through and through. I like the hustle and bustle of big cities and their cosmopolitan nature. That said, Tegucigalpa seems to be the sketchiest big city that I have visited in Latin America. There are legions of glue-sniffers and generally thuggish looking people all over the city. The cops seemed corrupt in a particularly aggressive way. This is the only place where cops have ever wanted to search my bags. I gave the cop a dirty look and told him to

go for it. He would not have found anything anyway. The cops also wanted to search the other tourists at the place where I stayed. I mostly avoided walking around at night, to avoid the drug addicted and uniformed thugs. Fortunately my hotel had cable, so I watched movies.

I finally managed to break free from the comforts of the city today. I didn't leave until the early afternoon but I am now officially out of the city. The place where I am camping right now has a lovely view of the pine forests outside of Tegucigalpa.

Day 172, 3-27-2008

kt: 63.8, ta: 2995, gps: N 14° 01.851' W 86° 34.244'

I committed the ultimate sin today: I accepted a ride from someone. There were extenuating circumstances, though. First of all, I only had another 15 kilometers to go until I reached the city of Danli, Honduras. Second of all, the rear tire, that I just recently purchased, has a manufacturers defect. The steel wire that gives the tire form separated from the rubber, causing the inner tube to poke out the side and hence, explode. I could not continue on like this because that would have destroyed all of my inner tubes. The holes that this left were un-patchable. As I was pondering my dilemma, a couple in a

truck pulled over and offered me a ride, before I even had a chance to flag anyone down. They were going all the way to the border, but I just wanted to go to Danli since it was a bigger city and I had a better chance of finding a replacement tire there. As I secretly suspected, I was not able to replace my tires in Danli, but the mechanic had a pretty ingenious solution. He used a needle and thread to sew my tire back together. I was skeptical that it would work, but he swore that he has done it before, and that it lasted for a long time. If they gave out a Nobel Prize for bike repair, I would nominate this

mechanic. When I tried to pay him, he told me that he just wanted a soda. I bought two big sodas for him and all of the onlookers at the shop because I was very grateful. I am going to look for new tires whenever possible, but I think that my tires will hold for now.

Since I was having a bad day, I decided to spoil myself by staying at a luxurious hotel for about $12 a night.

The place had nice large rooms with private bathrooms and hot water. There was even a large television with cable. I watched Kill Bill in Spanish. My favorite part was when they translated "My name is Buck and I like to fuck." to "My name is Buck and that means fun." I wonder how hard it is to get a job translating Hollywood movies into Spanish because I think I could do a significantly better job.

Day 173, 3-28-2008

kt: 57.2, ta: 2620, gps: N 13° 37.652' W 86° 28.590'

The highlight of my day, besides crossing the border into Nicaragua, was when two men attempted to assault and rob me. I say that they attempted to do this because they weren't actually successful.

When I was climbing a mountain, about four kilometers from the border in the countryside, the two men stopped me. One of them grabbed me from behind, and he held onto my buck knife, which I wear on the right side of my belt. The other stood in front of me, and threatened me with a rock. The man behind me had a knife of his own. I immediately placed my right hand on my knife's sheath and placed my left hand on his arm, so he couldn't just stab me at will. I essentially ignored the man with the rock because it wasn't a very large rock.

I placed all of my attention on the man with the knife, or rather on the knife, since this man was potentially more dangerous. We all ended up in what could best be described as a standoff for about a minute or so. We were all kind of waiting for someone to do something to break the stalemate. I lied and told them that I didn't have any money. The man with the rock said that he wanted my bicycle, and I told him no.

To steal my bike would be to steal my dreams, and I would rather die, than not be able to complete my dream of riding to Argentina. The standoff would have lasted longer, if a truck didn't drive by. The two would-be thieves ran for cover on the side of the road, and I immediately unsheathed

my knife, so I was better prepared for a knife-fight. The truck kept on going without stopping but I don't think that the two men were ready for a duel to the death. After I brandished my own knife, they kept their distance. After cursing them out, I decided it was best that I didn't stay around and challenge them, so I continued up the hill with the knife in my hand, looking back to make sure that they weren't following me.

I think that these men weren't very hardened thieves. They probably expected me to be a cowardly gringo, who would beg for my life, and give them everything that I had. They were wrong. From now on, I am going to watch my back more carefully when I am ascending hills because these men surprised me. If I were going down a hill, I would have zoomed by so fast that they would not have seen me coming. Considering things, I came out of this situation pretty well. I was unharmed, they didn't take anything, and I didn't have to stab anyone. I still haven't changed my opinion that the drivers here are more dangerous than the criminals.

When I made it to Nicaragua, it started raining but stopped long enough for me to reach the town of Ocotal where I found a room for about $2 a night. It started raining again shortly after I arrived in the city. I saw the sun setting while it was still raining for the first time of my life. It was incredible. The sun was almost a blood red color. I have watched many sunsets before, but I have never seen one quite like this.

Day 174, 3-29-2008

kt: 78.4, ta: 3670, gps: N 13° 05.055' W 86° 21.384'

Today was a delightfully uneventful day. None of my inner tubes exploded, I didn't get into any knife-fights, and I wasn't skullfucked by anyone. In fact, a Nicaraguan congressman pulled over in his S.U.V., handed me his card,

and told me to call him if I had any problems. I have a friend in high places here in Nicaragua now.

When I reached the city of Estelí, I had drank a lot of water because it was very hot and I ended up hanging

out long enough at a restaurant and then an Internet cafe that, before I knew it, it was only an hour before sunset. I then went downtown and found a cheap place to stay. Estelí has some interesting murals and public monuments. There is a statue of a Sandinista holding a machine gun in one hand and a Molotov cocktail in the other. There was also a mural that functioned as a public service announcement. It exhorted women to get regular pap smears for early detection of cervical cancer. I will take some pictures when the light is better.

Day 175, 3-30-2008

kt: 142, ta: 2658, gps: N 12° 26.206' W 86° 52.535'

I feel like I have been going through my own personal Trials of Hercules recently with the exploding tires and knife-fights and all. Today was no different. Before I left Estelí for Leon, a man told me that there was a more direct route to Leon that was all dirt road. He also told me that the main road to Leon had a lot of pot holes. I told him that I would prefer the road with potholes if there was pavement. I was second guessing my decision after I was actually on this road. It was mostly potholes and not much of a road. Combined with the fact that it was ridiculously hot and I there weren't any places to eat, it was a pretty hard day. I ate mostly cookies and almonds and must have drunk about 8 liters of water. I drank another 2 liters of soda on top of that. I used a sugar rush to ride the last 30 kilometers to Leon. I sweated so much that there were salt stains in my T-shirt. On top of the 140+ kilometers in 100 degree heat that I rode, I had to ride about a half kilometer through thick smoke from the fires that farmers set using slash-and-burn agriculture. I am going to enjoy the next few days in Leon.

Day 176 to 184, 3-31-2008 to 4-8-2008

I stayed in Leon

kt: 93, ta: 2386, gps: N 12°08.692' W 86°16.914'

I stayed in Managua

kt: 48.1, ta: 2109, gps: N 11°55.905' W 85°57.414'

I took the ferry to Ometepe Island

After traveling through Mexican colonial towns, Central American colonial towns seem pretty unimpressive. These cities have always been poorer, and hence, have less interesting colonial architecture. Moreover, it seems like every Central American town has been destroyed, at least once, by an earthquake. Granada, Nicaragua has been destroyed by pirate raids. That being said, I stayed multiple days in Leon because it is very hot and I was comfortable in the place that I was staying. I didn't do anything special; I just lazed around and did mundane things like file my taxes and watch movies. The main highlight of my stay in Leon was meeting yet another cyclist who is on his way to Southern Argentina. His name is Eric. He is from California and he left from Northern Alaska nine months ago.

The other highlight of my stay was the food. Though it is not quite as good as food from Mexico, its an improvement over from Guatemala and Honduras. I enjoyed manuelitas, which are like pancakes wrapped around cheese, and the tortas de lechuga, which is rice and beef wrapped in lettuce and then pan grilled.

I finally broke free from Leon and headed to Managua. I rode 90 kilometers starting at noon. On the road, I saw a pedestrian who looked like they had been killed by an overly aggressive bus driver. This seemed kind of ironic to me because, if anything, the drivers in Nicaragua seem to be infinitely more polite than other Latin American drivers. I even had taxi drivers yield the right of way to me. I was stunned. I think that this probably has something to do with the fact that the police actually enforce traffic laws here. Police even used radar detectors on the main highway into Managua.

It is really hot in Nicaragua. It feels like an eternal Texas summer. I am well accustomed to the heat but it, nevertheless, saps my energy. I find myself staying in cities for extra time just so I can watch T.V. shows about spoiled, selfish Americans spending thousands of dollars, so a plastic surgeon can suck minuscule amounts of fat out of them. I can't help but wonder about how the average Nicaraguan who is struggling to survive feels about Americans when they see these shows.

My guidebook says that Nicaragua is the second poorest country in the western hemisphere after Haiti. This isn't immediately apparent until you reach Managua. There are shanty towns constructed in the cities public parks, the roads have no labels, and there are holes that drop all the way into the city's sewer system as if people stole the lids and sold them for scrap metal. The poverty is not concentrated in any part of the city, because it is entirely decentralized, after having been destroyed more than once by earthquakes. The working poor of America have nothing on the working poor of Nicaragua. I would like to see an American survive by selling bags of water for ten cents each. As long as these conditions exist in Latin America there will always be illegal immigrants coming to the U.S. no matter how high we build a fence, nor how many laws we pass against them.

I spent several days in Managua running errands which proved to be quite tedious, due to the lack of proper road markings. I purchased a needle and thread to sew my tire back together if need be, sent a form to the I.R.S., and extended my visa in the immigration office.

Bureaucracy is the worst form of oppression. I would rather have my eyes gouged out by birds, take a tazer to the balls, or use sand paper as toilet paper. My personal version of Hell would be just like that of Sisyphus, but instead of having a rock to roll up a hill, only for it to roll down again, I would have a form that needed to be notarized an infinite number of times in an infinite number of government agencies. That being said, I thought I would be able to get my visa extension in about an hour which apparently was unrealistic, because that would be some kind of bureaucratic record. Not only did the clerk quit helping me to check text messages, but she actually left one line in a document unsigned so she could go eat lunch. I just said, "Fuck it." and went to go eat lunch myself. If I ever run amok I'll make sure to do it at some sort of bureaucratic office and only kill bureaucrats. The experience was so aggravating that I decided to stretch my errands out to two days instead of one.

I eventually left Managua for a one-day stop at Granada and the onward to the Island of Ometepe. I have heard good things about this place so I hope that I won't be disappointed.

Day 191, 4-15-2008

kt: 30.8, ta: 970, gps: N 11°26.614' W 85°49.566'

My gear and body are going through some wear-and-tear. The valve on my camel-back has a hole the size of a bird's eye, rendering it useless and forcing me to divert my trip through San Jose, Costa Rica to find a new valve or, if necessary, a new bladder. I can carry the same amount of water but I have to stop to drink it now.

I had a case of athlete's foot that turned into painful blisters between my toes and then a bacterial infection. I have finally solved this problem by lazing around my hotel room and only wearing flip-flops so my feet could breathe. Since I am going to go back to exclusively camping in Costa Rica, I figured it would be best to solve this problem now. I don't want to get my feet amputated because I have gangrene (I'm far from having gangrene).

While in Ometepe, I hiked to the top of the taller of the two twin volcanoes named Concepción. I managed to save $20 by refusing to hire a guide. After the fact, one of the guides practically begged me to tell other travelers that it was impossible to hike to the top without a guide. Seeing that it was his bread-and-butter, I acceded to this request. I would not particularly recommend this to the general traveler anyway because the trail is relatively dangerous and if you got hurt you might be stuck there for a couple of days. I however, am not stupid and have a G.P.S. device, making it nigh impossible to get lost.

The trail was steep and very rocky meaning that it was actually harder to descend than ascend. I conquered the mountain only to see a cloud-obscured sulfurous pit at the top and to be humbled later on.

During the descent I had to step very carefully because there was always the danger of losing my footing or getting my feet wedged between rocks and stumbling forward, thereby breaking my ankles. I descended slowly, stopped a lot, and planned almost every step. By the time I got to the bottom, I was stumbling forward and my legs were trembling from having to balance backward on such a steep slope. As an added treat, my quadriceps stiffened up over the next few days to the point that it hurt to walk or get up from a lying or seated position. The spasms were so bad that it hurt when I barely touched them. I looked like an old man inching around with muscle spasms in my legs and blisters between my toes. I am better now and my feelings of youthful immortality have returned.

While recovering from my various ailments, I mostly found myself lying in a hammock and reading or watching movies with the hotel crew. Oh what a thrill it was to see the retro-futuristic dystopian shoot-em-up Robocop dubbed in Spanish. I actually remember going to see that movie in the theaters when I was kid. It actually made me start thinking about the present state of the world. The prices of food and fuel (they are related) have been marching inexorably upward for the past year while we are most likely about to enter into a multi-year recession caused by the bursting of the international housing bubble. There are food riots in Haiti and road blockades in Managua to protest rising fuel prices. The Chinese and the Indians want to drive their cars everywhere and eat meat every meal just like the Americans and in doing so are proving just how unsustainable our lifestyle is with a planet of only six billion people on it. I hate to think about how bad these problems will be in 2050 when the world's population is projected to reach 9 billion people. In a few decades the Detroit City of Robocop will seem quaint compared to the reality. Make sure to stop and smell the roses now while you can, before global warming kills all of the rose bushes.

Day 192, 4-16-2008

kt: 59.1, ta: 2383, gps: N 11°03.142' W 85°37.565'

This morning when I woke up there was a man who had just gotten his passport and $600 stolen from the people he was sharing his room with. I think he was Costa Rican. I felt sorry for him because he was in a bad situation but I also feel like he could have been more careful. If I am in a shared room I sleep holding my wallet and passport, and my knife is never farther away than arm's reach. You can never be too careful.

I crossed into Costa Rica today. It was surprisingly more annoying getting out of Nicaragua than getting into Costa Rica. I had to stand in line and wait for the immigration officer to give me my exit stamp whereas when I got to the Costa Rican immigration office, I didn't have to wait in line or pay any money for my entrance exam. I have become a veteran border crosser at this point in my journey.

Costa Rica is supposed to be a lot better off than Nicaragua. This is not immediately apparent as you cross the border but becomes more so once you go further inland. The houses are constructed more or less like they are in the U.S. and not made of mud and scrap metal like they often are in Honduras or Nicaragua. There seem to be more trees than are on the isthmus in Nicaragua, but it is still hot and dry which should change as I enter more highly elevated land soon.

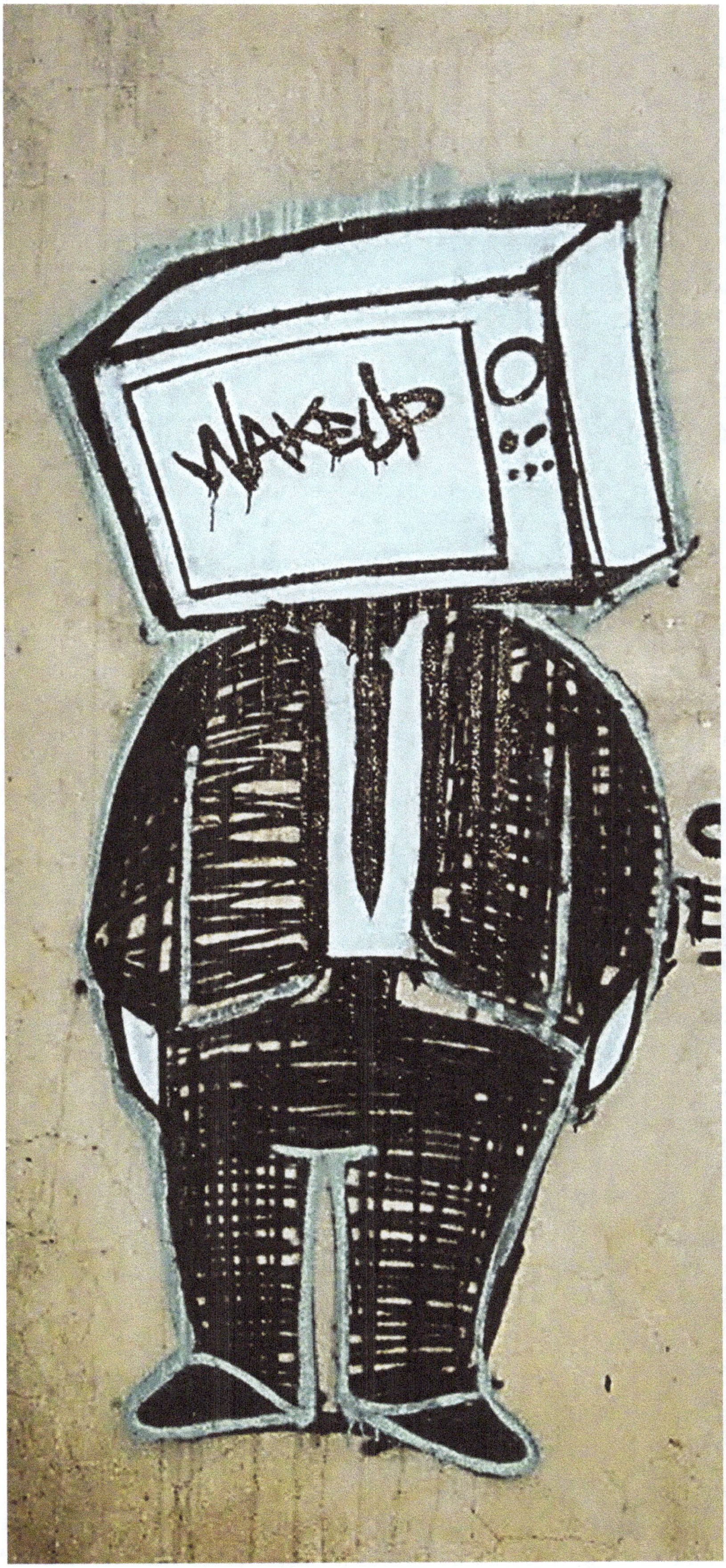
WAKEUP

La ignorancia es el peor pecado de un pueblo, y la mejor ARMA para un caudillo........

La vida dá vueltas..... y de ti depende que tu INTEGRIDAD esté intacta...

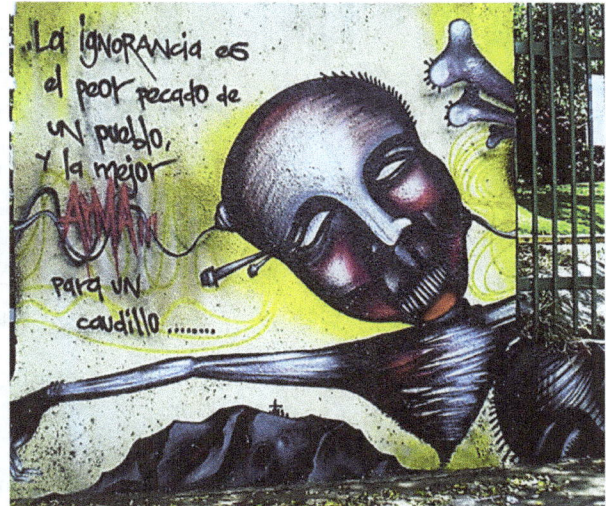

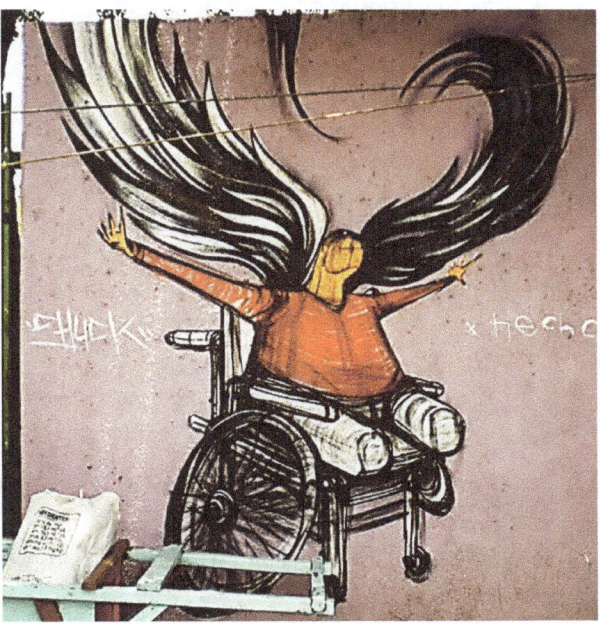

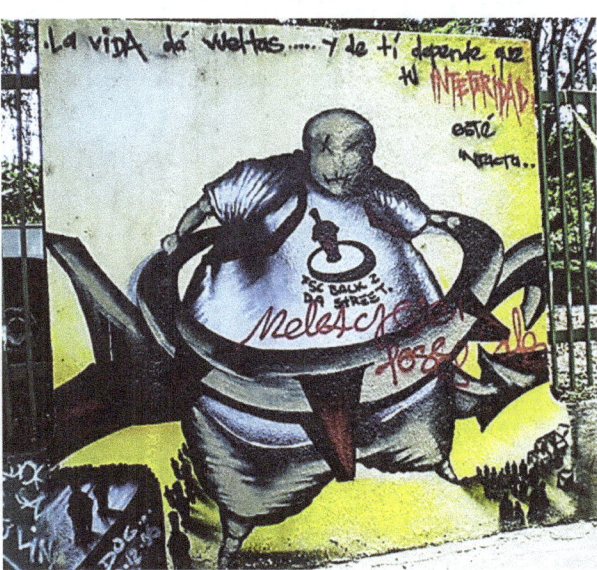

This morning, the morning before I left Rivas, Nicaragua, I went to the marketplace to eat breakfast. There was a crazy homeless man who seemed to get his kicks by touching people on the back of the neck. When he tried to do it to me earlier, I just turned around and said, "No!," thinking that he was trying to ask me for money. I don't like being touched by strangers at all.

Later that I realized that this was how he amused himself. I felt bad entertaining myself with his insanity but I couldn't help but laugh while watching the reactions of different people. Some people just ignored him and continued walking while others slapped his hand away.

The funniest moment is when a man reared back in a boxer's stance to fight him. When I asked some ladies at the bus station next to the marketplace what was wrong with him they told me he had smoked too much crack. Oh well, I guess he brought this on himself.

Day 193, 4-17-2008

kt: 82.8, ta: 1966, gps: N 10°31.544' W 85°15.755'

It was surprisingly cold when I woke up this morning. I was, after all, in the lowlands where it is quite hot during the day. The reason for the chilliness was the strong wind that was blowing from the mountains to my east towards the sea to my west. There were times when the wind was so strong that I had to ride diagonally just to ride straight and keep myself from being blown off the road.

My previous two days were meant to be light, therapeutic days to stretch out my still tight quadriceps. This definitely did the trick. I feel good as new and I could have conceivably ridden another 60 kilometers today if I hadn't taken my four hour lunch and Internet break.

I have seen a lot of people riding nice bikes here. This leads me to think that I should have no problem replacing my camel-back and finding new bike tires. I think that I will save this errand for San Jose as I am getting along fine with these tires right now.

Day 194, 4-18-2008

kt: 51.4, ta: 4372, gps: N 10°26.272' W 84°56.836'

Though beautiful in many places, the entire country of Costa Rica seems to be one giant tourist trap. The citizens of Costa Rica have devised numerous ways to get gringo money. I even see signs, in English, advertising time shares. Everything here is at least 50% more expensive than the rest of Latin America except, maybe, the Internet cafes. For this reason, I have decided to camp the whole way except for when I am in San Jose looking for bike supplies. Fortunately for me, there seem to be laws governing the offset between the highway and fences. I haven't had any problem finding good hiding places.

I spent most of my day charging up a hill, into a headwind. I knew I was in trouble when I saw a wind farm on top of the hill. I have a feeling that I am going to be charging into this headwind for the next couple of days.

The part of Costa Rica that I am traveling through is cowboy country through and through. When I stopped in the town of Tilaran, they even had some kind of horse parade. All the horses were trimmed and made-up while the men and women were wearing their cowboy best.

I decided to call an early day, not because I was tired, but because I liked the spot where I was at. My original plan was to ride to a hotel close to the bio-reserve of Monteverde, and use it as a base of operations to explore the park. My new plan is to ride to the park and back. I don't trust the accuracy of the Lonely Planet anymore, and I won't be gouged by a local hotel.

When I was riding up a hill today I found a new treasure: it is a motorcycle helmet, not one of those full-face helmets, but one that only covers the top of my head and has spikes on it. It has a faded sticker on it that says, "Ride it like you stole it." I usually don't like helmets but this one makes me look like a post-apocalyptic bandit in a Mad Max movie. Hell yeah!

Day 195, 4-19-2008

kt: 23.3, ta: 3196, gps: N 10°21.222' W 84°52.217'

I woke up with a sore throat, and afraid that I was coming down with a cold. This is not the greatest way to feel before you enter a dirt road. The useless Lonely Planet, of course, doesn't mention that it is an unpaved road. There are all sorts of travel trips for gay travelers, but none for cyclists. The funny thing is, I haven't met a single openly gay traveler, but I have met nine other cyclists. I am happy that there are tips for gay travelers; I just wish that they indicated unpaved roads on their maps.

The feeling crappy and riding on the dirt road, was all worth it, because I saw one of those gorgeous green-beaked toucans. Parrots are as common as pigeons, and monkeys are as common as squirrels, but toucans are relatively rare and elusive. Maybe some time shortly, I will get to see a quetzal. That would be something.

Days 196 to 198, 4-20-2008 to 4-22-2008

kt: 32.4, ta: 3252

I stayed in Tilaran

kt: 12.5, ta: 1145, gps: N 10°31.245' W 84°57.724'

I still wasn't feeling super-great on the day that I was supposed to go to Monteverde. Because of this, I ended up stopping and turning around about 8 kilometers before I got to the park. I was just going to turn around anyway and I was getting tired of the crappy dirt road. I had reached a point in the road where I couldn't start back up after I had stopped to take a rest. There are not a lot of things that are as frustrating as losing your traction while going up a 15° dirt road. I had already seen a green-beak toucan, a green toucanette, and some pretty scenery so I was happy.

Going back towards Tilaran was a lot easier due to the fact that the head wind was now a tailwind. The wind was so strong that there was actually one part of the road where I accelerated uphill without pedaling.

I still felt a little funky when I reached Tilaran, so I decided to stay at a hotel for a day. I had a slight fever and a runny nose so resting seemed like a good idea. When I took a shower, an entire river of dirt flowed off of my skin into the drain. It was satisfying to be clean again.

When I finally made it out of Tilaran today, another screw in my bike rack jiggled loose, and caused me to turn right back around. I found one screw but the other was missing and I thought it would be better to deal with this while I was close to civilization. I think that I had been missing one screw for a while because I noticed a strange feeling whenever I stood up while going uphill a couple of days earlier, but I couldn't figure out what was wrong with my bike. Since I often spend entire days on my bike, I am quite attuned to weird sounds and feelings,

but I can't always figure out what is causing them. I stopped and checked my bike many times but didn't notice the screw was missing until today. This was an easy problem to fix, but it delayed my leaving the city even longer.

I am camped right now on top of a hill in someone's ranch. How can I not camp at a place like this, when they make it so easy to enter their property, by giving me gates? Anyway, I plan to get up early tomorrow and leave before anyone notices anything. If there were no clouds, I would have an unobstructed view of Mount Arenal, the most active volcano in Costa Rica.

Day 199, 4-23-2008
kt: 71.8, ta: 4038, gps: N 10°28.731' W 84°56.200'

I rode along the northern edge of Arenal for most of the day today. There was a lot of tree cover so I didn't have to deal with the fierce headwind but the hills did add up. There were many signs, in English, proudly proclaiming the area as Costa Rica's "Lake Tahoe". Yuck!!

I saw so many "For Sale" signs, and ads for realtors, that I couldn't help but wonder if Costa Rica was going through a housing bust of its own. The lake isn't that great in my opinion. I would much rather live along Lake Atitlan in Guatemala than here. The only active draws here are the jungle wildlife and the very active Arenal which constantly puts on nighttime lava shows.

I saw more toucans today. I was also finally able to take a good picture of a monkey. He was perched on a branch right off of the road, just at eye level. When I got my camera out he just stayed there calmly while I shot my picture. That will never happen again.

When I was riding by the volcano, it started smoking real heavily. This excited me because I thought I was going to witness a major eruption and I have always wanted to see one. I didn't want to see anything of Krakatau magnitude, but I did want to hear explosions and feel the earth tremble. Alas, it was not meant to be. By the time I stopped my bike to take a picture; the angry volcano had relaxed a bit and was no longer pumping out large amounts of ash. Maybe, I will get to see something like this in South America.

After I arrived in the town of Fortuna, Costa Rica, I was very surprised to run into Sjaak, the very first cycle tourist whom I met in Zacatecas, Mexico. I thought he would be well into South America by now. I felt bad that I had to cut our conversation short, but the sun was about to set and I had to get out of the tourist-trap town. It is always a bad sign if you are in a Spanish speaking country and yet, all the signs are in English. There are also lots of expensive looking hotels with views of the volcano along the road. I got out of the city with about 30 minutes to spare, and am now camped on the edge of some kind of orchard. I cannot identify the trees which have all been planted in rows here. Maybe they bear some kind of nut. Anyway, I would have a good view of Arenal if it wasn't shrouded in clouds, again.

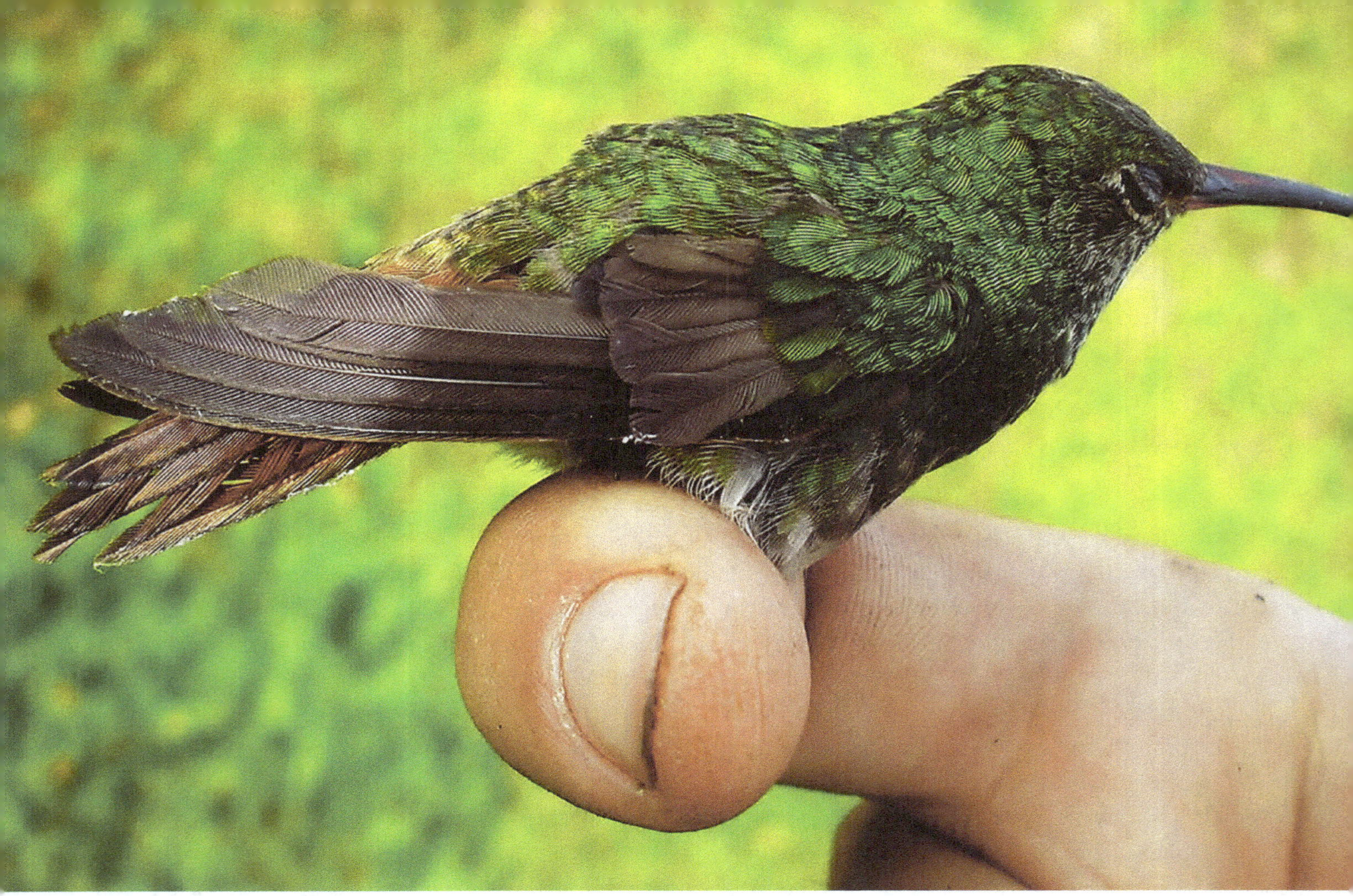
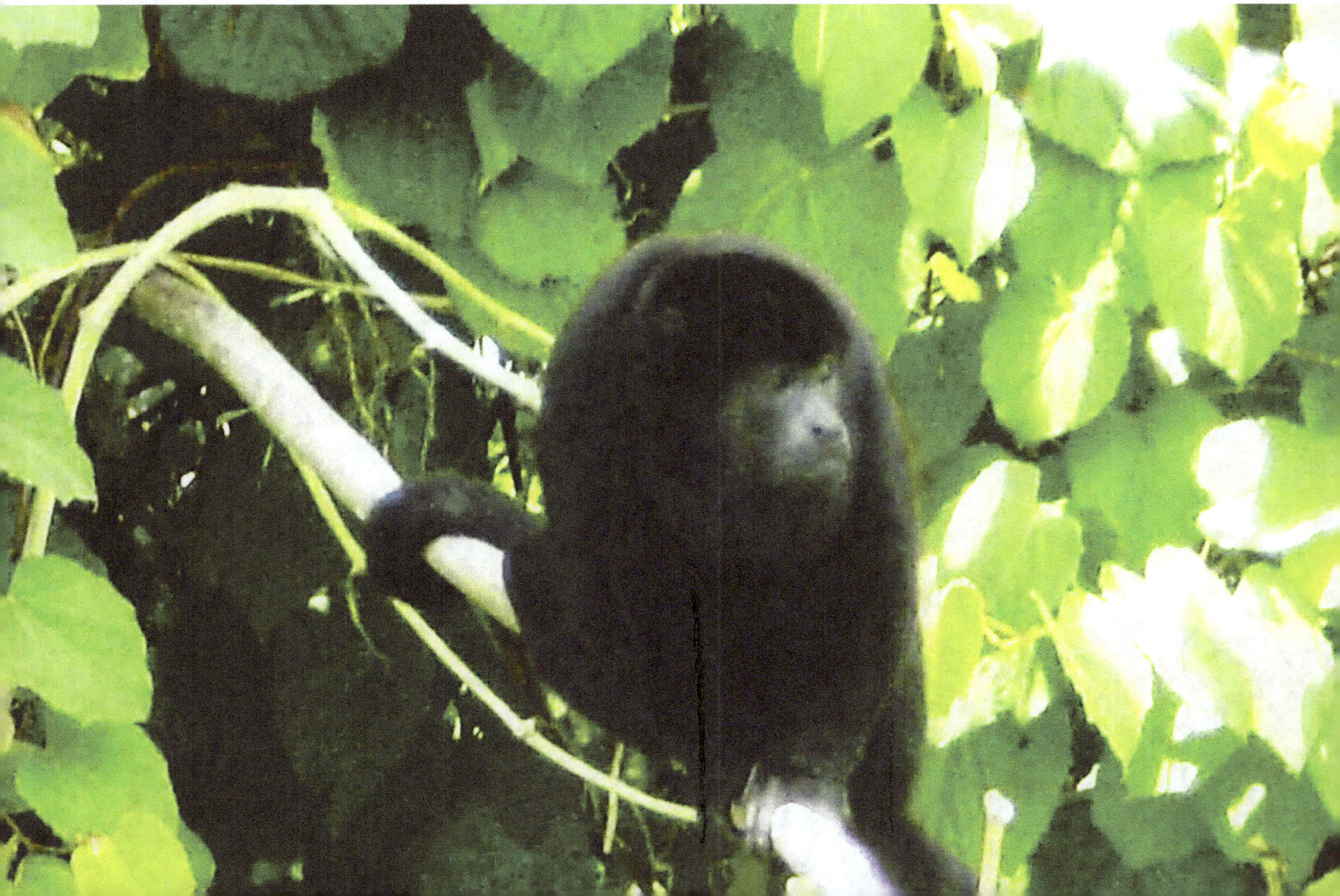

Hitchhiking and Knife-Fighting, & To South America Part II

Day 201, 4-24-2008

kt: 69.5, ta: 3615, gps: N 10°20.794' W 84°14.678'

I have been slacking off recently, but I have a nice punishment planned for tomorrow: I get to start my day off with at least 5,000 feet of ascent. Woo hoo! The mountains to my south look imposing and intimidating, being cloaked in clouds. A number of people tried to give me directions for an easier way to San Jose from Ciudad Quezada, but I paid them no heed because I would rather suffer a little and go on the more scenic, mountainous route.

There were a bunch of red-winged blackbirds on the side of the road today. They are supposed to migrate as far north as Texas but I have never seen one there before. Right now, I am camped above the Rio Toro underneath the bridge that passes over it. The rapids here have the muddy appearance of volcano run-off. The water has stained the rocks on the edge a coffee color. It really makes me want to take up kayaking.

Days 202 to 204, 4-25-2008 to 4-27-2008

kt: 74.2, ta: 7395, gps: N 9°56.277' W 84°04.480'

I stayed in San Jose

kt: 14.8, ta: ???, gps: N 9°50.927' W 84°04.976'

Near the beginning of my day riding towards San Jose, I found a hummingbird on the side of the road. It actually willingly perched on my finger when I went to pick it up. If it was sick, I didn't want it to die the undignified death of being splattered by a semi. Eventually, after I tried to get it to perch on a barbed wire fence, it flew off on its own as if nothing were wrong.

I knew that I was going to have to pay for my sin of sloth and boy, did I suffer. I actually ascended more in one day than I have ever done before. There were several times when I had to stop and ring about a pint of sweat out of my shirt. Despite my suffering, the ride was beautiful. The whole area between the town of San Miguel and San Jose is mostly undeveloped cloud forest. There is some development along the side of the road, but it is mostly untouched. I even passed by a couple of pristine waterfalls that are right next to the road.

I didn't get to San Jose until after nightfall because of my all-day-long ascent. Arriving in a large metropolitan area at night is not my favorite thing to do, but it is a necessary evil sometimes. I had to come to San Jose because I needed to look for replacement parts for my bike and camel-back. I did manage to find the hostel where I wanted to stay but not without riding through some sketchy areas of town filled with the usual suspects of glue-sniffers and thuggish looking people.

The place where I stayed is called Tranquilo Backpackers. It is in downtown San Jose and was a pretty good value for my $10 a night. They whip up a bunch of pancake batter every morning for all of the guest to make their own pancakes. It is kind of fun to see the disasters that some people cook up. They have free Internet and the first steel-stringed guitars that I have seen in all of Latin America. Most importantly, they have a kitten. I could see myself being comfortable at this place for a while but that $10 can add up fast.

As usual, I didn't actually leave the city until real late. I discovered some loose screws with stripped nuts that I felt that I had to replace. This of course, took more time to do than I anticipated because it was hard to remove the old screw. I also promised a guy from Singapore that I would fetch a pair of sunglasses for him because he liked the pair that I had just purchased.

That being said, I barely made it to the city. I am now camped in a banana/coffee plantation, hoping that I don't get discovered. Because I am crazy and a glutton for punishment, I think I am going to ride straight through the highest part of the country over the next couple of days.

Days 205 to 206, 4-28-2008 to 4-29-2008

kt: 16.1, ta: 1744, gps: N 9°46.527' W 84°04.247'

kt: 18.1, ta: 2796, gps: N 9°44.596' W 83°58.337'

I haven't traveled much in the last few days but I did read over 300 pages of a book to finish it. I've become a voracious reader on this trip. I have probably tripled the number of books that I have read since I graduated college four years ago. I have been reading so much that it has slowed me down every time I have a good book.

The mountains where I am at are covered in coffee plantations. If they aren't covered in coffee plantations they are covered in cloud forests. It is mostly cool and misty where I am at right now. I might top out at over 10,000 feet tomorrow, so I expect it to be downright cold. I will probably have to dig out my cold weather gear. I am already wearing my full length bicycle tights.

Yesterday, I passed the satellite dish that I believe scientists use to try to communicate with extraterrestrial life forms. It was huge, at least 50 feet across. Shortly afterwards, I saw a turquoise-browed motmot. It has a funny name but it is a beautiful bird. It is the national bird of Nicaragua but they live in Costa Rica, too.

My flashlight has become my latest gear casualty. It barely gives off any light at all and bleeds the battery after I turn it off. I don't think that there is a single piece of gear that I can't destroy on a bicycle tour.

Days 207 to 208, 4-30-2008 to 5-1-2008

kt: 89.4, ta: 4890, gps: N 9°22.461' W 83°42.183'

kt: 32.9, ta: 1075, gps: N 9°15.296' W 83°30.427'

Yesterday, I climbed to the top of el Cerro de la Muerte which means the Hill of Death. It seems like a pretty ironic name since the place is overgrown with plant life. I topped out just 8 feet shy of 11,000 feet. Even in the tropics, it is cold above 10,000 feet. The rain didn't make things any better. It was misty all morning but it actually started raining about 4 hours before sunset.

I had finally figured out a comfortable clothing arrangement until it started to rain. I kept my torso covered while I allowed my body to cool through my bicycle tights. The rain fucked that arrangement up. I was able to stay warm until I started to descend, but once I started, I got real cold, real fast. I had to stop at a restaurant and have some hot soup and hot tea. I didn't want to get hypothermia. I also put on some extra winter gear for the remaining descent.

The 8,500 feet of descent might have been a lot more fun if the roads weren't slick, and if I wasn't cold and wet. I had to hold onto my brakes the whole time, just to prevent myself from sliding out. I used my brakes so much that I had to stop just to give my hands a rest every once and a while. If the conditions were dryer, I would have zoomed down the entire mountain at 50+ kilometers per hour and would have had a hell of a time doing it.

The whole area that I rode through has an almost enchanted feeling. All of the forests here are as green as can be. Plants grow on plants, which grow on other plants. Occasionally a view of the mountainside, with clouds rolling up the hills, would open up. If I wasn't so cold and wet, I would have been mesmerized by the beauty. I pretty much decided that I was going to ride all the way to the town of San Isidro, Costa Rica, named for the patron saint of farmers. I wanted to stay in a hotel as soon as it started raining. Unfortunately, the sun set before I got there. All those years of riding my bike at night, ninja-style without

any lights or reflectors paid off, as I was able to successfully navigate the highway and avoid vehicles.

I only got a half-day of riding in, as I got enmeshed in the comforts of the city, as I have a tendency to do. With about three hours to go until the sun set, it started raining again. Rather than tough it out, I decided to set up camp early. I really get tired of waking up with wet shoes. Hopefully, I can make it to Panama with minimal rain.

Day 209, 5-2-2008
kt: 71.1, ta: 2321, gps: N 8°57.815' W 83°08.993'

I rather enjoyed a nice leisurely ride through many miles of virgin rain forests today. My favorite part was when the road followed the red-clay colored Rio General. There was even one spot where two twin 200-foot waterfalls flowed into the river. While I was relaxing by the waterfalls, I saw a coati. I should cross into Panama tomorrow. I am expecting more mountains and more cloud-forests. The road from San Miguel to San Jose, and then from San Jose to San Vito on the border, have been two of the more scenic routes that I have followed.

I read in the news that an Arkansas resident is going to give birth for the eighteenth time. I am disgusted, I don't care if the family is debt free. The average American consumes 32 times more resources than the average person in the developing world. Since the world's farmers sell their crops to the highest bidder, people like those are the reason that Haitian children eat mud.

I have also been thinking about Barack Obama's former pastor, the Reverend Jeremiah Wright. I think he is taking it a little far to say that there is a conspiracy to kill black people with A.I.D.S. but I think he has a point when he says terrorists attack us because we commit acts of terrorism. When our government assassinates a Somali warlord we say it is a necessary strategic elimination. When Hezbollah assassinates a Lebanese leader, we say it is terrorism. When we secretly fly someone to a country that uses torture and don't allow them to communicate with anyone, we call it extreme rendition. When the F.A.R.C. kidnaps someone and holds them for ransom we call it terrorism. I am not saying that these are not terrorist acts; I am saying that we commit terrorist acts, too. There can be no double standards. All is fair in love and war and war is hell. For every terrorist action there is an equal/greater terrorist reaction.

Day 210, 5-3-2008
kt: 51.3, ta: 4355, gps: N 8°49.079' W 82°51.783'

I planned to cross the border into Panama today but my plans were thwarted by dirt roads and rain. When I arrived at the border, the immigration offices for both countries were already closed.

Just to prove that things operate differently here in Latin America, I am camped at the police station. I asked permission and they said yes. I could have easily crossed into Panama illegally, but I am not anxious to find out what kind of bureaucratic delays this could cause. I plan to get my exit and entry stamps when I wake up tomorrow.

The rear hub on my bicycle is loose and it is making me nervous. If it wasn't a sealed hub, I would swear that I needed to re-grease and repack the bearings. My wheel jiggles from side to side. I can feel the play in the wheel whenever I go uphill. Hopefully, I will be able to tighten my hub and solve this problem tomorrow morning. If not, I can add sealed hubs to the growing list of bicycle parts that I have ruined in my eleven years as a bicycle commuter. I should be able to make it to David, Panama soon, where I should be able to get a new hub.

Day 211, 5-4-2008
kt: 54.8, ta: 4564, gps: N 8°40.140' W 82°37.916'

When I woke up this morning, I had to wait for the Costa Rican and Panamanian immigration offices to open, so I played with my rear wheel. I managed to tighten the two bolts on the outside of the wheel and this solved my jiggly wheel problem, but now it doesn't seem to spin as well. I think I am going to have to replace the hub.

I had to wait an extra hour for the Costa Rican immigration office to open. Even though the buildings are no more than 200 feet apart, they operate in different time zones. That was no problem, I just went and ate breakfast while I waited. It cost me $25 to enter Panama, about $20 more than I expected. I might as well throw my fucking useless Lonely Planet away because, although it is the newest addition, it is thoroughly outdated by the time it is published. This fortunately was no problem because I expected to have to pay the Costa Rican immigration office $26 and didn't have to pay anything. I should have plenty of money to make it to David, Panama.

Speaking of money, although the Panamanian standard of living is high, Panama does not suffer from the scourge of tourists like Costa Rica does. I immediately realized that the food was about 33% cheaper than in Costa Rica; it is better too. I probably rode through my last Central American rain forest today. It is replete with exotic plants, wildlife, and waterfalls cascading down cliffs on the side of the road. Tomorrow I should enter the Pacific lowlands where I expect to see a bunch of boring farms and ranches. Oh well, I should be in Colombia soon.

Day 212, 5-5-2008

kt: 70.2, ta: 1247, gps: N 8° 24.038' W 82°12.816'

Rain has been the story of my last week. It has rained 5 out of the last 6 days. It rained real hard today, I think that the rainy season is beginning. I remember when a friend of mine from high school and I would trade irreverent jokes. I would say, "When it rains, God is pissing on us,", and he would reply, "It only rains when the angels masturbate!" Ancient cultures prayed to the rain gods, but I wonder if the nomadic tribes were among them. Rain is great when you are inside by the fire and you have crops planted but not so great if you are on the back of a horse or on foot in an open plain with no trees. All the rain does then, is makes you cold and wet.

I have been a waterlogged nomad for the last week. At 11,000 feet, I had to take precautions against hypothermia. I also had to hold my brakes while riding downhill so my wheels wouldn't lock up and slide out from underneath me. A slide-out at 50 kilometers per hour can be deadly and, at the very least, could break my hip.

It only seems to rain when I'm climbing mountains, and its uncomfortable to wear rain gear, because of all the sweating underneath it. From now on, I'm going to do most of my riding before the afternoon, when the rain comes in the tropics. I am camped underneath a bridge right now, which means that I won't have to use my rain fly for my tent, and I'll wake up dry and happy.

Day 213, 5-6-2008
kt: 96.6, ta: 4133, gps: N 8°12.151' W 81°30.575'

I read in the news that the Vatican has given its official approval for the belief in extraterrestrial life forms, now if only it could approve of contraception...

It didn't rain today and for that I am grateful, but man was it humid. The air was so dense dense with moisture that it actually started drizzling without there being a cloud in the sky. I have actually seen this phenomenon a couple of times in Costa Rica as well. It did not rain but it might as well have, because my shirt, bike shorts, and socks were completely soaked with sweat. To make matters worse, I've developed a rash, caused by the excessive moisture and friction, in a sensitive and unmentionable area. All I can do is apply a lot of ointment to it.

Aside from the heat and humidity, I actually had a good day. I discovered a distinct form of Panamanian music called cantadera. When I heard the music, I had one of those reactions where I geeked out, and starting asking as many questions as possible about it. I plan to do some more investigation and buy some pirated CDs soon.

Day 214, 5-7-2008
kt: 103, ta: 2653, gps: N 8°08.214' W 80°41.078'

I had two wildlife highlights today: I saw a large butterfly with purple wings, and a live snake. I have seen plenty of snake roadkill but this is surprisingly, the first live snake that I have seen in Latin America. I did not see if it was a pit viper nor did I try to find out. I am not particularly afraid of snakes, but I am wise enough to let them run, since I do not carry anti-venom as part of my medical kit. Generally, if you make any noise at all when you walk, and watch where you step, you won't have any problem with snakes.

After I passed through Santiago, Panama today, the land flattened out and I had a nice strong tailwind. I was flying. If the land remains flat tomorrow, and I have the same tailwind, I might try to ride the entire 215 kilometers to Panama City. That is a big "if" though. If anything, I would like to ride over a hundred kilometers tomorrow, so I can get to Panama City before nightfall the next day.

Days 215 to 217, 5-8-2008 to 5-10-2008
kt: 64.9, ta: 1376, gps: N 8°30.834' W 80°20.954'
I stayed in Penonome
kt: 60.5, ta: 1520, gps: N 8°29.871' W 79°57.482'

Whenever I plan on a long day, something always ruins it. The strong tailwind shifted into a strong headwind, I had several flat tires, and my rash graduated from being merely irritating, to being painful.

I had the opportunity to learn how to sew my tires shut, when the steel wire that gives my tire form separated from the rubber in another spot. At first, it was frustrating trying to figure out the proper stitching, but I eventually figured it out. My rear tire looks bad. Not only have I worn off the treads, but I can actually see the thread mesh poking through the rubber. I absolutely need to replace my rear tire in Panama City, it will not last much longer. I also need to replace my rear cassette, chain, and brake pads. I rode around Penonome for a while, looking for replacement tires, but to no avail.

My bike is not the reason I stopped in Penonome. My rash in the unmentionable place, let's just call it a saddle sore, became so painful that it hurt to ride my bike. There is only one cure for saddle sore: get off the saddle, and don't wear tight shorts. I rented a room in the cheapest hotel room that I could find, and spent a lot of time watching T.V. in my room naked. The day of rest helped me, and I can now ride my bike without grimacing in lots of pain.

Panama actually seems to have a culture distinct from other parts of Central America: children here play baseball instead of soccer; lots of men wear distinct straw hats, that look like cowboy hats curved upward at the front; and there seems to be a lot more racial diversity here. There are blacks on the Caribbean side of all Central American countries, and there are Asians in all of the big cities, but Panama has sizable minorities of both in all of the towns on the Panamerican highway. Another thing that I noticed is that most of the general stores and restaurants are owned by Asians. There also seem to be a larger number of indigenous people in Panama than in the other Central American countries, with Guatemala being the obvious exception. The Kuna Indians seem to have the most style, out of all the Indians I have seen in Central America. I really appreciate all this racial diversity. It all contributes to a very unique culture.

I saw several items in the news of interest to me. One is that there is a church of the Jedi in Great Britain. The entire religion is based on the philosophical musings of Yoda, and the rest of the Jedi Council from the Star Wars movies. George Lucas should be proud that he unintentionally spawned a new religion.

The other article that I saw stated that the average American wedding cost over $28,000. I was disgusted, that is so wasteful! To put it in context, I would like to show how much money this would be, if it were invested over a 50 year period at a 10% rate of return, which is doable. I estimated up to $30,000 to simplify matters. When I punched the number into an interest rate calculator, it ended up being over three and a half million dollars! Considering that most marriages in the U.S end up in divorce, I would rather keep the money. I would prefer to have a pepper spray enema, than marry one of these selfish gold diggers.

Days 218 to 224, 5-11-2008 to 5-17-2008
kt: 89.1, ta: 3025, gps: N 8°58.976' W 79° 31.494'
I stayed in Tilaran
I stayed in Panama City for five days

I made it into Panama City with a few problems, but nothing I couldn't handle. I had to fix a spoke and my rash came back. When I reached the Bridge of the Americas, a cop made me get off my bike and hitchhike across. I was ready to ride across, but the cops seem to frown on that. There are some gnarly looking ghettos on the other side of the bridge, but I didn't have any problems there.

I haven't done anything special here in Panama City. I've just rested and surfed the Internet a lot. One day, I rode down to the ghetto, and bought a pirated copy of the new Indiana Jones movie. The quality of the movie is terrible, but the credits were in French which makes me think that a person snuck a camera into the french Canne's film festival and filmed the premier. Go pirates!

My bike was hurting. I replaced the rear tire, rear cassette, chain, brake pads, and the rear hub. I am proud to say that this is the very first time that I have destroyed a hub, its a major accomplishment.

Panama City is a very cosmopolitan city. There are also a lot of very wealthy people here. I saw lots of people driving Maseratis and Porches. On the other side of town, people live in buildings that are crumbling around them. There don't seem to be any bona-fide shanty towns though. If you come to Panama City, you can hobnob with millionaires in the banking district, or hang out with rasta dudes in the ghetto.

The place I stayed at in Panama City is nice. It is called Zuly's Hostel. Zuly is an African-Panamanian goddess, who isn't but a year older than me. The beds were comfortable, the rooms quiet, and we had free Internet and cable. My only complaint is that she cracks down on pot smoking, but that is mainly to protect herself.

The day before I left Panama, I was sitting at a lunch stop, when two other cyclists from Colorado rode up in a truck taxi. They had to hurry to the town of Puerto Lindo, Panama because their boat was leaving the next day. Being faced with the opportunity to leave Panama the next day, rather than sit around for a week or more waiting for a boat, I put my bike in the back and rode with them to Puerto Lindo.

The names of the two riders are Ralph and Pat. They are a married couple from Colorado, who are taking two years to ride from Prudhoe Bay, Alaska to the southern tip of Argentina. Being a gearhead, I had a bicycle-induced orgasm when I saw their bikes. They have two titanium soft-tail bikes, with front suspension, and mechanical disk brakes. My bike is nice enough, but I was having very unfaithful thoughts when I saw theirs. They have ridden offroad some, their bikes can devour dirt roads.

Days 225 to 226, 5-18-2008 to 5-19-2008
I stayed in Panama City one more day
kt: 38.7, ta: 1309, gps: N9°13.286' W 79°37.579'

I finally broke away from the clutches of Panama City today. If I wanted to wait around for the rain to stop, I would probably have to wait around for several months, so I decided it was time to go, rain or shine. It is raining right now, and my campsite is at a government building. It is an agricultural inspection post to be precise. I didn't ask anyone permission to be there, I just set up my tent. A worker found me a little later, but he said it was okay. He even offered for me to set up my tent under a roof, but I was already unpacked, so I politely declined. If I were in the U.S., they would have called the cops, and I would have spent a night in jail.

Days 227 to 228, 5-20-2008 to 5-25-2008
kt: 42.9, ta: 1613, gps: N 9°36.043' W 79°35.283'
I was in the Caribbean Sea on a boat to Cartagena

I have heard a lot of horror stories about drunken captains, and un-seaworthy boats, so I wanted to go to port before I agreed to get on a boat. That being said, the boat ride to Cartagena was at times a little unpleasant, but it was mostly a hoot. The unpleasantness was entirely due to my day-long bout of seasickness, and not the captain or the boat. I was a little disappointed that we were motor-sailing but the wind wasn't strong enough for us to keep our schedule. There is only so much food and fresh water that you can carry on a boat.

Captain Mark was a gregarious guy, with a with a lovely Colombian wife young enough to be his daughter. He spends most of his time on his boat in the San Blas Islands, a Caribbean paradise south of the hurricane danger zone. He makes money by delivering goods to islanders, and other boaters anchored at the San Blas Islands, and taking backpackers from Panama to Cartagena and vice versa. It seems to me that he lives a pretty idyllic life, though I am not ready to give up tierra firma and follow in his footsteps just yet.

We stayed at the San Blas Islands, as Captain Mark's house guests, for most of the time we were on the boat. This place really is beautiful, with crystal-clear blue water, and abundant sea life. I spent most of my time snorkeling and reading. The reefs in the San Blas Islands are not as impressive as those in the Bay Islands of Honduras, but it still had an impressive array of sea life. I saw lots of barracudas, sting rays, and eagle rays to go along with many of the fish that I saw in Honduras. I also saw dolphins and squid. My boat mates saw sharks, but I wasn't so lucky. We ate well while we were anchored at the islands, so my memories of this place are all good.

A Plague of Mosquitoes, Trigger-Happy Cops, & Majestic Mountains

Day 233 to 235, 5-26-2008 to 5-28-2008

I stayed in Cartagena

There's something about the humidity in Central America that causes excessive rubber rot, because I had to sew my new/used rear tire back together the day before I left Panama. I miraculously found two more new/used tires at a bike shop in Cartagena. This miracle, which now seems to be on the Jesus-walking-on-water variety, has probably given me at least another several thousand kilometers before I have to worry about my tires again. I should be able to make it through Colombia at least, without having to buy more tires.

After five days at sea, we finally arrived in Cartagena, Colombia. Cartagena is one of the more popular tourist destinations in Colombia. I would describe it as a small island of beautiful colonial architecture and fortifications, surrounded by a sea of slums. The hotel where I am staying is cheap and upscale compared to what I have gotten used to in Central America, but there are plenty of sketchy people in its surroundings. I am spending a few days here getting used to Colombia and running some errands before I start pedaling again. At the hotel, I smoked a joint with another person staying in the hotel, for the first time in over a month.

I then went back to my room and watched cable T.V. Here in Latin America, some of the cable channels show cherry-picked reruns of the American cable channels. I saw "That's My Bush" and "Breaking Bad" for the first time. Maybe it was the fact that I was stoned for the first time in a long time, but these shows seemed brilliant. In That's My Bush, the president was going to celebrate the arrest of the 100 millionth War on Drugs criminal at a White House Press Conference, when he accidentally ingests a couple of ecstasy tablets. The press conference quickly degenerates into a rave, with the president dancing like a club kid, and being as cuddly as ever. In Breaking Bad, an underpaid science teacher decides he is going to make some extra money by cooking up methamphetamines. I love it when Hollywood mocks the government. As long as the government persists in its quixotic attempt to fight the War on Drugs, there will be plenty of fodder for the screenwriters to ridicule the government with.

Here I am in Colombia, the front line on the War on Drugs. This is the land of the F.A.R.C., A.U.C., E.L.N., Pablo Escobar, and the Medellin and Cali cartels. Narco-terrorism was invented here. That being said, drugs seem pretty readily available here. Even though I got a stern warning from Captain Mark, I could have easily carried drugs on board in the Caribbean Sea, if I were discrete. The sea to the north of Colombia is one of the most heavily policed bodies of water on this planet, but they can do anything to stop the flow of drugs. For every time they stop a ton of cocaine, ten tons are probably making it through. There are people who openly smoke pot on the street here, and I have been accosted on more than one occasion, by people selling a variety of drugs.

As a pot smoker, I am indignant at amount of effort that all the governments of the world expend keeping pot illegal. Cigarette smokers blithely walk down the street sucking on their cancer sticks, and throwing their cigarette butts wherever they want, while drunks beat their wives and kill people in traffic accidents, but I have to hide in the shadows and constantly look over my shoulders if I want to smoke a joint. There are so many addictions that are worse than marijuana. Cocaine and heroin are obvious, but there are so many addictions that are legal and that are worse. Have you ever met someone addicted to sniffing glue or huffing gasoline? It is not a pretty sight. How about someone who is addicted to prescription pills, gambling, or sloth?

The worst addiction of them all is the addiction to all the matierialistic "stuff" that seems to afflict most Americans, and spreads like a cancer to the rest of the world. This addiction lead to the housing bust afflicting America today. Americans wanting to finance their increasingly expensive lifestyle fell victim to the lure of easy money, and easy credit, to take out mortgages which they couldn't afford. When the times were flush, and the house prices were rising, we were able to flip our houses, or take out home equity loans, so we could buy bigger cars and more stuff than we could ever reasonably afford. Now the economy has been worsening and our lifestyle is being exposed as unsustainable. The Chinas and Indias of the world want their share of stuff too, leading to the rise in almost all commodity and food prices, so they

can live like westerners. Those poor kids from the slums of the world that grow up to become drug dealers don't do it so they can provide their families with financial security and health care, they want the bling. Maybe we should end the War on Drugs, and start fighting the War on Greed.

I don't smoke cigarettes, I almost never drink alcohol, I don't gamble, I don't snort coke, meth, or shoot speed, but I smoke pot, and ingest an occasional few grams of mushrooms. I am not some retarded, drug-addicted loser, who can't take care of his own business. I graduated college with a degree in math, while working my way through school, and I speak two, soon to be three languages. I paid off all of my loans before I graduated school, and have saved up a shitload of money because I have a simple lifestyle centered around not owning a car. I have a rule, where I don't buy anything on credit, and I usually don't buy anything that I can't carry on my bicycle. This eliminates a lot of useless shit.

People probably say, "You must live like a monk," but I don't. I eat well, go dancing, enjoy being with friends, making music, cooking food, and general merriment. I am currently traveling on the adventure of a lifetime, because I have been afforded the opportunity by my own personal responsibility. I think it is fun to smoke a whole bunch of pot and spend four hours cooking. I can't think of many things more fun, and spiritually rewarding, than taking a bunch of mushrooms and climbing a tree. I harm no one with these activities, not even myself, and I am pissed off that my government wants to say that I am a criminal for this behavior. I will be forever defiant, until the government ends its insane War on Drugs.

The drug problem is like a poison ivy rash. The more you scratch, it the worse it gets. It itches so bad but you have to resist scratching. You have to treat it intelligently by applying ointment to the affected areas. I understand the visceral reaction people get, when they see someone who has ruined their life because of their addiction.

I watched my own father ruin his life because of his drug addiction. He chose being an addict over being a father. He started out as just a user, but quickly graduated to selling drugs to feed his own habit. People think, "We should lock up all the people who sell these drugs and turn our children into addicts." They never think that these people are victims too. They never think that they are fathers, or mothers, and that they are somebody's child.

Like the person who scratches his poison ivy rash, the government only gets temporary relief by attacking the supply of drugs. It would do a lot better by attacking the root causes of drug addiction, such as social inequality and a lack of education and opportunity among abusers. Only when the government tries an intelligent solution rather than a reactionary temporary solution, will we be able to win the drug war.

The group of presidential candidates is a little bit narrower now, but none of them have any positive, proactive solutions for ending the War on Drugs. With that being said, I am going to announce my candidacy for 2016, when I will be old enough to run for president. I promise that I will gather the heads of the D.E.A. and all the respective leaders of the drug agencies from the rest of the world, and anyone else who is responsible for this mess we have gotten ourselves into. We will have a summit about the War on Drugs. I will bake special brownies, and harangue all these people for their asinine drug policies. Afterwards, I will have a shaman administer mushrooms to all them, so they can experience what it feels like to dissolve their ego for the very first time.

Days 235 to 237, 5-28-2008 to 5-39-2008
kt: 33.5, ta: 537, gps: N10° 38.400' W75° 24.352' '

kt: 94.1, ta: 2137, gps: N10° 56.539' W74° 49.980'

kt: 78, ta: 984, gps: N10° 21.390' W74° 52.263'

As I expected, I didn't leave Cartagena until late in the afternoon. I headed to Barranquilla with a very important mission; I was to take a picture of the giant Shakira statue for my mother. At about an hour before sunset on my first day back on the road, I stopped at a town called Arroyo de Canoas. The locals there were friendly, they offered me a place to stay for the night. I gratefully accepted, because I was being swarmed by bugs at the time, and wanted to get away from them. You could bathe in mosquito repellent, and they would still viciously swarm around you.

I stayed in the room of Jonaton, the family's 17-year-old son. He's a big fan of telenovelas, so I watched a few with him. Most telenovelas are made in Mexico, but Colombia has its own homegrown telenovela called "El Cartel." I'm glad someone figured out that the drama that goes on in a drug cartel would make a good soap opera.

I was off to Barranquilla the next day, ready to fulfill my mission. I was making good time, until my rear tire deflated. As I suspected, the flat was caused by my faulty tire repair.

I learned that the trick of sewing tires back together only works with cheap tires, because they have more rubber. The stitching held, but the tire ripped even more, causing the flat. Oh well, I still have a back-up tire.

Only an hour and a half remained until sunset by the time that I made it Barranquilla. I had gained some intelligence as to the whereabouts of the statue. It was, I was told, on the outskirts of the city at the Metropolitan Stadium. It was getting dark and I was hungry when I decided it was best to find some food and a place to stay. The mission could wait for the next day.

The place I where I was camped at was an abandoned house, close to a highway intersection. It was far enough from the road so that I didn't have to worry about being bothered. Abandoned houses are great places to camp in the countryside, but not so great in the city, because they become de facto public toilets. There were no shit stains on my tent when I woke up, and I was happy for this minor miracle.

Fortunately for me, the statue of Shakira was on the way to the highway to Medellin. It was not as impressive as I had hoped. I took a few pictures and took off.

It is hot, humid, and flat in this part of the country. There are ranches as far as the eye can see. Insects plague me everywhere I go. I can't wait to be in the mountains, but they don't start for another 300 kilometers. I would happily give up the flat terrain to be rid of insects.

Day 238, 5-31-2008

kt: 93.1, ta: 2646, gps: N9° 39.812' W75° 07.967'

Last night, I was unpleasantly awoken by a cop and four soldiers, when they shined the lights of their patrol truck on my partially obscured tent. I quickly put on my sweatpants and said, "Buenas noches," to indicate my friendly nature, but to no avail. The cop imperiously barked, "Venga aqui con las manos arriba." I apparently didn't come out of the bushes fast enough, for the cop then demanded, "Venga ahora!" several times. Since I didn't want to get shot, I quickly explained that I was unarmed, that I was barefoot and had to put on shoes, and that I had to unzip my tent which was hard to do in the dark. I held my hands high when I came out of the bushes, trying my best not to get shot. All four soldiers had their machine guns trained on me.

They let down their guard a little bit when they realized that they had their guns pointed at a half-naked, flip-flop wearing, gringo. The cop was still annoying though. He interrogated me for a few minutes as if he was trying to catch me in a lie. He told me that my name didn't sound American even though he was holding my passport. I told him that I was a fifth generation American, with a funny name. He asked me when and where I arrived, and told me that my passport had a different date stamped on it. I told him he probably was looking at my Panama exit stamp. (I checked later and I was right. He was indeed, looking at my exit stamp.) After I passed his interrogation, he directed me to a hotel and told me my campsite wasn't safe. I wanted to tell him that I felt safe until they pointed their fucking machine guns at me. Thanks Big Brother.

I went to the hotel and put my sleeping pad on the dining room floor as instructed by the hotel owner. He didn't charge me for this impromptu arrangement. I didn't want to unpack everything after I had been forced to repack it in the dark. The mosquitoes devoured me, but they started doing this during my ordeal with the law. I managed to get some sleep, but only after the hotel owner turned on the fan for me.

It is a good thing that I am pretty proficient with my Spanish, or this could have been an international incident. I figured that I would write down a few useful phrases for someone else who finds themselves in the same situation. "No tengo armas," means "I do not have any weapons." "No disparen," means "Don't shoot." "Venga aqui con las manos arriba," means "Come here with your hands up." Understanding and being able to speak these phrases might save your life.

Sometimes the governments of our world make us choose from a false dilemma between liberty and security. They do their best to spin everything to seem like such a dangerous place. An adroit politician can make fascism sound like chocolate cake. Y'all like chocolate cake don't y'all? What would we ever do, without Big Brother there to protect us? I am not afraid of this world. I would choose liberty every time. I am old enough to make responsible decisions about my security, and I am willing to reap the consequences if I am wrong. One of the great problems without world is that there are too many cowards who would choose security over their freedom. These are people who vote for neo-fascists. The flat land is starting to turn into rolling hills today. Soon enough, I will be in the mountains. I can't wait!

Day 239, 6-1-2008

kt: 74.8, ta: 2491, gps: N9° 13.722' W75° 24.863'

My day was more of the same today. It is still hot, and there are still lots of rolling hills. There do not seem to be any good roadside camping spots here in Colombia, or at least, not in this part. I am especially paranoid, after my rude awakening two nights ago. My campsite tonight is in a graveyard. This is surprisingly, a first for me.

There are two political issues that can whip me into a loquacious fury. One is the Drug War and the other is the issue of immigration. As far as I am concerned, the only Americans that have any right to complain about immigrants are full-blooded Native Americans, and they don't exist anymore because they have all been killed off or bred with Europeans.

The federal government, and some state governments, have recently started taking more aggressive actions against immigrants. They have been raiding workplaces, arresting immigrants, and charging them with felony identity theft, because they are using real Social Security numbers.

I read comments from many Americans that say something along the lines of, "They get what they deserve because they are all breaking the law." I disagree with that statement, because the laws were passed with racist intent to begin with. We did not have any immigration laws, minus the Chinese Exclusion Act, until after World War I. Being heavily influenced by the ideas of eugenics that were in vogue at the time, Congress passed the Johnson-Reed Act of 1924. A better name for this act would have been the "No More Mics, Spics, Dagos, Kikes, Niggers, or Gooks Act," because it effectively limited legal immigrants to Western Europeans. It created a quota of no more than 2% of any nationality that currently resided in the United States.

Since Southern and Eastern Europeans only started to come to the United States at the turn of the century, the numbers that were allowed to legally immigrate were severely restricted. Africans, Asians, and Latin Americans were not even listed in the quotas, so it was assumed that

the government didn't want any of them. The U.S. government so enthusiastically enforced this new law, that it turned away entire boatloads of Jews during World War II, knowing very well that they would surely be killed off by the Nazis. In 1952, and again in 1965, the U.S. Congress amended the original act, so that it broke down the quota between hemispheres insteac of by country.

It also allowed for war refugees to immigrate to the United States. I like to call these amendments the "No More Poor Uneducated Mics, Spics, Dagos, Kikes, Niggers, or Gooks Acts." They provided no quota for skilled and educated immigrants, but still severely restricted immigrations from the huddled masses. They should have torn down the Statue of Liberty when they passed these laws. Maybe they should change, "Give us your poor, tired, huddled masses...." to "Fuck all you Mexicans!" because that would be more of a reflection of the current sentiment. Notice that no one wants to build a wall on the Canadian border.

I wonder what would happen if the U.S. government sent all of the "illegal" Mexicans back home. Mexico already has significant unemployment and underemployment, and sending back 10% of the population would only exacerbate this issue. This is a recipe for revolution. They could then all immigrate to the United States as war refugees. Maybe they could all get jobs, as drug mules and assassins working for the cartels, and thus avoid unemployment.

Day 240, 6-2-2008

kt: 84.8, ta: 2344, gps: N8° 34.639' W75° 29.072'

It rained very hard in the graveyard last night. I discovered the rain-fly for my tent is practically useless if the wind is blowing hard. The center of the storm passed right over me. The thunder and lightning were simultaneous. There was nothing I could do in my drizzling tent, but cover my body with my rain jacket, and cover my sleeping bag with my body to keep it dry. I managed to get some sleep, dreaming of cops with machine guns.

In Colombia, the truck drivers drive older rigs than I have seen in Central America. I have seen some that look like they are at least fifty-years-old. Many of them were hauling hefty payloads too.

The people in the towns are crazy for their small motorcycles, which are barely powerful enough to keep up with the cars on the highway. Today, I saw two men carrying a hog-tied pig on their motorcycle. In the larger towns, there are so many motorcycles that it reminds me of pictures that I have seen of Bangkok.

I popped a spoke today. I'll fix it tomorrow. I hope that it doesn't become a chronic problem.

Day 241, 6-3-2008

kt: 61.8, ta: 1554, gps: N8° 08.174' W75° 24.723'

As is usually the case whenever I have to fix something on my bike, the spoke repair took longer than I anticipated. I had to remove the tire, remove the rim tape, put in a new spoke, true the wheel, put on new rim tape, put the tire and inner tube back on, and pump up the tire. After I finished pumping up the tire, the prestivalve shot off to God knows where, and I had to repeat the last two steps. I noticed that the bike shop in Panama City gave me a 36" spoke hub for my 32" spoke rim. This concerns me a little bit, because there are gaps in the rotational symmetry of my wheel. I am worried that this will lead to uneven spoke tension and, hence, more broken spokes. I will probably try to swap out hubs in one of the big cities.

Between the late start, and the long Internet/lunch break, I didn't get very far. I am hoping to make it to a point where I can finally see the Andes tomorrow.

Day 242, 6-4-2008

kt: 97.1, ta: 2483, gps: N7° 33.088' W75° 22.841'

I can finally see the northernmost part of the Andes, though they are still about 50 or 60 kilometers away. Hopefully, I will reach the base of the mountains by midday tomorrow, and make it up to at least 4,000 feet where it will be cool at night and devoid of mosquitoes. I have grown tired of the heat, the plague of flies, and the lack of good campsites. I probably won't pass the tree line until I am somewhere in Peru.

There was another unexpected road hazard today. A dump truck rode under some electricity wires with its back still propped up, and almost took down the wires with the poles. It is a good thing that I was paying attention. I quickly rode to the other side of the highway to avoid any live wires or downed poles.

I found another bridge to camp under tonight. This is good because it looks like it is going to rain again tonight as it has been prone to do recently. There are literally hundreds of wasp nests above me on the roof of the bridge. This is good, because I like wasps, and I am not allergic. Maybe they will eat all of the mosquitoes.

The river I am camped next to is one of the first clean rivers I have seen in a while, so I took a bath. This is nice, because I haven't bathed since Cartagena. When I get to Medellin, in probably three days, I am going to shower to my heart's content.

Days 243 to 246, 6-5-2008 to 6-10-2008

kt: 65.1, ta: 4533, gps: N7° 07.067' W75° 28.045'

kt: 75.2, ta: 6553, gps: N6° 38.860' W75° 27.610'

kt: 81.1, ta: 2641, gps: N6° 12.446' W75° 34.529'

I stayed in Medellin

I am now in the Andes. The road that I followed into Medellin is quite lovely. It starts out by going along a ridge. Huge green gorges open up to each side. There are lots of waterfalls, right by the side of the road. It is already significantly cooler too.

The locals have a novel way of hitchhiking on the long uphill parts of the road. I see rigs passing by with people hanging off the back, like they are spider-man. There are people on bicycles hanging on to the corner of the rigs as well. I don't do this because I think it is cheating.

When I was taking a break from a long climb, my Belgium friend Gwen rode up the hill. We rode together for the next two days. Having a riding partner actually makes me move faster, because I feel guilty if I take too many breaks. We made good time on those long ascents.

Just so no one thinks I hate soldiers, I actually camped with a bunch of soldiers at a checkpoint on the road. It was close to sunset and I didn't see any good prospective campsites, so I straight up asked them for permission to camp with them. This helps avoid mis-understandings that lead to getting machine guns pointed at me. In the morning, Gwen and I took some great photos with them. They even brought out their fully loaded grenade launcher for the photo shoot and let me hold it.

After staying in the town of Santa Rosa de los Osos, Gwen and I parted ways because I wanted to sleep in, and he didn't. Santa Rosa is a nice place, and I am surprised there are not more tourists there. It has a special dish called an "arepa de queso," that I really liked. It is a pan grilled hunk of cheese covered in a sweet milk sauce.

In the morning, I wondered around the central plaza, and watched some people trying to catch a stubborn cow. It was pretty hilarious watching the cow run around, block traffic, and overpower two people trying to rope it.

I finally left Santa Rosa around midday, but I made it to Medellin because there is a very large descent to the city, on the way from Santa Rosa. I must have passed at least 20 semis on the way down. The metropolitan area of Medellin is pretty large. It seems like there are probably about 5 million people living in the general area. I am now resting and relaxing. It is nice to enjoy a little down time, every once and a while.

I read the other day that the state of Florida did a study that concluded that prescription drugs were responsible for at least three times as many deaths in the state as all illegal drugs combined. Alcohol and cigarettes also kill more people than all the illegal drugs. Guess how many deaths were attributed to marijuana? Zero. Our nation's drug policy is a fucking joke.

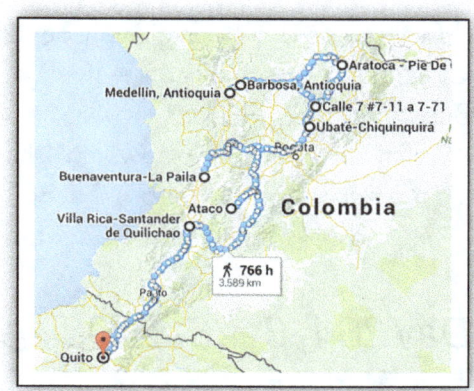

To the Land of Toilets that Flush in Both Directions

Days 249 to 263, 6-11-2008 to 6-25-2008

I stayed in Medellin for 5 days

kt: 41.5, ta: 2624, gps: N 6° 32.323' W 75° 05.291'

kt: 50.8, ta:1302, gps: N 6° 27.308' W 75° 18.470'

kt: 37.9, ta: 2074, gps: N 6° 30.145' W 74° 49.243'

kt: 80.7, ta: 2618, gps: N 6° 28.619' W 74° 14.093'

kt: 70.6, ta: 1393, gps: N 6° 51.636' W 73° 45.993'

kt: 59.7, ta: 2053, gps: N 7° 06.284' W 73° 24.533'

kt: 60.1, ta: 4836, gps: N 7° 06.561' W 73° 07.058'

I stayed in Bucaramanga

I ended up staying in Medellin a bit longer than I expected. The weather there is perfect. This is the reason it is called "The City of Eternal Spring." I didn't really do much, other than go see some bands during a free music festival. Medellin has some talented musicians though I guess this is to be expected from such a large city.

Sometimes its kind of weird staying in a hostel. I go from speaking Spanish exclusively to exclusively speaking English. It is actually quite possible to travel through out Latin America with very little Spanish. All you have to do is hop from one hostel to another.

I think of travelers as a small community of people. It is surprising how often I see some of the same people in different cities. I even hear about news affecting travelers through word-of-mouth. Case in point: when a jeep carrying a bunch of Japanese tourists collided with a jeep carrying a bunch of Israeli tourists, killing all but one. I heard about it from other travelers first.

The mountains between Medellin and Bucaramanga are not as tall as I expected. What is strange is that I prefer taller mountains, because it is a whole lot cooler. I seem to get a new rash every time I enter tropical lowlands. This time it is on the back of my thighs which is more pleasant than other places I have had them.

I followed several river valleys from Medellin to Bucaramanga. The Medellin River is a large raging torrent that doesn't seem like it could ever be tamed. It goes through a concrete channel when passing through Medellin, picking up a lot of trash along the way. It may be an ugly river, but I was nevertheless awed by its power. The Nus River is much prettier and cleaner than the Medellin River. At its most beautiful point, it comes cascading down the side of a mountain right outside of a town called Cisneros. There is another nice river gorge right outside of Bucaramanga, but I don't know its name.

The other items in the news that I thought were interesting were the separate reports that Barack Obama wants to expand government subsidies for faith based programs, and that he now supports warrant-less wiretapping, and he has voted to grant immunity to the telecommunications companies that acted in collusion with the Bush administration in allowing illegal wiretaps to occur. I don't know why the left of the Democratic Party likes this guy so much. He is just as bad as the Clintons.

Day 264, 6-26-2008

kt: 25.8, ta: 1560, gps: N 6° 55.777' W 73° 00.839'

There have been several items in the news that have caught my eye. The first is that the Colombian government managed to rescue Ingrid Betancourt and a little more than a dozen other prisoners from the F.A.R.C. She was by far, the most high profile kidnaping victim that was held by them, and was a major bargaining chip for the release of F.A.R.C. prisoners held by the Colombian and U.S. governments. Now the F.A.R.C. can focus on what they do best which is trafficking cocaine.

Day 265, 6-27-2008

kt: 46.3, ta: 4543, gps: N 6° 41.182' W 73° 02.033'

In my travels, I go through many places that seem ordinary, for lack of a better word. For example, the cattle ranches throughout Latin America are often very much the same. They are sometimes on flat land and sometimes on rolling hills. Regardless, they are always in a place where all or most of the trees have been cut down. Cattle ranches dominate the areas which I have traveled through on most of this trip. Needless to say, I have grown bored of riding by so many cattle ranches, not to mention that this makes finding a decent campsite harder to do.

The Chicamocha Canyon is not an ordinary place, not by any means. The peaks of the mountains rise imposingly high above the valley floor. Large parts of the mountains remain untouched because their slopes are too steep for farming, ranching, or building just about anything. The road that travels through this area winds down into, and then back out of the valley. It is stunningly beautiful here and hence, well worth the seemingly never-ending ascents.

It is these ascents, coupled with the daily rain showers that begin around 3:00 p.m., that make me question my undying faith in the viability of commuting by bicycle in mountainous areas.

The fact is though, that the era of cheap petroleum is coming to an end and the people that live in these areas are

going to have to come up with something to replace internal combustion transportation. Doing this without contributing to global warming will be a challenge as well. If we use electric cars we will be consuming more electricity and hence putting more carbon dioxide into the atmosphere, as much of that electricity will come from natural gas or coal burning power plants. The same is true for hydrogen fuel cell technology because of the fact that hydrogen may be universally abundant, but it is almost always chemically bonded to another element and requires energy, hence electricity, to separate the hydrogen from its chemical bonds and make a usable fuel.

Generating the electricity we consume now is difficult, if not impossible, using non-atmosphere-altering, renewable energy sources. Imagine how difficult it will be doing this if all of earth's petroleum dependent planes, cars, trucks, trains, boats, war machines, construction machinery, and agricultural machinery were plugged in to the grid. Nuclear energy is not a viable option. If it were, the nuclear powers of the world would have no problem with Iran developing their nuclear energy program.

It all comes back to reducing our energy consumption and I think more widespread use of the bicycle can help us do that. Sooner or later, people are going to have to give up their cars, as it will be prohibitively expensive, not to mention damaging to the environment to continue using them. If $4.00 a gallon gasoline is enough to make Americans give up their

trucks and S.U.V.s just wait to see what will happen by 2050 when the earth's population is supposed to reach 9 billion people, and gas will cost who knows what? At least some of those 3 billion extra people will probably want to drive, effectively negating the gas savings from switching from an S.U.V. to a car. I keep pedaling away, astonished by the insanity of it all. If people ever wonder why I am crazy enough to ride my bike as far as I have, this is why. I don't ever want to own a car. I don't want to be part of the problem, but rather part of the solution. I don't want to be part of a dying tribe, but rather a part of a flourishing tribe. With all of these future energy challenges we face, there is a reason to be optimistic. All the scrap metal coming onto the market from all of the soon-to-be obsolete tanks should actually bring down the cost of producing a bicycle. I wonder how many bicycle frames you can make using the metal from one tank.

In the U.S. a woman recently died in a hospital waiting room, while waiting for medical assistance. This contrasts with a woman in Ibague, Colombia who gave birth on the street, because she couldn't afford to do so in a hospital. Having no access to health care is one of the dangers that much of the world's poor suffer from. We should all be so horrified of these events happening, that we work to increase the availability of health care everywhere. I can't believe that there are people who believe that the for-profit health system actually functions.

Days 266 to 268, 6-28-2008 to 6-30-2008
kt: 46.2, ta: 1567, gps: N 6° 28.136' W 73° 15.732'
I stayed in Socorro

When I was in Socorro, I found myself watching the National Geographic Channel on television. Don't get me wrong, the National Geographic has long been a respected institution, but there are some shows on that channel that make me want to spit. I was especially disgusted by the show about Ewan McGregor and his friend who are traveling through Africa by motorbike. I have respect for people that go on motorcycle tours but I don't have this same respect for Ewan McGregor. He is taking not one, but two, Land Rovers along for support. He went through a simulated hostage experience, and has a personal trainer, but he didn't seem to want learn any basic first aid or take any language training. Moreover, his handlers did all the paperwork in advance. Even if you do all of the paperwork in advance, you will still be taken for a loop

at every border crossing. I also think that he exaggerates the dangers of his undertaking. My favorite quote of Ewan McGregor is, "I feel like I am on a ride with my mates." You are on a ride with your mates, dipshit! I could cycle around the world five times with the amount of money he is probably spending on his three month trip.

I ended up staying in Socorro longer than I originally planned because my right hip stiffened up to the point where I was walking with a slight limp. Waking up with gastrointestinal issues, the day after a full day of rest, caused me to rest one more day. I left Socorro this morning with the same sore hip. I plan to take it easy today and try to stretch out my hip by riding my bicycle. All in all, this is not a serious problem, but I am being extra cautious since I should be doing some grueling mountain climbing in the next four days.

I am currently traveling through a part of the world that has a bad reputation for violence, but its been mostly tranquil thus far. Yes, there are soldiers and police everywhere, but Coca-Cola deliverymen don't have shotgun-wielding security guards, like in Guatemala or Honduras. I personally consider the Mara Salvatrucha to be a bigger threat than the F.A.R.C.

Days 269 to 272, 7-1-2008 to 7-4-2008

kt: 44.9, ta: 3517, gps: N 6° 08.802' W 73° 20.883'

kt: 49, ta: 3053, gps: N 5° 55.752' W 73° 37.076'

I stayed in Barbosa

kt: 49.9, ta: 3837, gps: N 5° 37.063' W 73° 48.939'

It took a while for my hip to finally loosen up. This is a recurring problem that I have had to deal with in the past, but this is the first time that I have had to deal with this on the road. When my hip stiffens up it never seems to be caused by any external injury. It usually happens when I sleep in a bad position. Anyway, after taking it easy for the last couple of days, my hip has finally completely loosened up. The bicycle is such a wonderful invention. It is like a leg stretching machine.

Spending time in the small mountain towns in Colombia is a very eye-opening experience. It seems like the American media is always pushing the idea that the rest of the world is so poor and dangerous. The truth of the matter is apparent, if you spend any time at all in small Colombian towns. Children run around unattended. Everyone seems to be well fed and well clothed. Whole towns walk around the city centers and socialize with their neighbors. Everyone seems to know everyone else. I feel safer in these places than I feel in many places in the United States. Sometimes, I can't help but think the whole idea of American exceptionalism is a load of shit.

At 8,500 ft its surprisingly chilly. Its always surprising to need a jacket when you are in the tropics. I finally topped out today on my way to Bogotá. I am in the town of Chiquinquira and I will head to Bogotá soon.

Day 273, 7-5-2008

kt: 35.2, ta: 1229, gps: N 5° 25.986' W 73° 45.276'

I have been slacking off way too much. I have not even come close to my maximum capabilities for at least two weeks. Because of my laziness, I am going to have to extend my visa in Bogotá. Tomorrow, I will make myself ride to Bogotá no matter how many hills are in the way.

Days 274 to 279, 7-6-2008 to 7-11-2008

kt: 97.1, ta: 2483, gps: N7° 33.088' W75° 22.841'

I stayed in Bogotá

Coming into Bogotá from the north, I began to wonder when I was going to reach the city. I kept on seeing signs that indicated that Bogotá was less than 10 kilometers away but it still seemed pretty rural. Then as I topped out over a hill I saw it: a damned big city! I entered the city around 186th street, and the place where I wanted to stay was at 16th street, so I still had some riding to do. About 30 blocks away from the hostel where I wanted to stay, my front shifter broke. This is not as bad as breaking my rear shifter. I was still able to ride up hills and I made it to the hostel, albeit more slowly.

Bogotá is a massive city, filled with street performers, graffiti, big buildings, and lots of traffic. The graffiti and street performers are both of high quality. It is amazing how well the people juggling for change can juggle. Most of the graffiti is really colorful and psychedelic. Even though it is illegal, many people brazenly smoke weed in the streets. There are a whole bunch of rastas that sell stuff in one of the central plazas. I almost bought a Marcus Garvey hat but then I thought it would look funny to see a white boy wearing a black power hat.

Day 280, 7-12-2008

kt: 67.8, ta: 2043, gps: N 4° 21.704' W 74° 22.819'

When I finally left the city after six days of chilling out, I still had to ride over 20 kilometers, just to leave the metropolitan area. After topping out at just over 9,000 feet, I descended over 8,000 feet the next two days. Some of the scenery along the highway, outside of the town of Melgar, Colombia, was so spectacular that I had to stop just to take it in. It is no longer cold but uncomfortably hot. The mosquitoes are back in force. I can't wait to ride into the mountains again.

Day 281, 7-13-2008

kt: 91, ta: 1947, gps: N 4° 13.825' W 74° 50.480'

By the time I finish this trip, I will probably have replaced every single part on my bicycle at least once. I was expecting to have to pay $100 for a new pair of shifters but this ended up costing $400 after labor was included. My new shifters are much nicer than my old ones. For all you gear-heads out there, I upgraded from Shimano Tiagra to Shimano Ultegra. The shifting on my bike is much smoother now. I was also lucky to find new bike tires, after going to about a dozen bike stores. My tires are already going bald again, so this is a relief.

Days 282 to 284, 7-14-2008 to 7-16-2008
kt: 64.2, ta: 3022, gps: N 4° 26.290' W 75° 14.159'

kt: 39.6, ta: 3994, gps: N 4° 26.095' W 75° 27.954'

kt: 50.3, ta: 3905, gps: N 4° 29.181' W 75° 41.967'

I just spent the last two and half days climbing uphill. Austin doesn't have hills that come even close to the hills that I have to climb in Colombia. The longest I have to spend climbing any hill in Austin is no more than 30 minutes. The first 4,000 feet of climbing in the tropics is always the hardest to climb. Not only are you ascending but you have to do so in tropical heat. On the first day of climbing, I had hit my wall by the time I reached the city of Ibague, Colombia. I ended up staying in Ibague for the night because I wanted to recuperate my strength for the strenuous climbing that I knew lay ahead.

As usual, when I stay at a hotel, I didn't leave Ibague until midday and I didn't get as much riding in as I wanted to. I ended up not finding a good campsite until after dark. After worrying my poor little head off, I lucked into finding an abandoned house on the side of the road. I felt very fortunate, because almost all of the land on the side of the road is sloped. All of the flat land is already monopolized by houses.

I finally made it to the top today, at about 10,800 feet. It was cold and windy at the top. The wind was so strong that it redirected me several times when I was going downhill. Believe me, I do not like being redirected by wind when I am moving at 60 kilometers per hour. It is always very scary. The descent was long and I must have passed at least 30 semis on the way down the hill.

When I reached the town of Calarca, Colombia at the bottom of the hill, I was given a total rock star treatment. A news crew happened upon me, interviewed me, and then I must have been surrounded by 20 people, all of them asking questions at a restaurant that I ate at. I don't mind being a rock star for a day or two, but I sure do love my anonymity and privacy.

Days 285 to 287, 7-17-2008 to 7-19-2008
kt: 67.4, ta: 1908, gps: N 4° 12.286' W 76° 09.016'

kt: 117, ta: 2081, gps: N 3° 26.794' W 75° 32.416'

kt: 54.7, ta: 948, gps: N 3° 01.266' W 76° 29.959'

I am in sugarcane country. There are warning signs for el tren cañelero or sugarcane train. At first, when I saw these signs I was confused because I didn't see any tracks, but then I saw a semi with four trailers full of sugarcane and I

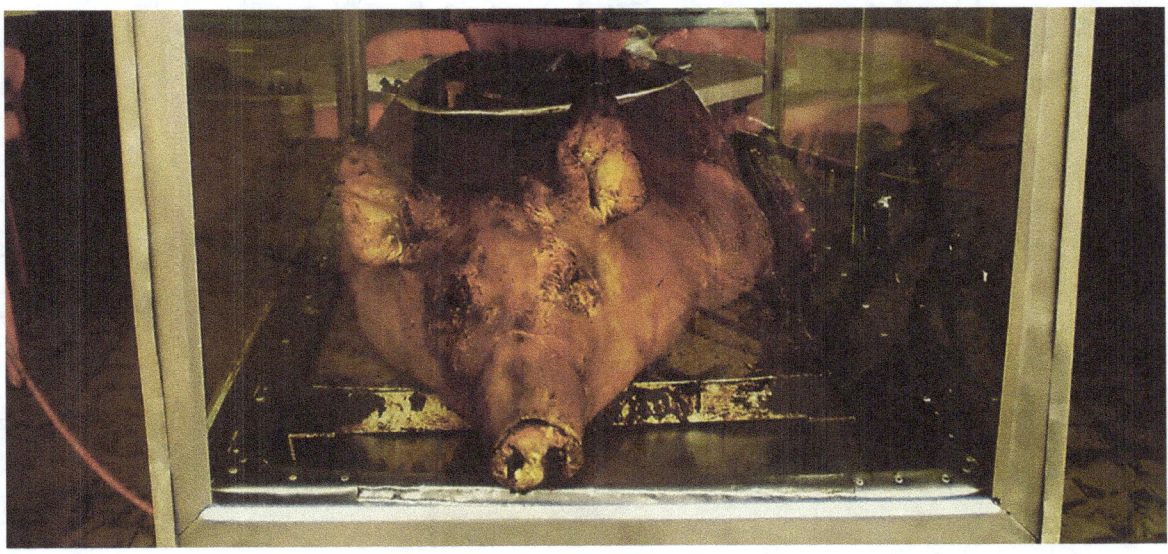

the people at the place that had the food, gave me some sugarcane to chew on. Sugarcane is so ubiquitous that everyone seems to just have some lying around.

The day before yesterday was one of those days where mechanical issues slowed me down. My rear gears were slipping so much, that I saw it as necessary to stop and try to fix this issue. After fiddling around with the limiting screws on my derailers for at least an hour, I was able to solve the problem. When I came into Cali, Colombia, I had ridden 110 kilometers by 2:00 p.m. I was hungry because I hadn't eaten in the last 80 kilometers. My breakfast was delicious, and filling enough that I was able to ride a long distance without eating again. I had lechona for the first time. Lechona is a whole pig that is stuffed with rice and more pork and then baked. Mmmm!

My lunch was the typical fair which includes soup, meat, rice, beans, fried bananas, a salad, and a drink, which is usually limeade but can often be something more exotic such as maracuya juice. The main thing I like about these meals is they are large, and pack in a lot of calories and liquids for me to make it through these long, hot days. After eating lunch, I was headed to an internet cafe to look for a place to stay for the night, when I ran into a couple of teenagers who were smoking weed. They got me high and helped me find more weed.

The place I stayed in Cali is in a nice neighborhood that has a park on a hill overlooking the city. The park is filled with people on Friday nights. There are aspiring musicians playing music for their friends on the hillside, little children sliding down a sidewalk in milk crates, comedians, and lots of merchants selling their wares. When I was smoking out on the hillside in the morning, some woman found two boxes filled with kittens. They were all healthy and cute as hell. I helped the woman carry the boxes to a dog groomer, where they were going to stay for a while.

I didn't leave Cali until midday but I wanted to stay longer, so I could explore the zoo and find cool graffiti. Alas, I do not have that much time remaining on my visa, and I don't want to pay 30 dollars for another two months when I would only be in Colombia a few more days. I'm trying to cross the border with Ecuador at the beginning of August. Today clouds started rolling in after dinner, but I was able to find a good place to camp with enough time to watch the storm before it hit. A thunderstorm in the mountains is often a beautiful thing if you aren't in the middle of it.

figured out what it was. Sugarcane is grown everywhere here, as far as the eye can see. I have really come to enjoy a drink here called "guarapo," which is made of pressed sugar cane juice, squeezed lime juice, and cooled with ice. For a little more than 50 cents, it is a very tasty, cheap, and refreshing beverage. While eating my dinner today,

Day 288, 7-20-2008

kt: 82.5, ta: 5831, gps: N 2° 26.780' W 76° 36.519'

Riding along the highway, I see many different kinds of buses. By far the king of style among all the buses is the "Colombian chiva." They are dripping in style, so much so that they put even the Guatemalan chicken buses to shame. Made using American buses, no younger than 20 years old; the roof is reinforced; the walls and seats are removed and replaced with bench seating with no doors; there is an extra-heavy duty reinforced bumper; and the whole body of the bus is painted in intricate patterns. As the buses pass by, there are often people or merchandise hanging off the bumper. I once even saw one pass by with a dog curled up on the bumper. There is a large bamboo beam that goes across the roof so a tarp can be hung over the roof which carries all the luggage that ranges from sacks of potatoes, to motorcycles, and everything in between. Sometimes they are rocking some bad ass cumbias when I pass them. Sadly, they are mostly a relic of the past, and they have been largely replaced by more conventional buses.

Days 289 to 295, 7-21-2008 to 7-27-2008

kt: 57, ta: 3263, gps: N 2° 12.146' W 76° 48.920'

kt: 54.8, ta: 2150, gps: N 1° 56.684' W 77° 08.195'

kt: 49, ta: 2856, gps: N 1° 40.570' W 77° 19.759'

kt: 51, ta: 5576, gps: N 1° 26.271' W 77° 16.763'

kt: 38.3, ta: 4534, gps: N 1° 11.490' W 77° 16.766'

kt: 78.4, ta: 6593, gps: N 0° 49.819' W 77° 37.960'

kt: 12.6, ta: 891, gps: N 0° 48.117' W 77° 43.320'

The part of Colombia that borders with Ecuador is spectacularly beautiful. The mountains are massive and they are cut through by many deep river gorges. This does, unfortunately, mean that there's a lot of hill climbing, but I can deal with that. Considering I'm no more than 100 kilometers from the equator, its surprisingly cold.

I met yet another person who is riding his bicycle to Southern Argentina. His name is Tom Snyder a.k.a. the bicycle comedian. I personally think that riding a bicycle is more fun than funny, but he has made a living as a comedian for the last couple of decades, and I respect that. He usually rides from gig to gig around the world on his bicycle. In his act, he rides up on-stage. He has amassed an impressive number of miles on his many journeys. It was fun riding with him. We split up at the border, because I knew that having overstayed my visa, that I was going to be delayed at the border and I didn't want to get him in trouble.

I tried to make it to the border on time, but the mountains slowed me down. When I arrived in Ipiales, Colombia, on the border with Ecuador, I thought that I had already overstayed my visa, so I just got a hotel room and decided to deal with it the next day. When I arrived at the border crossing, I found out that I had overstayed my visa by exactly one day, and that this was going to cost me $100. Doh!!! To officially deal with this problem, one has to pay a fine at a bank, and receive a stamp in the passport. However, since it was a Sunday, and all the banks were closed, I took the unofficial route, and bribed the border officials to erase all the records of my being in Colombia, so I could receive my exit stamp before I entered Ecuador. I am not happy about dropping a C-note to deal with this, but I figure my idiotic government will find some way to devalue my savings by at least that amount in a couple of weeks anyways.

Day 296, 7-28-2008

kt: 59.5, ta: 3341, gps: N 0° 30.680' W 77° 55.320'

I had a miserable, rainy start for my day today. At 9,000+ feet, the rain is always cold. After sitting in my tent for a while, I finally decided that the rain wasn't going to let up any time soon, so I put on my rain gear, packed up my gear, and rolled up my wet tent. There is a phenomenon that I am finding thoroughly annoying: all of the zippers on my rain gear have become so calcified that none of them work. I can usually get the zippers to work after some effort, but this morning, I ripped the handle off of one of my zippers while trying to close my pocket. To add to the pleasure of the day, I pulled a muscle in my left thigh, after I slipped under my bike, before I had even started riding for the day. It was not a bad pull though, and the sun came out around midday, so I was able to enjoy my ride.

One of the things that I love about Latin America is that you can blatantly trespass on someone's property and they are cool with it. After I pitched my tent tonight, a man with a rifle walked up. I was startled because I thought that I was well hidden. I showed him my hands and told him that I was unarmed. I then told him that I saw clouds coming in from behind and I had to quickly choose a place to erect my tent for the night. He told me not to worry and to sleep well. This was nice because I was planning to pack up my stuff and leave before sunrise. This way, if its raining in the morning, I can take my time.

Days 297 to 298, 7-29-2008 to 7-30-2008

kt: 65.2, ta: 3577, gps: N 0° 21.607' W 78° 07.282'

kt: 37.5, ta: 2522, gps: N 0° 10.257' W 78° 12.414'

Though I love long, fast descents, the change in temperature can be annoying. When I woke up two days ago it was cold and I didn't want to get out of my sleeping bag. After zooming down a mountain, I was in a desert valley, and I had to strip off all of my winter gear and my full length tights. I then ascended back into the mountains and had to stop again because it was getting cold. I stopped in the city of Ibarra, Ecuador because I had an upset stomach, and I didn't feel like dealing with digestive issues while camping.

Day 299, 7-31-2008

kt: 89.8, ta: 6075, gps: S 0° 12.187' W 78° 29.233'

I am camped at 9,000 feet again, and it is cold again. I should make it to Quito tomorrow, and I'm hoping I don't have to deal with any major elevation changes. I don't know when they decided it was their official hat, but the indigenous Ecuadorans like to wear a hat that looks like a cross between a fedora and a stove-pipe hat. After passing through mostly black areas in sugar cane growing regions I am just to the north of Quito, where everyone seems to have a more indigenous appearance.

Ecuador is dirt cheap. If you spend more than $2 on a meal, you should expect a feast. The hotel I stayed at in Ibarra was a "luxury hotel" that cost $7 a night. It was a pretty nice place that would have easily cost at least $60 a night if it were in the U.S. If an Ecuadoran was working in the U.S. for $6 an hour, their first two hours would probably pay for all thier monthly rent, daily expenditures, and the rest would be icing on the cake.

I finally crossed the equator on the way to Quito. There are no official markers on the highway, which was surprising. I spent yet another day going through large temperature changes, as I would go from higher elevation to lower elevation and back again. My friend Luis

was ironically, in the city I had just left from in the morning. So when I called him from Quito, I realized I had to get a hotel for the first night. I met Louis when I was going to the University of Texas, and he was also attending school there. He is from Guayaquil, Ecuador originally, but moved to Quito about three years ago. He is currently opening up the first head shop in all of Quito. He has told me that he has the only store in the country that sells bongs. Right now at his place, there are hundreds of bongs and pipes, spread all over his tables.

I am happy to report that one can find pretty good weed in Ecuador. It doesn't smell or taste as nice as what I am used to smoking in Austin, but it has no seeds and packs a punch. We have been smoking out of a bong which he smuggled into Ecuador from the U.S. by airplane. He left it at his mother's house for the longest time, and told her that it was a flower vase. He told me that he

thinks about 5% of Quito gets high, so he may be on to something by opening up his head shop. I have never had so much hope for capitalism to succeed.

We made some tea out of San Pedro cactus, and went wild. San Pedro cactus has trace amounts of mescaline, which also is the psychoactive substance in peyote, in the skin. San Pedro grows all over the place in Ecuador and many people have it their doorways because it is the "guardian of the doorway to heaven." Preparation requires a lot of time, and a lot of patience. I spent several hours peeling the outer layer of skin off the cactus cylinders, and despining them, before we boiled the skin several times to make a very concentrated tea. The trip was strong, compared to the peyote I ate in Mexico, which surprised me because the mescaline is more concentrated in peyote. We are talking about going camping with a bunch of this tea. All good fun.

Day 359, 9-29-2008

gps: S 1° 4'3.95" W 78° 10'55.89"

Hola Friends, maybe I will eventually come back to the US, but my trip looks like it is going to be closer to three years long, rather than just two years. I was going to post to my blog again, but then I decided that I didn't feel like it anymore. I feel as strongly as ever that I don't want to pay

any taxes to the U.S. government, in light of the pending bailout of those fucking frat boys, who are destroying the economy. I believe that the collapse of the U.S. Empire is an inevitability, and I for one am going to cheer it on! I will probably be better able to find a job in Brazil anyway.

Still Losing the Drug War, Desert to Mountains

Day 389, 10-29-2008

gps: S 4°53'31.03" W 80°41'2.72"

Right now, I am sitting in an Internet cafe in Sullana, Peru, relaxing from the desert heat and reading archived news from the New York Times. Sullana has a reputation that precedes it, as a city where there are a lot of drug addicts who smoke base, the chemicals used to extract cocaine from the coca leaf. I was warned at least five times before coming here that it was a sketchy place. The streets here are overrun with mototaxis, as the three-wheeled, motorized pedicabs are called.

As cab drivers are universally shady people, I made a deal with one of the drivers to take me somewhere, where I could buy weed. I paid the driver a little more than the going rate to take me somewhere to make the purchase, and then return me to where we had left from.

While buying the "grifa", which I have learned is pretty much universally used throughout Latin America as slang for weed, one of those fucking base smokers jumped in the cab to grovel and beg me for money, or some of my weed. I politely said "No, I'm sorry" while I allowed the driver to play bad cop. After not listening to his repeated requests to get out of the mototaxi, the driver threatened the base smoker with a knife, and he got out.

I was carrying my knife, but I prefer not to use it to threaten people, unless I am threatened first. As I stated before, the base smoker was groveling to me rather than trying to threaten me, so I didn't consider him to be very menacing, just annoying.

The Drug War is still waged internationally by the U.S. government and their allies, but it still hasn't eliminated my ability to find marijuana in various cities throughout Latin America. I didn't get a whole lot of pot, but I only spent $10 on the whole transaction, including the cab ride. The fact is that I should be able to go to any store that sells cigarettes and alcohol and buy marijuana for even less than that. I shouldn't have to dodge crack-heads, and go to dangerous neighborhoods, just to buy weed. Marijuana is unfairly compared to harder drugs such as methamphetamines, cocaine, and heroin when placed into the same category as an illegal drug.

Corruption linked to the Drug War has been in the news recently, as it always seems to be, as history repeats itself ad nauseam. There is a scandal which has grown to implicate several generals in the Colombian army, as well as a larger contingent of mid-ranking and lower level soldiers. It appears that these military personnel have been involved in the abduction, murder, and cover-up of what could be several hundred cases, in which poor, sometimes homeless men were promised jobs in the military, only to be taken to areas that were officially combat zones between the government and the leftist rebels, killed, and then disguised as rebels. In the Colombian military, promotions are often largely based on successful body counts of rebels, so several of the mid-level officers received promotions as a result of these war crimes. As

the Colombian army is in a war with rebels who traffic cocaine, any corruption in the military is inextricably linked to the drug war.

While corruption is metastasizing throughout the Colombian military, there was news from Mexico that several people who work in the Mexican Attorney General's office have been caught accepting bribes from drug traffickers, to pass them information about raids and other drug trafficking related intelligence. This hearkens back to the glory days of the Mexican government's corruption, when three successive heads of the nation's chief anti-drug agency were implicated in taking bribes from drug lords. They were Javier Coello Trejo , Mario Ruiz Massieu, and General Jesus Gutierrez Rebollo. It was during this time that the transit routes for the Colombian cartels began to shift through Mexico from the more traditional Caribbean routes.

Javier Coello Trejo is infamous for other reasons, other than accepting bribes to provide information to drug lords. When he was Mexico's equivalent of Drug Czar, several men specially vetted and picked to be in his personal security contingent were implicated in a rape scandal. It turns out that they were using government owned police cars and machine guns to abduct, rape, and even kill Mexican women in the southern part of Mexico City. Many feminist groups charged that these crimes would have gone completely unpunished if it wasn't for the fact that several rich girls with political connections were raped by this gang of thugs. There were also allegations that at least one of these policemen was a rampant coke-head.

Eventually, Mr. Coello was caught accepting bribes and was forced to resign.

His successor was Mario Ruiz Massieu. He was caught trying to launder $9 million in Texas, but wasn't forced from office until he was bizarrely implicated in a cover up of the assination of his brother, Jose Fransisco Ruiz Massieu. Raul Salinas de Gortiari was eventually convicted in ordering the hit. Mr. Salinas was, of course, the older brother of Carlos Salinas de Gortiari, the president of Mexico during that time. Raul Salinas had amassed an illegal fortune of at least the $120 million, that he had unsuccessfully tried to transfer to Swiss bank accounts. Carlos Salinas's younger brother was eventually assassinated in Mexico City, during the time that I was living there, for unclear motives- probably related to the drug trade. Mario Ruiz Massieu eventually committed suicide with an overdose of painkillers while under house arrest in New Jersey, while awaiting a U.S. money laundering trial. In his suicide note he implicated Ernesto Zedillo, then the current president of Mexico, in the corruption scandal. The Mexican government, of course, vociferously denied these accusations.

The Ernesto Zedillo regime appointed General Jesus Gutierrez Rebollo as the new head of the government's anti-drug division. This was a break from the past, as a military man was given a position which had previously been a traditionally civilian post. The military was seen at the time as being less corrupt than other sectors of the government and the move was hailed by the U.S. Drug Enforcement Agency. General Barry McCaffrey, the U.S. Drug

Czar of the time, praised General Gutierrez as a man of "absolute, unquestioned integrity." He had a reputation for major drug busts of powerful trafficers.

As it turned out, he had been on the payroll of Amado Carrilo Fuentes, the nation's most powerful drug lord of the time, for seven years. He shared information with Carrillo and only busted his competitors. At the time, Amado Carrillo Fuentes was estimated to net $10 billion a year. The General also had a penchant for illegally disappearing those who were accused of drug trafficking, even if there was no case against them.

Under provisions of the Foreign Assistance Act, the U.S. president has until March 1st, every year, to certify a government as being cooperative in the U.S. Drug War. Nations that are de-certified are no longer given U.S., I.M.F., or World Bank assistance. The president also has the option of de-certifying but continuing such assistance on the grounds of the wellbeing of a country being of "vital" interest to the U.S. government. None-theless, the U.S. continues to certify Mexico and Colombia, just like it did at the height of their corruption, despite endless years of repetitious subterfuge. These governments don't want to kill the goose that laid the golden egg. When cocaine brings in money from both the U.S. government and the private sector, there is just too much money at stake for the Mexican or Colombian government to ever want to truly do away with drug trafficking. There is too much poverty in both of those countries to ever pull the rug completely out from under their economies.

I don't think that the likes of Barry McCaffrey and John Waters, are so stupid to be so naive to government involvement in the drug trade. I think that they have known all along and are probably complicit in the respective Mexican and Colombian schemes. I consider them to be terrorists for their connections to all of these aforementioned people. It is time to end this government sponsored terrorism by ending the drug war.

Day 418, 11-27-2008

kt: 44.9, ta: 3517, gps: S 8° 6'44.53" W 79° 1'48.08"

I am in Trujillo, Peru right now. I got a new tattoo recently and I will send pictures in the future. As my blog is a cumbersome burden I have decided to abandon it in its current form. I will now write a lot less but I will still keep track of my daily statistics out of my own curiosity.

Day 419, 11-28-2008

gps: S 8° 6'44.53" W 79° 1'48.08"

I have spent the last three weeks in Trujillo trying to transcribe my blog. The desire is just not there to do this task. You can tell when you don't want to do something when you can find almost anything to distract from the task at hand. Anyway, I came to the decision that I would write less and try to focus on quality over quantity.

Walking around the streets of Trujillo is like walking around the track of Mario Kart, except the battle carts have been replaced with a whole bunch of little taxis. By an unofficial count, I would guess that close to 90% of all vehicles on the streets are taxis, colectivos, and buses. The taxi drivers are of course, a menace. I have no doubt that they would run over their own toddler or grandmother if they got in their way. The other day I was impressed by the method that a man in a wheelchair used to cross the street. When he wanted to cross the street, he blew a whistle. My faith in the taxi drivers' bloodthirstiness was shaken when they actually braked for him. Most of the time, the taxis are empty, but not in the morning when they bring people and their goods into the market to sell their wares. I even saw a taxi with a whole bunch of 2X4's strapped to the top and a cement mixer hitched to it. In Latin America, you have to hustle for your money in any way that you can think of.

The place where I am staying is close to a large number of different schools. Their students flood the area dressed in the various uniforms that indicate where they attend school. The other night, when I was sitting at an Internet cafe, I witnessed an interesting urban phenomenon that I was previously unaware of. I saw about 40 kids all dressed in one uniform run past the front door, while being chased by another group of equal, or larger, size that was wielding large rocks the size of my head. Outside, there was smashed glass everywhere. It turns out that Trujillo is filled with adolescent soccer hooligans. When I asked the lady who worked at the Internet cafe how often this happens she just shrugged and said it happens daily. All the street vendors outside kept on selling what they were selling as if nothing happened. The cops were able to break it up pretty quickly, so I guess it wasn't too bad.

Day 433, 12-12-2008

gps: S 9°32'7.94" W 77°31'49.95"

I just arrived in the town of Huaraz, Peru. It is a lovely place indeed. There are about a dozen snow-capped peaks just outside of the city to the east. Getting here was not the most pleasurable experience, as I had ascended to a height of 13,877 feet (a new personal best) on a dirt road, with a badly cracked rear rim. I passed through a number of villages that didn't have any places to eat, other than stores that only sold cookies, potato chips, cans of tuna, soda, and coca leaves. I pretty much had to force myself to suffer food rationing, and I went to bed with hunger pangs a number of times. Coca leaves are known to have a hunger repressing properties, and I took advantage them because of the lack of food.

I also left the wonderfully dry desert for the cold rains of the mountains. The rain actually turned the road into nothing more than a mud pit at a number of places. I even had to get off my bike and push it for a small stretch. Descending into Huaraz during a torrential downpour was downright hellish. Just outside of the city, I was trapped between a bus and a semi, on a road that could best be described as a mud cascade, since it was unpaved and had no gutters. When I finally got to the city, I had to change out of my wet clothes so I wouldn't get sick. I am now happily dry, comfortable, and well fed at a hostel where I plan to relax for the next couple of days.

It is amazing how much contrast there is between the mountains and the desert here. When you are high in the mountains it is lush and green. The coastal deserts are almost completely devoid of native plant life. I went through long stretches of road where there is nothing but miles and miles of sand. Fortunately, because of the strong Antarctic wind coming from the south, it is not the hottest desert I have passed through, at least not until the coastal mountain ranges near Casma, Peru block it off. Camping was easy, as there are almost no areas that are fenced off. I would just go about 100 meters off the side of road and camp behind a sand dune or some other obstruction.

The stark emptiness of the desert is quite incredible. I can only describe the moments where the sun strikes a wind-swept sand dune as moments of perfect beauty. I took some pictures but, as usual, they don't do any justice to the beauty of the places where I was.

Even though the desert is devoid of native plant life, there are parts of it where they have used irrigation to grow rice. I was completely astounded by this, as rice is one of the most water intensive crops that one can grow. It seems to me that a country that has managed to grow rice in the desert shouldn't be so poor. Despite the cultivation of water intensive crops in the desert, Peru still manages to consume six times less water per capita, than the United States. I protested this fact my not showering for a month. In the desert, unlike the jungle, I don't get skin rashes when I don't bathe. I love being dirty. It makes me feel like I am embracing my caveman roots.

I encountered one of the very first locals I have happened upon, which didn't seem too friendly to foreigners. As I rode by and said, "Buenas tardes," to indicate my friendliness. She said something in Quechua to her dog,

which then started chasing and barking at me. Her tone was aggressive which made me think that she was saying, "Sick him, Sick him." and she did absolutely nothing to restrain her dog, unlike most people with over-exuberant guard dogs. I just ignored her dog until it went away, but I almost sassed her for her rudeness.

If you have any kind of phobia of dogs, you should not ride a bicycle through Latin America. There are legions of dogs, which roam the streets in every part I have passed through. As there are no leash laws, domesticated dogs and stray dogs mingle at every corner, often chasing passer-bys on bikes and motorcycles. I am not afraid of dogs at all. As an animal that travels upright, humans have an evolutionary advantage over dogs. Not only do we scare them because we appear bigger to them, but we can also pick up rocks and throw them. Since I carry a large buck knife, I know that no dog is my match in a fight. One of the funniest moments involving dogs, that I have seen, was in the city of Sullana, Peru. There was a large pack of about 10 dogs roaming the streets and fighting amongst themselves to establish dominance. It seems that a bitch had wandered into their midst and they were fighting for the first dibs to inseminate her. The locals just laughed at this, and shrugged, as if it is an everyday occurrence.

Day 444, 12-23-2008

gps: S 10°44'14.79" W 77°14'59.37"

This last week, I learned that rain at 10,000 feet may be unpleasant but rain at 13,000 feet is downright hellish. It is freezing cold and usually mixed with hail. Yesterday, I had had my share of rain and was very happy to find a building that was under construction where I could pitch my tent. Having a roof is a luxury which I don't always have on the road. It was nice to let all of my gear dry.

I had formerly had a high opinion of Peruvian roads. That was before I did extensive riding in the mountains of Peru. The roadway I rode on today was under construction, to put it politely. There were long stretches where the road was nothing more than a mud pit. Fortunately, I was wearing all of my rain gear as a precaution from my unpleasant day yesterday. I managed to become completely covered in mud which happens more often than one might think.

While descending, I couldn't help but think, "At least I'm not climbing this road." Sure enough, I met another cycle-tourist going the other direction. She was Ani from Switzerland, the first solo female cyclist I have met thus far. Girl power bitches! I warned her about the lovely road conditions that lay ahead and we parted ways.

Neither the Chinese nor Indians seem to know anything about making inner tubes. The Indian inner tubes that I used almost always have a bulge somewhere which drives me fucking crazy. While annoying, the Indian inner tubes function at least. The Chinese inner tubes don't have the bulge, but they have an even more annoying problem. They slowly leak air and when you try to pump them up, the valve snaps in half. I had this happen to two different inner tubes within days of eachother. As I had used up all of my cheap Chinese inner tubes, I actually had to jump on one of the colectivos with my bicycle and all my gear.

The first few colectivos didn't stop. It seems that they didn't want to carry my bicycle which is unusual, since I have seen hog-tied sheep riding on the top of them. As I had descended into the desert, this was a somewhat worrisome development. Finally, one of them stopped for me, and we were off to the coastal city of Barranca, Peru, where I am now.

By some Christmas miracle, I managed to find some new inner tubes. I got them at the bike shop right across from the collectivo station. They are shraeder valve inner tubes, not that cheap Chinese presti-valve bullshit. Tomorrow, I am going to start heading the next 200 kilometers to Lima, where I have a friend waiting for me and I should be able to find a replacement for my ailing rear rim. Hopefully, Santa will give me a shitload of weed this year, instead of the diarrhea I got last Christmas.

The Plight of the Palestinians, Santa Claus, and Lima, Peru

Day 452, 12-31-2008

gps: S12° 5'16.62" W77° 2'12.79"

I was cut off from the news for a couple of days, but when I reentered civilization from the desert again, I was horrified to see that the Israeli government had unleashed a massacre against the Palestinians in Gaza, in what seems to me, to be a typical Israeli overreaction to Palestinian violence against Israeli citizens. They responded to the Palestinian's firing of mortars, which are essentially high hifalutin bottle-rockets compared to the Israeli weaponry, supplied by the U.S., by launching a full-scale air assault on the Gaza Strip.

Seeing the typical pro-Israeli bias in the U.S. press, I can't help but ask a question: if a child walked up to a full-grown man and started punching him, and the man responded by stabbing the child in the throat, who is more culpable; the child who did the provoking, or the man who did the stabbing? The fact is that Palestinian actions are a nuisance, while the Israeli actions are far more serious and far more worthy of condemnation.

Let's have some fun with numbers. First off, according to The Economist, about 420 Palestinians have been killed by Israeli operations in the Gaza Strip, before the current slaughter of its caged inhabitants. Of those 420, about a fifth of them are believed to be civilians. The current death of Palestinians during the last couple of days is about 390 and rising. Does anyone want to guess the number of Israelis killed by these rocket attacks all year? The number of Israeli deaths comes to a grand total of five, four of those being during the current Israeli offensive. According to an article in MSN, about

700,000 Israelis live within range of Hamas's homemade rockets. So that means, for the year, the chances of an Israeli being killed by rocket fire is about 5 out of 700,000. I thought to myself, "That is funny, the population of Austin is about 700,000." and I couldn't help but wonder what the murder rate of Austin is. With a quick Google search, I found out that in 2003, there were 27 murders out of a population of 682,316 people. That means your chance of getting murdered in Austin is higher than your chance of being killed by rocket fire in Israel. Austin's murder rate in 2003, by the way, was about half of the national average. It is a tranquil city. I could probably walk up to a crack-head at 12th and Chicon, slap him in the face, and live to tell about it. I doubt that all of the Israeli citizens are as terrified as the stock Israeli citizens the American press interview, just as as the average Austinite isn't too worried about being murdered.

I hope that one day, the Israeli government will realize that the only military solution to Palestinian problem is the final solution of turning the Gaza Strip and the West Bank into giant death camps, marching all the Palestinians into gas chambers, and threatening nuclear annihilation to anyone who challenges them. I also would hope the Israeli people haven't developed the cognitive dissonance required for such an atrocity. To bring about real, lasting change, the onus of responsibility lies on the shoulders of those most powerful. I think that more carrot, and less stick is in order. If the Israeli government did the mature thing, eased the economic blockade of food and medical supplies, and promised further enticements for the Palestinians, provided that rocket attacks cease, or at least, slow considerably; I guarantee that it would be more effective than the current slaughter, which will lead to more tit-for-tat recriminations in the future. The fact that the U.S. government is again towing the official line that the Palestinians are the culprits, and the Israeli government is blameless and angelic is not helping anything. The U.S. government should immediately end all support for the Israeli military and demand a cease-fire, because it is the only nation the Israelis will listen to. For some reason, I doubt it is going to happen. The incoming Obama administration is probably not going to bring real change to this conflict, as he has been silent about it, and his incoming Secretary of State is a war hawk.

In other news, the U.S. has had its first official Santa massacre. This seemed like such an inevitability to me, as the U.S. is the only country that, individually and collectively, makes Israel seem like a model of self-restraint. I can only imagine what was going through this guy's head. He must have thought something like, "I can't believe that evil bitch is divorcing me, I know what I can do. I think I will kill her, and every single person who was invited to her Christmas party. I can dress as Santa to stay in the holiday spirit!" He was a laid-off aerospace engineer (read military subcontractor) so I can only guess that he was probably of the Fox-News-watching, jingoist variety of person that plagues American society. I predict there will be more Santa massacres, so much so, that they will probably compete to be the deadliest Santa killer ever. Right now the bar is set at nine. Maybe the Easter Bunny and Jesus can get in on the act too.

I am in Lima, Peru right now, staying at the apartment of a friend of mine. Lima is massive and hot during the day right now, as it is summertime. This place abounds with beautiful architecture and lovely graffiti. My friend, his name is Marco, lives in one of the nicer parts of town and I can tell y'all, it is a completely different world than most of Peru. The area of town he lives in is like a nice neighborhood anywhere in the U.S., except you still can't drink the water. After not seeing a white Peruvian in all of Peru, I see them on a daily basis here. The streets here are well paved and there are lots of parks. I am going to spend the New Year here, and explore the city after my bike is fixed.

Day 481, 1-29-2009

gps: S 13°25'31.91" W 76° 8'12.16"

I am taking a break in the city of Chincha, Peru. The coastal desert of Peru is FUCKING HOT once you leave the north. I think that the real reason I stayed in Lima for as long as I did, is that I knew that I was going to have to reenter the desert. I was born and raised in Austin, Texas and I have endured many a summer without using an air conditioner, so I am usually not one to complain about the heat, but this has taken things to a whole new level. The desert here is devoid of plant life, and shade here is like gold. Once you leave the shade, it is like walking into an oven. The sun is powerful here. At the end of the day, I can say I know what it feels like to be a barbaqued piece of meat. I am unusually exhausted, and it feels like leftover solar radiation is still emanating from my skin. I keep most of my body covered, except for my limbs, but sun burn is creeping in on the back of my neck and on my face. I should be veering off the coast in four or five days, but until then, I am in a boiling inferno. I can´t wait to encounter the cold rain and hail from the mountains. Why would I put myself through such suffering? Because I feel like such a stud after challenging the desert.

Day 487, 2-4-2009

gps: S14°50'21.42" W 74°56›24.60»

I finally made it to Nazca after crossing some more brutal desert terrain. Yesterday, I saw a new form of heat rash, which I have never had before. Little bubbles form on the skin. They don't hurt and you can pop them like blisters. I also had to combat against the heat suppressing my appetite. After riding on a 50 kilometer stretch which resembles some kind of martian landscape except it is hotter, I could not get myself to eat a portion of food, which is normally easy for me to eat. This came back to bite me later, as I ran into an energy wall due to lack of calories, and I could not make it to Nazca yesterday as planned. Feeling exhausted, I ended camping on the land which holds the famous Nazca lines. I didn't even pitch my tent: I just rolled out my sleeping pad and unpacked my sleeping bag. I still have problems with a suppressed appetite, but those should subside with a day or two of rest which I plan to take. After following a desert route almost exclusively since I entered Peru, I will be happy to see cooler weather, but I will miss the stark desert landscapes which vary from barren, multicolored mountains, to massive sand dunes.

I was tempted to say that I was a fan of Michael Phelps, before his recent photos of him sucking on a bong because of his A.D.H.D., which I was also diagnosed with when I was a child, and normally, I would be more of a fan of someone who is publicly outed as a pothead, but Michael Phelps' response is about as cowardly and money-grubbing as

can be. He essentially said, "I am sorry and I will never do it again. Now please give me my money back." I remember when he got busted for D.W.I. (a much more serious offense) and that story didn't have half the legs of this story. The companies that gave him endorsements read like a who's who list of those responsible for the obesity epidemic: McDonald's, Nestle, Kelloggs, etc. I would argue that thier products are many times more harmful than marijuana.

The fact is that many world-class athletes smoke marijuana. An N.B.A. player by the name of Charles Oakley once caused a controversy, when he said over half of basketball players smoked marijuana and many played high. I can list a number of football players just from the Dallas Cowboys, who have gotten in trouble for drugs in the past. I have smoked with professional B.M.X. riders and I know that getting high is prevalent in a large variety of sports. The fact that these are world-class athletes provides anecdotal evidence that marijuana does not have the same damaging effects of tobacco.

Just once, I would like to see an athlete speak out against marijuana prohibition. I would also like to see them reject all the junk-food and soda endorsements out of principle, but this is wishful thinking. Fortunately, there have been a few athletes with the courage to speak out on the subject of marijuana prohibition. Mark Stepnowski, a member of several Super Bowl Championship winning Cowboys teams, is a rare exception to many athletes. He never got in any trouble with the league while playing football, and promptly became the executive director of Texas N.O.R.M.L. after retirement. I was hoping that Michael Phelps would say something like, "Fuck you and your junk-food money, you fucking hypocrites. Marijuana prohibition should be ended, and I stand by that statement." But alas, Michael Phelps is just another piece-of-shit, corporate whore.

Day 516, 3-5-2009

gps: S13°31'32.26" W71°59'14.50"

The road from Nazca to Cusco is long, desolate, and spectacularly beautiful. It transitions from a dry, hot, and mostly lifeless desert, to a cold and wet mountain eco-system filled with vicuñas, vizcachas, and alpacas. After riding in an oven for so long, I now had to ride through a giant refrigerator. The top is particularly beautiful. I passed dozens of small, natural lakes filled with fish, and exotic waterfowl, all backed by snow-capped mountains. With the exception of the road, most of this area is untouched by man, left to the whims of nature.

The road keeps climbing and climbing, and then climbing some more, after all of the previous climbing. When I

finally topped out, I rolled over 14,900 feet, only to discover that the top was a actually a large rolling pampa, and I topped out over 14,900 feet four more times over some 40 or 50 kilometers. It was sleeting and snowing at the top, but the frozen precipitation didn't stay frozen, so I didn't get to travel through quite the winter wonder-land that I wanted to. Being that the pampa at the top was so large, I ended up camping at 14,600 feet which is most definitely cold. The next morning, something disastrous happened: my tent broke. Like almost all tents, my tent has collapsible poles which form an exoskeleton to the structure of my tent. Without the exoskeleton intact, the structure fails, and this was exactly the problem that I faced. I was still in the middle of nowhere when my tent failed, but I thought that I could MacGyver a solution to this problem, so I wasn't too worried about my situation yet. That same day, I finally reached a point where I descended more than I ascended, after "only" 250 kilometers of mostly uphill riding. I still couldn't reach civilization though. I was still at over 13,000 feet, with a little more climbing to do when it started to rain, so I decided to figure out how to make my tent stand up. I ended up doubling over a bicycle spoke with a piece of fence I had clipped off, and inserted them into the broken pole, with the hope of erecting some semblance of a shelter from the cold rain. Inside the tent. I covered my sleeping bag with a large plastic tarp I had acquired, and hoped that the tent wouldn't collapse from the wind that was making it lean to one side. Getting

wet, and getting all of my winter gear wet in this kind of environment, would lead to disastrous consequences.

I was able to tough out the night and stay dry, but I knew that I was going to have to do something about my tent soon, or I would have to catch a ride to the nearest city and try to find a solution there. When I made it to the small town of Challhuanca, I finally made it to a place with ferreterias and Internet, let alone electricity and plumbing. When I was able to check my email after a long absence from civilization, I discovered some very unpleasant news. Someone had, somehow, stolen my debit card number, and was using it to make cash withdrawals in Virginia, unbeknownst to me. The bank had in response, frozen my bank account and filed fraud documents, so I could recuperate the money that was taken from me. This was especially worrisome to me, not because of the identity fraud, but because my debit card is my only convenient access to my bank account, and I was running low on cash after going for a long time without having access to an A.T.M. machine. To make matters worse for me, the simple hardware solution I had devised for fixing my tent only made the problem worse, and rendered my tent completely useless. I had encountered a problem which I couldn't fix on the fly, and I had to do what I least like to do on this trip: hitch a ride.

The ride from Challhuanca to Abancay was mercifully cheap, only costing $3 for almost 150 km of road. Defeated by the force of entropy, I had to accept the boxed-in view of beautiful mountain scenery from inside a cramped

van, instead of the panoramic views I was so used to. In Abancay, I talked with my mother and clarified exactly what was happening with my bank account, and whether I could still use A.T.M. machines.

Fortunately, I was able to get more cash out of the A.T.M. machines, I just couldn't use my card as a credit card. I was able to contact the bank, and make transactions. As Abancay is not a good place to deal with the ongoing banking and tent issues, I caught another ride to Cuzco, since it has more developed tourism infrastructure, and is the location of a U.S. Consular office. I have been stuck in Cuzco for about a week and a half now, impatiently waiting for a new debit card and replacement poles for my tent. I can't wait to get back on the road again.

As a tourist who has had the unique opportunity to pass through parts of Peru with absolutely no tourism infrastructure, I have seen what I think is the authentic Peru. All the tourist areas like Cuzco, Huaraz, Nazca, Huacachina, and parts of Lima have these superficial facades of luxury that are hard to find elsewhere. More-over, the people in these areas seem to smile at you, as if their smile were only part of an elaborate mask. In all of my travels thus far, I have discovered that one is much more likely to be assaulted, robbed, or conned in these areas, than outside of them.

The tourist areas stand in stark contrast to the countryside. The people in these areas are poor, but they seem like they are but a stones-throw from sainthood, because they are so honest, friendly, and uncorrupted by civilization. I saw many people dressed in indigenous clothing, and living a way of life similar, no doubt, to how they have lived for

thousands of years, herding alpacas. When the herd would get to close to the road, the alpaca shepherds would hurl a rock towards the edge of the road with a sling weapon, which they have probably used for thousands of years. The people in the mountains are mostly bilingual, speaking Quechua amongst themselves and Spanish among strangers. There were places that I stopped to eat something, where large groups of children would come stare at me in amazement. This was annoying, but in all fairness to the kids, I was probably the first blue-eyed devil they had ever seen in their lives. Now that I am in Cuzco, I miss traveling through the countryside. I have to worry that people I encounter are just masked con-men trying to liberate me from my money. I don't mean to say that Cuzco is a shithole or anything.

There are some very nice restaurants that are very cheap compared to the U.S. or Europe. There is also a small measure of authenticity to the city. One can go to the central marketplace and purchase not only San Pedro cactus but also pure powdered mescaline and ayahuasca. I haven't found any fresh milk yet, but I am still looking for it. In the countryside, the milk is so fresh and unprocessed that Bessie is mooing out back, and you can see curds floating in the top. Once I finally hit the road again, I hope to pass through more places that are similar to the small villages between Nazca and Cuzco.

My thirtieth birthday is fast approaching at the end of this month. I am not ecstatic about the prospect of turning thirty, but aging is a fact of life. Like many thirty-year-olds I am taking stock of my life, and the world around me. Many of my friends are getting married and having children, and

that it is kind of alarming. I remain blissfully single. I have come to several conclusions about what kind of paths I am going to pursue from this point in the road. Since I generally prefer traveling of the Odyssian variety, rather than the wam-bam-thank-you-mam variety, I have decided that I don't have enough time to get married, have children, get a soul-crushing job in corporate America, and buy a house with a white-picket fence in suburbia.

I will never work more than 40 hours a week from now on. All the time wasted while working is better wasted traveling, or pursuing your passions. In some ways, I am a little boy who refuses to grow up. In other ways, I am a fully mature, grown man.

While America was spending money like a junkie with a stolen credit card, I was saving money. I paid off my college debt a week before I graduated, from the money I earned while working the entire time I was in school. Yes, I have no personal career ambitions, but I don't have to, since I have no debt at all. My ambition is to live as stress-free a life as possible, and to spend as much time as possible pursuing my passions. The American Dream was never a dream to me, but always a nightmare, even before it was exposed as the sham that it is. Rather than focus my energy on consuming resources, I am going to pursue leisure and savor every last moment I have on this planet. I am only hoping that the prolonged recession that we are going through helps people realign their priorities away from consumption,

and towards leisure. It would be nice to feel like I am part of a community, rather than feel like an outsider, as I do now.

One of the things that I'm extremely passionate about is music. For me music is a holy, sacred thing. To me, all of the modern commercial pop acts aren't just making bad music. They are committing blasphemy, by soiling the airwaves with the audial flatulence they have the gall to call music. I love the way good music inspires people across borders. It has no respect for the artificial boundaries that humanity has created. I love it when someone in some far-flung corner of the globe hears music from another part of the world, and wants to recreate the sound, and then make it their own. Rock and roll may have been born in the United States, but it in no respect, belongs to it. In that same respect, I'm completely inspired by Latin music in general, but more specifically cumbia. I think I am going to make it a point of mine to spread my love for this beautiful music, as much as I can. I am even thinking of trying to start a cumbia band, when I return to the states a couple of years from now.

My minor obsession with cumbia has caused me to spend countless hours on-line trying to find out information about my favorite cumbia bands, and the evolution of its sound. Sadly, there don't seem to be a lot of good sources for information about cumbia on-line. I have, nonetheless, been able to get to the point where I feel that I have a pretty good understanding of the roots of cumbia, and I would like to share that with all of my loyal readers. In the

interest of brevity, I will shortly discuss some of the better known pioneers of cumbia through the 1970's.

Cumbia had developed over centuries on the northern coast of Colombia, but was considered a lower class music, until the great maestro Lucho Bermudez recorded, in the early 40s, the first commercially successful cumbia named, "Prende la Vela." It was through the efforts of the first generation of cumbia band leaders and composers that cumbia became more than just a regional music. Besides Lucho Bermudez, other noted musicians and composers from this first generation of cumbia include Jose Barros and Pedro Laza. I think I should point out that Colombia was an important center of Latin music at the time, and still is. Lucho Bermudez was from Colombia, but he lived in Mexico and Cuba, where he met such Latin music greats as Perez Prado and Celia Cruz. Sonora Matancera, the famous Cuban group where Celia Cruz got her start, recorded at least one composition by Jose Barros. Cumbia was still relatively isolated to Colombia until the sixties, when groups like Sonora Dinamita and Los Corraleros de Majagual toured Latin America, spreading cumbia's popularity. I like the name of the Corraleros so much that I want my band's name to be,

"Los Fumaleros de Ganjamual." By the end of the decade, Peru had taken the cumbia and created a very new sound. As far as I know, the Peruvian cumbia bands were the first such bands to use an electric guitar in cumbia. The sound of Peruvian coastal cumbias sounded like a fusion of surf music (The Ventures and Dick Dale, not the Beach Boys) and cumbia. Los Destellos is probably the best known of these Peruvian cumbia pioneers, but there were many other bands providing their contributions to cumbia.

In the eastern part of Peru, there was yet another subgenre of cumbia that was created during the sixties. It is the cumbia amazonica of Juaneco and Los Mirlos. I still can't verbalize the difference between their music and that of the other Peruvian cumbia bands, but it is definitely different than the rest.

Cumbia, to this day, continues to grow and branch off into new music, but its sound still has links to the early days of the cumbia. Discos Fuentes, which was responsible for the recording of a large majority of early cumbias, is still in operation today. Like all music, there is a lot of bad, commercialized cumbia out there, but there are also many groups still producing a lot of good music.

Day 526, 3-15-2009

gps: S 14°48'10.20" W "71°25'18.62"

I am in a town called Espinar, nestled in the altiplano between Cuzco and Arequipa. After getting hailed on the

last two days, I decided it was time for a break, so here I am. I have rain gear and a helmet to mitigate the effect

of the hail, but it is still not any fun to deal with. I have also learned that a good 30-minute hail storm will decrease the temperature significantly.

With all that said, I am ecstatic to report that my tent is functioning well, and that my engineering solution seems to have done the trick. All I can say, is that if you need epoxy putty to be pliable, use the stuff that is an actual putty instead of a paste before it dries. I am hoping that my tent will not require any more fixes but, if it does, I have an extra pole to fix it with. I have so far used my tent for every night except one, since I left Cuzco, and it has rained almost every night. Staying dry and warm when it is cold keeps my spirits high.

I went through the usual remote rural areas to get to Espinar. The people here don't have a lot of material possessions, but they eat well and they have electricity. This was evidenced by the numerous hydroelectric power stations and ample flocks of cows and sheep.

This doesn't stop children from begging me aggressively for money. As I ride by, the children beg me incessantly for "propinas." Considering that the word propina means tip, I wonder what they expect to be tipped for. I have been able to leave these kids behind, but their aggressiveness is worrisome. Some of the kids were carrying shovels which could readily be used as weapons. I have also read stories from other cyclist about the kids throwing rocks when they don't get their "propina." It is

a small step to go from aggressively begging people for money, to assaulting them. Rest assured that I have no qualms about beating one, or several, of these children mercilessly, if they became threatening in any way. When I am on my own, I have to follow the law of the jungle, instead of any ethical code. Fortunately, I have been able to avoid having to do that, but I have definitely heard stories about large groups of adolescents who roam around looking for people to assault and steal from. They are colloquially called "piranas" because of the nature of their attacks. I am continuing on, but I am weary of others, as I am definitely an outsider here. I hear Quechua more commonly spoken here than Spanish. One of the aggressive panhandlers seemed to barely speak Spanish at all. He first started speaking to me in Quechua and, when I asked him if he spoke Spanish, said in broken Spanish, "What a pretty bike. Sell it to me." When I politely refused he started asking me to give him money and even ran aside me while begging. I left him behind, but I am questioning whether my policy of civility towards all needs a little revision. I think that instead of meekly saying, "I am sorry. I don't have enough money for you." I should say something like, "I will not give you any money and if you don't want any trouble with me, you should leave me alone." I am inherently a nice person but I also have a mean, vicious side, and I'm not afraid to flash my teeth if necessary.

15,821 Feet, A Swiftian Economic Proposal, Colder Than a Snowman's Pecker

Day 530, 3-20-2009

gps: S 16°23'52.16" W 71°31'22.30"

As the title to this blog post suggests, I have broken my previous altitude record on this most recent leg of my journey from Espinar to Arequipa. The night before I broke my new altitude record, I found frost covering my tent and bicycle, for the first time since Northern Mexico. I was at only 13,000 feet then. Previously, when I topped out on a mountain pass, I was rewarded with a long downhill. Alas, the altiplano is cruel, and rewards me with several days, to a week, of cold wet riding. At 15,000 feet, its cold, even if it is sunny. Most of the time I spent in the altiplano was on a dirt road, albeit a high quality one, without the wheel destroying washboard grooves and massive rocks jutting out of the road. Nonetheless, the road slowed me down. I spent three days over 14,000 feet. The first day, I topped out over 15,000 feet. It began to snow, right when I reached a small village. The one and only lodging in town only charged $3 for one of its beds, so I jumped at the chance. I slept in late, knowing it would be as cold as a witch's titty in the morning.

I was so happy when I finally reached asphalt, even though I was still at a very high elevation. The headwinds were fierce and cold. There were times when my feet were really cold, despite the fact that I was wearing a double layer of socks. The small town of Imata had plenty of restaurants but no lodging. There were two little kids that told me that their family had lodging, and I trusted them because I thought they were too small to have truly sinister intentions, but they started acting real suspiciously which made my

spidey senses tingle. They led me to the back of a house on the main road, and told me to knock on the gate. When I knocked on the gate, the kids ran to hide. When I asked them why they were doing this they did not provide me with a satisfactory answer, so I decided to leave them. I would rather camp in the freezing weather than wait around to see what nasty surprises were in store for me. Fortunately, I was able to find lodging that night at the local police station. They had an extra bed and everything.

The next day, in an attempt to avoid camping in freezing weather, I rode over 130 kilometers and ascended almost 4,000 feet to the city of Arequipa. Despite all the ascending, I finally got the long downhill stretches I had been pining for. There is nothing quite as exhilarating and adrenalizing, as lane splitting between semis, on a long downhill stretch. I am going to rest here in Arequipa for the next couple of days, but I know that eventually, I am going to have to bite the bullet, and do some more camping in freezing weather. It is only going to get colder as I travel farther south.

As one who comes from the radical non-consumption camp, I have to admit that I am disgusted by almost all of the U.S. government's attempts to bolster the economy. I personally know several people who have been laid off recently, but I think that we should nevertheless embrace the Great Recession, as pundits are calling it now. There is something terribly wrong with an economic system that depends entirely on the profligate consumption by a few rich countries, of products created by a slave-like underclass of third world workers. I want to live in a world where a 20 hour work week is considered full time. Also, I'd like to see the industrial countries of the world significantly decrease their carbon footprint. In that interest, I have compiled a disparate list of companies, entire industries, government policies, and whatnot that should be downsized; if not outright eliminated, along with a short justification for each one. This list is by no means comprehensive, and I might add to it in the future:

The Big Three automakers do not deserve any sympathy. They have done their best to destroy public transportation infrastructure, and fight any increases in mileage standards for cars, for decades. They also effectively receive a massive subsidy from the U.S., state, and local governments in the form of highway building projects and free parking. The government should actively try to change consumer behavior by tolling all highways, eliminating free parking, and taxing gasoline. Moreover, the funds taken from these measures should be used to subsidize public transportation. Also every highway in the U.S., that has more than one lane for each direction, should sacrifice a lane for high-speed rail. The only legitimate argument that the car companies have is that their impending bankruptcy will cost the U.S. government even more money, than they are currently burning, because of a U.S. law that insures the pension plans of companies that go bankrupt. My re-

sponse to this: change the law. All of the other automakers will happily build more U.S. factories, to supply cars to the largest car market in the world.

Golf is an industry that I would like to see collapse completely. In a world where fresh water is an increasingly scarce resource, we have no room for implacably thirsty golf courses. The massive amounts of fertilizer that they use also pollute the water table,s further damaging fresh water supplies. The golf course in the middle of Yosemite National Park still pisses me off! Also, I strongly dislike the elitist, racist, and sexist tendencies of golf clubs. Membership fees are exorbitant for all but the well-to-do. The golf course in Augusta, Georgia, where the Masters are held, still excludes women. Did I mention that golf is not even a sport? Baseball is another sport I would like to see collapse. This is just a personal prejudice of mine I admit, but one has to admit that there is something inherently unfair about a professional league, where the team-that-shall-not-be-named spends up to ten times as much as all other teams on players. Put all those steroid junkies out on the street.

I would love to see military spending reduced if not slashed drastically. Unfortunately, the Obama administration seems to be doing very little, in this department. We should immediately eliminate all expenditures on weapons development, as we have no equal on the battlefield when it comes to technology. I would also like to see an immediate

withdrawal from all foreign war zones, and a selling off of all international military bases to our allies. All foreign military support should also be eliminated. Israel does not need our military support, and all of our military initiatives in Latin America seem to fail miserably, especially when one does a cost-benefit analysis. We should stop the drug war, as it does more harm than the drugs themselves. The illegal drug industry is also recession proof. As this is a favorite subject of mine to rant about, I will not beat this dead horse any more.

Junk mail is an absurd waste of resources. I would guess that most Americans do not read about 95% of their mail. I don't even check my mail anymore. There should be a do-not-mail list, as well as the do-not-call list. Also, anyone with an Internet account should automatically be weaned from receiving any bills in the mail by law. This would save countless trees and fuel. Yes, we would probably have to lay off massive amounts of postal workers, but they are redundant anyway.

I would love to see a massive grass-roots rebellion against planned obsolescence. It is an open secret that iPod batteries die after two years, and you have to re-place the entire iPod. This is just one example of many. We as consumers should stand up to the corporations that make shoddy products.

Since more Americans are being laid off, we should collectively have a lot more time to cook. In this spirit, I would love to see consumers shun prepackaged T.V. dinners and canned food, in favor of fresh, local ingredients. If more consumers shunned these products, fresh produce would become cheaper because consumers would no longer have to compete with massive corporations' bulk buying power for fresh food.

I would love to see the entire jewelry industry go down. These shiny little trinkets are useless, and do nothing for anyone. The entire gold industry is one of the most environmentally destructive industries there is. For each ounce of gold that the mining companies extract, they extract 30 tons of ore, and bake it in cyanide. There is no environmentally friendly way to do this. Also the diamonds that people purchase fund bloody insurgencies throughout the world. The advertising industry is another harmful industry. They create demand for products, where there previously was none. Fire the whole lot of them. The wedding industry needs some serious downsizing. I still can't believe how much money Americans waste every year on their weddings. Also, their inevitable divorces cost even more than their expensive weddings.

We should truly harness the power of the internet to eliminate the real estate industry. They get 6%, just because they had an effective monopoly of real estate listings. The internet can change that. I also have a personal hatred for air conditioners. They actually increase the temperature outside wherever they are in use. Also, as most of the electricity in the U.S. is provided by natural gas burning power plants, the use

of air conditioners contributes to global warming. If you can't stand the heat, stay in the north, you fucking Yankee!

People should stop paying for cable television. It is obscene that people pay a premium for these channels only to have infomercials on every one of these channels for about 8 hours a day. Night owls and early birds should know this well. We should be able to selectively choose which channels we want to have, and pay for only those channels, as most cable subscribers don't even watch half of the channels they have. Moreover, we should have the option of paying a onetime fee for sporting events, or other shows we would like to see. I recently discovered that I can watch many sporting events on the internet on live-streaming web sites.

I would love to see massive layoffs in law enforcement. The problem is not that we don't have enough police officers, but that there are too many laws that they have to enforce. Ending the drug war would eliminate the need for at least half of these police officers, not to mention prosecutors, defense attorneys, judges, and jailers. There are also a lot of other laws that we could eliminate. I personally hate noise ordinances. Why is it that the cops are called almost every time anyone throws a party, but I can't call the cops when the sound of leaf blowers and car alarms disturb me?

I am sure that I could think of a lot more industries to eliminate given the time. We could then spread the remaining jobs among everyone else and work towards achieving the 20 hour work week for everyone. With all this free time, we could then rededicate ourselves to our hobbies and passions. Maybe we could even spend more time with our families and friends.

Day 533, 3-23-2009

gps: S 16°24'46.39" W 71°31'3.17"

I believe that the vast majority of people on my email list are intelligent enough to know that the following is satire, just by looking at the title of this blog post. I, however, do not have that much faith in America as a whole, as the quality of our educational system has declined dramatically, while our armed forces have gotten all of the funding. I would love it if this blog post went viral and pissed a whole bunch of dumbasses off, so feel free to forward it to friends -- or better yet, enemies. As a cynic, there is nothing I enjoy laughing at more, than a bunch of apoplectic idiots. I hope all is well.

News about the economy is getting scarier by the day. The American spending glut that fueled not just the American economy, but the world economy as well, is over now that the bills for the debt that fueled our historic consumption are now due. The government has run up a deficit of well over a trillion dollars this year, in a desperate attempt to get people to start spending their money again, but to no avail. Despite the trillions of dollars being spent, no new jobs are being created, as we have in fact lost millions of jobs in the last year. This creates a vicious cycle as even people with jobs are even more likely to stop spending money, for fear of losing their jobs in the future, which leads to even more job losses. There must be some way to stimulate the economy.

The solution lies in class warfare. We wouldn't even have to spend more than the cost of bullets, since there are already 200,000,000 estimated privately owned firearms in the United States. I propose that we put them to use. Yes the rich own a portion of those firearms, they also have the police and the military at their disposal, and they would ultimately win a class war against the poor and middle class, but at a great economic cost. It is precisely this cost that would stimulate the economy.

Fear is what is largely driving this recession, but we can harness fear to provide an economic stimulus. As of 2006 there were an estimated 2,700,000 millionaires living in the United States, using net worth valuations which excluded the value of their homes. The number has no doubt dropped since then, but let us just walk through some math assuming that there are still around 2,000,000 such millionaires remaining. These people have enough available money to start spending it now, but aren't because they don't want to rub other's faces in their financial security, so they have been avoiding the usual ostentatious displays of wealth that they're accustomed to.

However, if they legitimately feared for their lives, they would no doubt begin to spend their money on security for themselves. As the police and military forces would be overwhelmed just by the sheer number of firearms in this country, they would no longer be able to provide around the clock protection for the rich and therefore, the rich would have to hire private security. Since the only way to ensure their safety is 24 hour surveillance, this would

create the need for many armed security personnel. Each week is exactly 168 hours long, so to have at least one armed guard around the house one would have to contract at least 4 full time employees, and one part time employee, in order to avoid having to pay overtime. As the rich have larger properties to protect, no one security guard would be able to protect more than four houses at a time. Using these numbers one could calculate that this would provide 4.2 X 500,000 = 2,100,000 new full-time jobs to the economy (the .2 trailing the 4 is for those 8 hours left over, after the four full time employees have been allotted their 40 hours a week). Moreover, these are higher quality jobs, as armed security personnel require a variety of special licenses in order to be able to carry firearms on the job. Also, the ultra-rich would no doubt hire 24 hour security detail to escort them throughout their days. Assuming that only 100,000 of these 2,000,000 would qualify as ultra-rich, we get that they would hire an additional 4.2 X 100,000 = 420,000 armed security guards as their personal escorts. These security guards would be even more highly paid as they would have to be highly trained in counter-assassination and counter-kidnapping tactics, in addition to their usual licensing requirements. That is 2,420,000 new jobs created thus far.

There is no doubt that the U.S., state, and local governments would, at the least, match the number of new private security hires with police and military new hires. That is 4,840,000 new jobs thus far. No doubt all the new private security, police, and military trainees would need instructors to train them in the counter-assassination and counter-kidnapping tactics, as well as general firearm use

for their licenses. Assuming that we would need at least one instructor for every 10 cadets that is an additional 484,000 jobs. These jobs would be permanent as security, police, and military personnel need to renew their various licenses and training. That brings the total of new jobs added to 5,324,000.

All of these 5,324,000 new employees would need to be properly equipped with weapons. As the U.S. gun manufactures currently produce and sell about 4,700,000 guns every year in the United States, the capacity to produce and sell weapons would need to be expanded by 112%. It has been estimated that at least 500,000 people are employed in gun manufacturing and gun retail. As both the gun manufacturing and retail jobs are already highly mechanized, the companies would have no choice but to hire about 112% more workers. That means there would be an additional 500,000 X 1.12 = 560,000 new jobs added. The total is now comes to 5,884,000 permanent new jobs. Gun manufacturers would no doubt have to build new factories, gun retailers would have to build new display rooms for their weapons, and the instructors would most definitely need additional training facilities all the new trainees. All this new building would stimulate the construction industry which is currently reeling from the housing bust. This would put more construction workers back to work, albeit only temporarily as this would only be a one-time expansion. All these new workers would undoubtedly spend their hard-earned money on their mortgages and rents, either directly or indirectly helping decelerate the foreclosure crisis which has led to the downward spiral in house prices that we have been experiencing as of late. There is no doubt countless new jobs which would be added to the economy as these security personnel spend their money. Before we know it, we would have replaced all the jobs that have been lost in this recession. If you don't have the guts to kill a rich person, there are other ways to do your part. Armed kidnapping will more than suffice, as would arson, which would have the added benefit of further stimulating the construction industry, as the houses are replaced. Rich people would now be so fearful that they would probably even be willing to take on debt to pay for all their security upgrades. So all of you that were hesitant to engage in class warfare before, because you feared being seen as a communist, can now do so with a clean conscience- knowing that you are helping stimulate the economy. You would be a true capitalist patriot!

Day 546, 4-5-2009

gps: S 15°50'43.05" W 70° 2'3.69"

Unfortunately, it looks like waking up and finding frost on my tent and bicycle is going to become more of the norm, rather than the exception, as I continue to advance southward. I purchased some new heavy-duty socks in Arequipa for when I am asleep in my tent. I wear three layers of socks when it is real cold. I have been blessed with sunny weather all the way from Arequipa to Puno, where I am now. All in all, I would take the sunburned face from the nose down, and the chapped lips, over having to ride through cold rain and hail. At higher elevations the U.V. rays are noticeably stronger as I have to wear my sunglasses to prevent snow-blindness, and cover my body more, to prevent sunburn. Despite the sunny days, it still freezes at night. I rewarded myself for reaching Juliaca with a nice warm hotel room and I intend to do the same here in Puno. A fun fact: I always thought it was strange how my "Army Field Guide to Survival" recommends to always have matches in a waterproof container, rather than a lighter. I have since discovered that lighters barely function, if they function at all, at higher elevations. My theory is that the thinner air does not provide enough oxygen for the combustion reaction.

Recently, President Obama rejected yet another call for legalization of marijuana from an internet forum. The person who posed the question, unfortunately, only reinforced the popular image of the idiot stoner. He suggested that legalizing marijuana would be some kind of panacea for our economic woes. President Obama was right to ridicule this line of reasoning, but he is wrong to reject the call for the legalization of marijuana. I have read a somewhat dubious statistic in Foreign Policy Magazine that 60% of the Mexican cartels revenue comes from marijuana smuggling. I don't believe this statistic, because almost everyone I know who smokes weed, smokes hydroponic weed with an American provenance. Nonetheless, legalizing marijuana would remove a major revenue source from the Mexican cartels, not to mention, empty our jails, and free up law enforcement resources to focus on real crime. I think, as more and more states face potential bankruptcy, that marijuana will become more or less decriminalized, as a fiscal measure to free up prison space, especially in local and county jails as there are over 700,000 arrests every year for marijuana possession. Currently, all these people have to spend at least one night in jail. The illegal drug industry is one of the few truly recession-proof industries, so people will keep buying these drugs.

I was pleased to discover, after leaving the wilderness, that gay people can marry in Iowa now because of a new court ruling. It pleases me that the Christian right is losing the culture wars in the U.S. In the last ten years the percentage of people that claim to be atheist has risen from 5% to 15% of the U.S. population. I only hope this trend will accelerate in the next ten years. I envision an atheist majority like in Germany. For the record, I do not consider myself atheist or agnostic, but I am definitely not Christian. You could say that I am an animistic pantheist. The Incas worshiped the sun. Since the sun melts the frost off of my tent and warms me, I would say that I am a sun worshiper too. I strongly dislike the Christian church, and I would say that I have declared open war on Christianity, after a Brazilian archbishop recently ex-communicated a nine-year-old rape victim and the doctors who performed a life-saving abortion on her, but not the pig of a stepfather who continually raped her. I can't wait for the next pair of proselytizers to knock on my front door. I am going to tear them a new asshole.

Day 551, 4-10-2009
gps: S 15°50'43.05" W 70° 2'3.69"

Peru is one of those places that strikes you as just another poor place, but them grows on you, as you scratch the surface and discover that the richness of the culture more than makes up for the poverty of worldly possessions. I've had the good fortune of getting to know a number of Peruvians, who have turned me on to some of the more beautiful aspects of Peruvian culture. Even now that I am going to be in Bolivia in a couple of days, I am still discovering new things about Peru. I am going to really miss Peru, as I have completely fallen in love with it.

When I first arrived in Puno, I made friends with a photographer who is just a little bit younger than me. He saw me on my bike and realized I was confused about where I was, and decided to help me find the place I was looking for. Usually, upon arriving in a new city, I am extremely wary of strangers as my white skin attracts all sorts of conmen and charlatans, but I could tell that Giorgio was not using subterfuge to try to liberate me of my possessions. I have only known Giorgio for a few days but I am so glad to have met him. He is one of the people who have helped open my eyes to the beauty of Peru, by introducing to me to new things. I also got to spend some time cooking with Giorgio and friends of his, as well as go on some bike rides with them. All in all, Giorgio and his friends have shown me a wonderful time in Puno.

As some of you are probably aware, this week is Semana Santa, or Easter week, for those who are ignorant of Latin culture. To understand Semana Santa, it is important to understand that Easter is much more important than Christmas here, as far as religious holidays are concerned. When I was working in Mexico, I got the day off for Christmas, but two weeks off for Semana Santa. All throughout the Catholic world, but especially in Spanish-speaking countries, there are all sorts of parades and pilgrimages honoring the last living days of Jesus.

Here in Puno, there is a large procession to the top of a hill, where there is a giant cross. People then light candles at the top and make their way back down the hill. My new-found amigos puneños and I decided that it would be a fun idea to drink a bunch San Pedro cactus tea, and go on the procession in a happily altered state. Maybe we could speak to God that way. Despite the rain and the cold, the hill was packed with the faithful, and it was still a beautiful ceremony.

In the past I have made some pretty damning statements about religion and, more specifically, Christianity. However, I do appreciate some of the symbolism and the beauty of some religious ceremonies. Catholicism has so much history and tradition (not all of it good) that I would have to choose it over other forms of Christianity, if I had a gun to my head. Evangelism doesn't hold a candle to Catholicism, when it comes to integrating beauty into its ceremonies. It is just a cheap, tacky, plastic church for cheap, tacky, plastic people living in a cheap, tacky, plastic society. Catholicism gave us Michaelangelo's Sistine Chapel while Evangelism gave us Pat Boone, and ugly suburban mega-churches.

Ganjobiciclatolicismo is the name I have given my own religion of one in the past, and I thought I might expound on it, since I am the high priest of it after all. As a true cultural syncretist, I have decided that I am going to borrow some of the symbolism from Catholicism, since not every single aspect of it is bad. As a non-Christian I have to say that I nonetheless, like the concept of human sinfulness. I only wish more people could see their own sinfulness, instead of the sinfulness of those around them. During the procession to the cross on top of the hill, one thing that I saw that I really liked, were people carrying stones up the hill and placing them on the various prayer stations before they reached the cross at the top. My friends explained to me that the rocks were symbolic of the people's sins and that carrying this burden up the hill was seen as a form of penance. This really jived well with me, since I had already kind of thought of myself as performing some kind of penance by hauling my bike with all of its gear up the sides of massive mountains. So there you have it. I have a way of paying penance in ganjobiciclatolicismo.

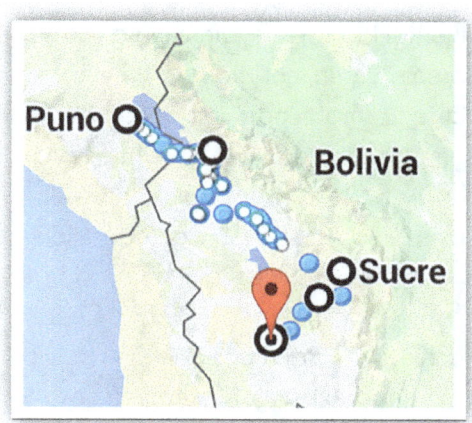

Bolivia, Web Piracy, & the Ganjobicicletholic Church

Day 559, 4-18-2009

gps: S 16°29'56.44" W 68° 8'46.49"

I finally left Peru two days ago, and I am now sitting in an Internet cafe in La Paz. I arrived here last night after a long, tiring day. La Paz sits in a large valley, which makes it difficult to navigate for someone who is visiting for the first time. After blatantly disregarding a sign that prohibits cyclists from entering the highway that descends into the valley from Barrios Altos, I arrived in the hotel zone of La Paz about a half-hour later, ready for the embrace of a nice, warm bed.

My first impression of Bolivia is that it is dirt-cheap, aside from the $135 dollars I had to pay to enter Bolivia. I actually paid $140 since I didn't have any change. The immigration office claimed to not have any change, and I didn't protest the extra $5, as I saw it as a fee to expedite the process. I have heard from other Americans entering Bolivia that they have been given a hard time by the authorities. Aside from paying the money and filling out a long immigration form, I found the process to be relatively painless. My first meal in Bolivian territory cost 5 bolivianos and my first stay in a lodging cost 12 bolivianos. The current boliviano to dollar ratio is 7 to 1. There don't seem to be many places to spend my money here, so I wouldn't be surprised if I spend less money in all of Bolivia, than I did to enter it. I should mention a certain caveat: the 12 boliviano lodging did not even have a collective bathroom for its guests.

Bolivia is the only country I know of where the president goes on a hunger strike when he doesn't get his way, legislatively speaking that is. I am a fan of Evo Morales. I think he is overplaying his hand with a lot of the social reforms that he is trying to enact but overall, I like him. There are not enough presidents in this world who are single, and Evo Morales is one of them. He has made his sister the official First Lady of Bolivia. His life story is pretty inspiring for me. He grew up in a family where the vast majority of his brothers and sisters didn't even reach adulthood. He is a polarizing figure, as evidenced by the recent attempt on his life in the Santa Cruz region, but I believe he really cares about the long neglected Bolivian indigenous majority. I hope that he succeeds in elevating the indigenous poor of this country.

Recently, it was in the news that the proprietors of Pirate Bay have been convicted in a Swedish court of making copyrighted material available for illegal downloading. I have high hopes that they win their appeal, as I would like to see the recording industry go bankrupt. The music industry has been producing too much homogeneous shit for too long. I am tired of hearing songs that range from clichéd love songs to celebrations of self-indulgent narcissism. The copyright laws, which grant protection to a copyright holder up to 150 years after the death of the original artist, need to be changed too. Even if the proprietors of Pirate Bay lose their appeals, I hope that pirates of the world unite to bring those motherfuckers to their knees.

I have been thinking a lot about creating the Ganjobicicletholic Church. The Native American church won the right to use peyote a long time ago from the U.S. Supreme Court, so I figured why not use religion as an excuse to smoke pot? The question is, how does one create an officially recognized religion? My solution is to apply for I.R.S. tax-exempt status. In order to do this, I will have to submit Articles of Confederation, and a Constitution, among other things, to the I.R.S. I figure if the Jedi Church can get official recognition in Great Britain, then I should achieve official recognition in the U.S.

The next step is creating an official mythology and rituals of the Ganjobicicletholic Church. I figured I'd just borrow from other religions to create a patchwork from thier positive aspects, kind of like Unitarian Universalists. We will worship the sun, the moon, the winds, and nature in general. Prometheus, the bringer of fire in Greek mythology, will be re-branded as the bringer of technology. As fire can grow out of control if one isn't careful, so can the use of technology, as evidenced by global warming. It will behoove us, the members of the Ganjobicicletholic Church, to limit our use of technology in order to achieve a greater balance with nature.

Regarding rituals, I can think of a few that we will borrow from other religions. I like the Day of the Dead which is practiced in Catholic Latin America, but not much elsewhere. Honoring our dead ancestors is a positive thing as far as I am concerned. I also like the Muslim idea of a once-in-a-lifetime religious pilgrimage. Instead of going to Mecca though, the end point of a pilgrimage will be discretionary as long as the pilgrimage is made using only human and sail power. Every full moon, we will have a feast and smoke-out, which culminates in a large group bike ride afterwards. The use of hallucinogens will be encouraged with proper supervision.

Day 564, 4-23-2009
gps: S 16°29'56.44" W 68° 8'46.49"

If there were a movie called "Leaving La Paz" it would be just like Leaving Las Vegas but replace alcohol with marijuana. I am too high to be pissed off about anything. On the contrary, there is a lot of good news in the world today. I am most excited about the U.S. Supreme Courts recent decision in Gant vs. Arizona, that limits a police officer's ability to search one's vehicle during an arrest. It has been standard police procedure for almost the last three decades to immediately search the car of someone upon arrest. The lesson is, if the police pull you over, park in a place where you can get out, if you think that you'll be arrested. As long as you're seperated from the car, the police can't search it. I didn't think I would hear a progressive ruling from the Supreme Court for at least a generation. I leave La Paz tomorrow. I expect to have to eat lots of cookie and tuna on the road.

Day 569, 4-28-2009
gps: S 16°29'55.76" W 68° 8'6.74"

I spent a week in La Paz. There is something I like about big, massive, congested cities. La Paz has its charming idiosyncrasies that make it an interesting place to stay. My favorite thing is that they have zebras directing traffic. Yes, zebras! Other cities have traffic cops, and there are some of those, but the local government decided that people dressed in zebra suits would be more effective at directing traffic.

What did I do in La Paz? Not much. I just enjoyed eating good food for good prices and indulged in my newfound cappuccino addiction. I never drank coffee until I passed through Colombia, and then I got spoiled by the good stuff. A cup of cafe con leche with a little bit of sugar is a cup of heaven, as far as I'm concerned. After you leave Colombia, you can only find good coffee in the big cities; everywhere else you can only find that powdered, instantaneous shit. Cappuccino is the closest I have come to recreating that perfect cup of cafe con leche. Knowing that, as soon as I left the city, I was going to have to endure freezing temperatures and monotonous food, it was easy to stay a week.

I did do one touristy thing while I was in La Paz. I road on El Camino de la Muerte or Death-road, if you like. Back in the day, it used to serve as a highway between La Paz and Coroico to the east. With 100+ fatalities every year it earned the moniker El Camino de la Muerte, after a U.N. study determined that it was the world's most dangerous highway at the time. The Bolivian government has since built a new highway, and the Death Road has become nothing more than a high-hifalutin mountain bike trail. Apparently there are still some fools who die on the mountain bike tour, but I was not one of them. We were babysat a little too much by the tour guides to my liking, but I compensated by smoking copious amounts of marijuana during the 10,000 foot descent. Even though we had our nannies with us, the tour was still fun. It was nice being able to hurl down the side of a mountain, without carrying half of my body weight in gear. I consistently stayed at the front and only had to ask the tour guide in front to move faster once.

After studying a map of Bolivia, I've decided on a rough course of where to go. I am in Oruro right now and I plan to traverse Sucre, Potosi, el Salar de Uyuni, and Tarija in that order. Once I get close to the Salar de Uyuni, I will be in a very remote part of the country, so I am mentally preparing myself for the monotony of eating nothing but cans of tuna and cookies and riding on dirt roads for days on end. It should all be worth it though, as the Salar de Uyuni is best described as an extraterrestrial, altiplano desert. If I play my cards right, I should be able to pass through the town where Butch Cassidy and the Sundance Kid were killed, on the way to Argentina. I had back-to-back one hundred kilometer days on the way to Oruro from La Paz, so there is a possibility that I will complete my tour of Bolivia in less than a month.

George Bush really opened up a can of worms with his excessive use of the word terrorist, to describe pretty much anyone that disagrees with the dominant imperialist agenda, whether it be religiously fanatic Muslim suicide bombers in the Middle East, left-wing narco-rebels in Colombia, or now, animal rights activists. What the hell does terrorist mean anyway? If the definition of terrorist is someone who terrifies in order to coerce change or adherence to the status quo, than I propose that the U.S. government qualifies. We are, after all, the only country to ever detonate a nuclear bomb on a civilian target.

The government of Evo Morales has taken a cue from the Bush school of rhetoric. He blithely calls the supposed international assassins that his government filled with bullets, "terrorists." I usually support Evo Morales's actions, but this goes too far.

Even if the government has incontrovertible proof that these men intended to assassinate the president, these men should have been arrested and not killed while sleeping during a S.W.A.T. style raid. The pictures of the so-called "terrorist" ringleader naked and bloody in his bed, belie the government's case that they were planning actions. If the government really had proof of their intentions, they should have tried much harder to arrest these people and bring them to justice. Extrajudicial assassinations of terrorist subjects set a bad precedent, but I can only say that the Bolivians are learning from us.

Day 581, 5-10-2009

gps: S 19° 2'31.79" W 65°15'21.13"

I am now resting in Sucre, Bolivia, after riding on what was probably the worst dirt road I have ever ridden on in my life. I will likely have nightmares about this road, 20 years from now. There are many parts of the road with rocky, 30 degree inclines, some of which go on for miles at a time. Pretty much all of the switchbacks were at these inclines, and also had loose dirt which added yet another layer of difficulty to this road. Sisyphus has it easy. The strange thing is that I actually preferred ascending, over descending, because I was afraid of damaging my bike. I have no doubt that this road has snapped car axles in half, and destroyed transmissions. If I was lucky enough to ride on a flat part of the road, I was pretty much guaranteed to be riding through a glorified sand pit. If there was a creek or river, there was probably not a bridge. I suspect that the road is impassable during the rainy season. There was very little traffic, and only a few towns where I could stock up on food and water and eat prepared meals. Most of the people who go from Oruro to Sucre take the longer, paved route via Potosi, but I did not heed the warnings of those who told me that it was a bad road, because I did not want to backtrack. I ended up needing just over a week to ride the 320 kilometers of dirt road between the town of Huanuni and Sucre. The upside to riding on this road was that it was indeed beautiful. The mountains seem to be painted every color that you can imagine a mountain would be. They're jagged and steep. I rode on many a mountain ridge with 1,000 foot drop offs.

The views were stunning. One night, when I was camping on the side of the road, I even got snowed on. The flurry only lasted about 30 or 40 minutes, but left a pretty healthy blanket of snow on my bicycle, tent, and my surroundings. Despite the beauty of this part of Bolivia, I was happy to make it out of the wilderness, as the road was definitely testing my morale. My bicycle is happy to be done with that road too, and is due for a tune-up.

One casualty of the road was my G.P.S. device. I had already noticed that my G.P.S. wasn't accurately recording elevation gains when I was in Peru, but I could live with that. I had also noticed that it would automatically shut off when I was going to down long descents. It took me a while to realize what was causing this problem. I would usually hit some kind of bump or pothole which would jolt the batteries loose for a microsecond and break the circuit, therefore shutting it off. This was a manageable problem before but this road was so rocky that I decided it would be better to just turn it off and use it more sparingly. This means that I am no longer recording my total ascent or kilometers logged, but I am saving a lot of batteries this way.

I was lucky, or unlucky enough, to witness something that few gringos ever get to see, while passing through the towns on this road. I happened to pass through these towns during the festival called Tinku. Apparently, the townsfolk all get together and beat the shit out of each other, but I didn't witness any of that: What I saw was everyone getting dressed up in traditional clothing and parading around town, rhythmically stomping their feet, and playing charangoes and sanpoñas. I was even awakened during one night while camping, by people stomping through the countryside with their charangoes.

The downside of Tinku, is that it is pretty much an excuse like most holidays in Latin America, for the men to get ridiculously drunk. In most of the towns I passed through, at least half of the male population was falling down drunk before noon. This created a volatile situation for me, as I had to deal with pushy drunks trying to get me to drink with them, in every town. In one town, a group of them even surrounded me when I was going up a hill and tried to get me to drink with them. I am damn near a teetotaler, and particularly despise drunks, so I politely declined to drink with them telling them that I was allergic to alcohol, but they were un-swayed by

this argument and annoyingly persisted in trying to get me to drink. One of them was particularly belligerent, and stole the sunglasses off of my bike before I was able to ride off. I then got off of my bike, and politely but insistently asked for him to give me my glasses back. I knew that it was wise to pursue a diplomatic solution to this standoff, rather than stab 5 or 6 drunk guys in the throat over sunglasses, so I maintained this strategy until one of the more reasonable drunks intervened on my behalf. At this point I rode off and put as much distance between myself and the drunks as possible, because I knew that once I was out of sight they'd forget that I had even passed through.

One consequence of riding through the Incan nation, as I like to call the Bolivian, Ecuadoran, and Peruvian Andes, is that the iconic image of the masculine cowboy on a horse herding his cattle has now been indelibly replaced with that of an indigenous woman, wearing a bowler hat, following her cows around and cursing at them in Quechua, when they don't move across the road fast enough. I have a similar image now for shepherds as well. When I hear, "The lord is my shepherd," I can't help but think of the little Incan lady cursing and throwing rocks at her sheep. I occasionally see a man with his cows or sheep, but it is almost always a woman. God only knows where the men are. After Tinku, I am starting to think that they are off drinking somewhere.

I was cut off from the rest of the world during my week on the nightmare road, because there was no internet access in most of the towns I passed through. When I finally got to Sucre, I wasn't shocked but nonetheless pissed off, to find out that the scandal involving the Colombian army's deceiving and murdering of indigent people to pad the numbers of rebel kills has only grown. According to the B.B.C. there are now over a thousand cases pending against the army, for these unspeakable human rights violations. The Colombian government, of course, claims that most of these cases were actually rebels, but I think they are lying. I am so angry about this, that I actually going to write a letter to my Congressmen and Senators, urging them to end Plan Colombia and demand an international investigation with prosecutions of all those involved. I don't think that this will actually do anything, but I don't want to feel powerless in light of these crimes against humanity, perpetrated in the name of the holy drug war.

Day 598, 5-27-2009

gps: I stayed in Sucre, then Potosi

My timing for being in Sucre couldn't have been any more serendipitous. The city celebrated its bicentennial of independence for the entire month of May. There have been free concerts and parades all over the city. I got to see the Bolivian super group Kjarkas play a free concert. Noticeably absent from the festivities is the Bolivian president Evo Morales, who despite his nation-wide popularity, is persona non grata in Sucre. The reason is that Sucre is constitutionally the capital of Bolivia, but La Paz is where the center of the executive and legislative branches are. As anyone who has held power is loath to let go of it, Sucre has been the site of various protests against Evo Morales, even blockading the airport runway and preventing his plane from landing in Sucre on one occasion. You can see signs scrawled in graffiti that say, "Sucre capital of Bolivia." I think Evo Morales knows that even showing up in Sucre would piss a lot of people off.

I ended up lingering in Sucre longer than I expected, partially because I'm lazy, and partially because I had an accident between myself and a car the day I was leaving. I left the accident with only bruises to my pride and body but my bicycle required a new wheel and a new part machined for my saddlebags. I take partial blame for the accident, as I was being a little too aggressive in challenging a yellow light. What I forgot was that, as my light changed from green, yellow, and then to red, the other light also changed colors at the same time.

As these are old single lane colonial streets, I thought I could easily beat the yellow light. What I didn't anticipate, was that any driver away from the intersection would anticipate the green light, and accelerate on their yellow. This led to me slamming into the side of their car that I didn't see coming. I could tell the driver felt a little bit guilty himself for, even though he stopped to check and see if I was alright, he was quickly gone. I am sure that I probably left a big dent in the side of his car, as two hundred pounds of flesh, bones, steel, and rubber, hurling into anything is sure to leave a mark. I might have even perforated the steel as my metal-spiked helmet impacted with the car first. I am now almost completely healed, and my bike is in optimal condition. It didn't even cost me that much to buy a new wheel and machine a new part.

I'm in Potosi now, site of the greatest theft of mineral wealth in the history of mankind. I have read that Potosi supplied half of the world's silver, for over two centuries. The Spanish, ruled by the Habsburg dynasty during most of this time, mostly squandered this wealth on wars and luxury goods, and were then in decline by the end of the 17th century. The Cerro Rico, or rich hill, which looms over the south of the city, has also swallowed literally millions of lives. Most of the estimates I have seen range from 4 to 8 million deaths. To put that in perspective the current population of Bolivia is around 9.1 million.

Day 608, 6-6-2009

gps: S 20°27'37.59" W 66°49'30.03"

I am in Uyuni, Bolivia now. It is fucking cold. It reaches -10F at night. I am camping in this weather. I finally sent a letter to my elected representatives and to the president regarding Plan Colombia. I have enclosed the letter and I would encourage yall to write your own letters.

If yall are feeling lazy, feel free to copy and paste. I don't think these shitheads are going to do anything that would affect the status quo, but I don't want to feel powerless. At least I have a voice, right. I hope all is well with everyone.

Love, Ezra

Day 613, 6-11-2009

gps: S 20°27'31.80" W 66°49'29.01"

The highlands of Southwestern Bolivia are unbelievably cold. I have read that the temperatures drop to -25C. which is close to -10F, for those of y'all that are afraid of conversion. I actually had to go to the trouble of buying a new blanket, which is about 2 centimeters thick. It goes on top of my sleeping bag, while I sleep inside with 4 pairs of socks, three pants, 3 shirts, a sweater, and 3 wool hats. Don't feel sorry for me, because I sleep comfortably. Without the blanket, though, I was freezing my ass off at night. I don't carry a thermometer with me, but I can assure y'all this is the coldest weather that this Texas boy has ever experienced. Anecdotally, I have camped next to ponds which freeze so thoroughly that I can put my entire weight on the edge without breaking the ice, and no less than a softball-sized rock thrown at an upward angle breaks the surface. The water in my camel-back tube freezes, and I have to insulate all of the water I am carrying, so it doesn't freeze solid.

My tent no longer zips shut, but this isn't much of a problem right now, as it is too cold for any insects or other critters to intrude upon my space while I sleep. I already wrote a letter to R.E.I. that was persuasive enough for them to refund my money for the tent, and I have ordered and sent a new one to my friend who lives in Buenos Aires, where I plan to stop on my way to Brazil.

Braving the cold is not without its rewards. This part of Bolivia is beautiful. If the southern coast of Peru is a Martian landscape, the Salar de Uyuni is a Venetian landscape, beautiful in its stark white infinity. I had to wear my sunglasses the whole time, because it is more than sufficiently bright and reflective to cause snow blindness. I rode out to the "Isla de Pescado" or "Isla de Inkahuasi," if y'all prefer. The cacti on this "island" are incredible, reaching up to 12m and living for hundreds of years. Most of them are massive, moreso than the same variety in other parts of Bolivia. The trip to the Inkahuasi was definitely worth it.

I have previously mentioned that the Salar de Uyuni holds over half the world's lithium carbonate deposits. This metal is essential for both laptop batteries, and for the batteries in electric cars, as it is the lightest compound from which batteries can be manufactured. So far, these supplies continue unexploited, as I hope the Evo Morales administration is driving a hard bargain to any company which wishes to access these deposits. The developing world has long suffered economically from the exportation of raw materials, and the importation of manufactured goods leading to trade deficits which always benefit the more advanced economies. Evo Morales should offer access to these deposits for no less than having the multinationals build battery manufacturing plants for laptops and

electric cars. In fact, he should hold out until the companies offer to build laptop and electric car factories in Bolivia. Until then, I hope the natural beauty of the Salar remains untouched.

I finally encountered a road which caused me to hitchhike out of a situation, without experiencing mechanical problems. Heading south from the Salar, which has a wonderful hard, and flat surface; the roads can only be described as a washboard, covered with 3 inches of sand. After moving maybe 10 kilometers, in about 5 hours, I hitchhiked the fuck out of there at the first chance I got. The road from Uyuni to Tupiza isn't a whole lot better, but I doubt it will drive me to the fits of rage that I was experiencing on this glorified sand pit. Bolivia is beautiful, but it has the worst roads I have experienced by far. I can't wait to get to Argentina where I already have friends waiting to share barbecue with me.

If anyone wonders why I don't like cops, the case of a 72-year-old Austin woman who got tazed by a trigger-happy cop should illustrate why. I actually read about this in the B.B.C. so the rest of the world is learning how brutal these Texas pigfuckers are. Ever since the vast majority of American police departments were equipped with these "non-lethal" tazers, the incidences of abuses have steadily risen every year. Because they are "non-lethal" police use them much more excessively than they would ever dare use a gun. You mouth off to a cop, you get tazed. You move suddenly, you get tazed. You have

dark skin, you get tazed. The federal government should make very strict guidelines for when a police officer should be allowed to use his/her tazer. I would suggest that they only be allowed to use their tazers when the "suspect" is exhibiting violent behavior.

I had a dream last night that was so vivid that, dare I say, I think it was a vision. Many saints have visions of bleeding Jesus, or weeping virgins, but the late, great comedian Bill Hicks appeared to me in my vision. In the dream, I had gone to a KKKristian church for the sole purpose of mocking them and laughing at them. After making loud fart noises and laughing hysterically at the verbal flatulence coming out of the pastor's mouth, a raging redneck dragged me out into the church lobby and threatened to pummel me, when a plastered Bill Hicks showed up, shooed the redneck away, put his arm around my shoulder, and told me to, "Keep up the good work!" I have interpreted this as an endorsement of the Ganjobicicletholic church. In my authority as the Grand Supreme High Archbishop of Austin, I have decided to mark this miraculous vision by canonizing Bill Hicks. He will, from now on, be referred to as Saint Bill Hicks by all Ganjobicicletholic practitioners. It has been decreed.

On a more serious note, I have been trying to form a new political manifesto that best represents my beliefs. I have fulminated many times on this blog about my objection to the drug war, racism towards immigrants, the bloated military budget, etc. but I have never tried to formulate

an overreaching political agenda. My main objection to national politics is that they are so myopic. The problems that we face in the world affect us all, and not just each individual nation. We need solutions that encompass the whole world, and not a patchwork of solutions for each nation. Nationalism replaced the obsolete system of feudalism, but it has now become obsolete itself. We need to form a political party with an international perspective to confront the problems that our world faces today.

I believe that every human being has a fundamental right to education, health care, access to clean water, access to nutritious food, shelter, and to all job markets. The right to make money is subordinate to these rights. I was tempted to include security on this list, but I fear that this has too much potential for abuse and misinterpreted by governments. I will now elaborate on these rights:

Education is the great equalizer. It is the only thing that can enable someone to rise from poverty and improve their lot in life. There have been studies that have shown that birth rates decline when women have real educational and economic opportunities. I would define the minimum standards of education as being trilingual (not bilingual), with an emphasis on the use of technology, and access to higher education for all. I prefer trilingual education for several reasons: there are already children who grow up bilingual, and it would allow the entire world to have a common language, without forcing the extinction of less commonly spoken languages. For example, a Peruvian kid could learn Spanish, English, and Quechua; an Israeli kid could learn Hebrew, English, and Arabic; and a Chinese kid could learn Chinese, English, and some other regional Asian language, depending on where they live in. Not only would this give everyone on the planet a common language, with which we could resolve our differences, but it open up our cultural perspective to better understand the cultures of others.

Access to health care, clean water, nutritious food, and shelter are really one and the same problem. Take away any one of these and the others fail. A child without proper shelter can't really defend against mosquito-borne malaria, just as a child without access to clean water really can't defend against typhoid. We all know that a lack of access to proper nutrition can lead to a number of ailments. The reason why the right to make money has to be subordinate to these rights, is to prevent companies from hoarding water for industrial purposes. Water intensive industries, such as nuclear power production, have to be subordinate to agriculture which, in turn, has to be subordinate to the right of everyone to have access to clean water. Health care should emphasize preventative care rather than reactionary care.

Access to all job markets means that all borders should be open everywhere. This would allow people to leave areas, due to drought, famine, poverty, government corruption, or anything else that might disadvantage these populations, to search for jobs elsewhere. The only legitimate use of a border, in my opinion, is for epidemic control. An American has no inherent right to jobs, over people from any other part of the world, and vice versa. Borders only serve to lock poverty into certain regions, while other regions benefit from pseudo-slave labor of their poorer neighbors. Remittances sent home from immigrants to their home countries are worth ten times as much as all foreign assistance, and do more to alleviate poverty than anything else. Moreover, there are people from the developed world, such as myself, who prefer the cultures and the climates of the developing world.

I admit that I'm an idealist, but I am also pragmatic enough to know that this vision will probably not be completed within my lifetime. In response to this, I would say that I am on a hundred-year plan. I am doing my part by learning new languages, and living and working in parts of the world other than the United States. This international political party would have a difficult time establishing a foothold in the United States, since the two-party monopoly has a stranglehold on power, but it could be a force to reckon with in parliamentary systems, where governments have to create coalitions.

Some of these plans are expensive but could easily be paid for if we collectively cut our military budgets. Even countries like Bolivia waste money on their militaries. I have passed by way too many military bases in this country. The fact is that Bolivia would get their asses handed to them in a conventional war with any one of their neighbors, except maybe Paraguay. I am not so naive to think that world would function in the absence of security forces, but I think that these security forces should be international in nature and should only be used in the face of humanitarian crises. In future blog posts, I will try to focus on ideas I have for implementing these changes to our world political structure.

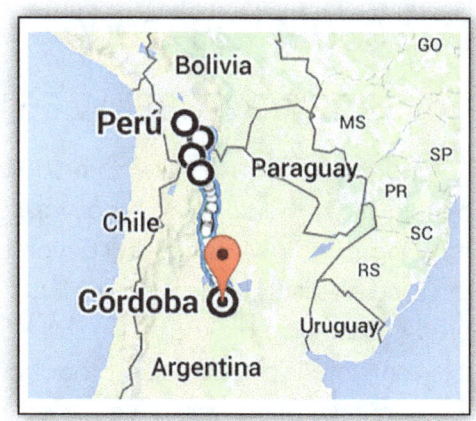

Bienvenidos a Argentina & The Amerikkkan Cult of Mediocrity

Day 620, 6-18-2009

gps: S 21°26'14.02" W 65°42'58.45"

After 5 days and 4 flats between Uyuni and Tupiza, I'm ready to get out of this country. Don't get me wrong, Bolivia is an incredibly beautiful country; a geologist's wet dream, where every other hill is a different color, but I'm tired of shitty roads and the cold, I repeat COLD, nights. One morning recently, I camped in a valley that was still above 13,000 feet. This was problematic because it takes longer for the sunshine to reach every corner of the valley and hence, stays cold longer. It was so cold that the small streams in the valley froze solid. I tested the hardness of the ice by smashing rocks the size of my head to pieces on it. I was so happy to finally reach civilization again, that I am staying in Tupiza for three days, before I ride the final two or three days to the Argentinian border.

I am looking forward to riding on paved roads again in Argentina, as I have recently discovered a couple of cracks in my third rear rim. I am also looking forward to the Argentinian barbeque's, as I have recently been partially starving myself, as there are no places to buy food. I go to sleep at night salivating and fantasizing about food I want to cook and eat. The parrilladas await me. Sorry vegetarians, I am going to eat so much meat that y'all might as well put me on a cholesterol I.V. drip. I already have friends and parrilladas waiting for me.

On a manliness scale of 1 to 10, an intercontental bike trip is probably somewhere between a 9 and 10, so I am not afraid to say that I love ballet. It is so funny how one's perspective can completely change over time. I remember when I was 9 and my mom tried to put me in ballet lessons. This experiment didn't last long, as I steadfastly remained in the corner of the studio and refused to participate. My mom also draged me to see Gregory Hines and Mikhail Baryshnikov in the movie White Nights. As a kid this pissed me off, but I had the unusual privilege of seeing the movie for a second time last night. Dance movies are one of my guilty pleasures, and I have a serious man-crush on Baryshnikov.

His dancing seems to defy the laws of physics. Gregory Hines was no slouch, but Baryshnikov is fucking spectacular. Most of the music in the movie is shit, since it comes from the 80s (yeah I know, it was the golden era of heavy metal and punk, but the rest of the music is shit) but I was turned on to the music of Vladimir Vysotsky, which is worth checking out. This is another reason I can't wait to get out of Bolivia. I need to indulge my high-speed broadband addiction and watch as many videos of Vysotsky and Baryshnikov as possible.

Day 630, 6-28-2009

gps: S 22°39'47.88" W 66°14'12.14"

Bolivia is beautiful, but I am so happy to be out of that country. I will miss the breathtaking scenery and the anything-goes lawlessness, but beyond that I can't think of anything else that I will long for. I will not miss the sand-covered, washboard dirt roads, the shitty cans of "tuna", and the complete lack of decent broadband network. There were so many times when I wandered into a town looking for food, only to be disappointed by the selection of items. My typical conversation would go like this:

"Is there a comedor in town?"

"No."

"Is there Internet?"

"No."

"Is there even a store."

"Yes there is."

"What do they sell?"

"Cookies and soda."

"What kind of cookies do you have?"

"We have shit cookies with vomit cream filling."

"You don't have chocolate?"

"Nope."

"Well, thanks anyway, bye."

I am still pissed off that Bolivia even has a military, since they would get the living shit kicked out of them by any one of their neighbors, except maybe Paraguay. Chile, Argentina, and Brazil would defeat them in a matter of days, while Peru might take a week. In my past post I said nationalism is obsolete, but I should have been more direct; it is fucking stupid. If I were in charge of Bolivia, I would fire every last soldier, and hire a bunch of construction workers to pave Bolivia's pitiful roads, and lay broadband wires in all of the cities that don't have any Internet access. Not only is a Bolivian military useless, but they are potentially harmful, as the recent coup d'état in Honduras should prove my point.

A friend of mine, who has crossed the land border from Bolivia into Argentina, described crossing the border as "leaving Kansas for Oz." That description is not too far off. The difference is just about as stark as leaving Mexico for the U.S. Actually the difference is more stark, because Mexico has well-paved roads. Everything here cost more, but the quality of what you are buying more than makes up for the difference in price. I have spent more on food, but I have eaten some amazing meals. The sheer size of the barbecue platters here makes my eyes pop out! The pizzas, pasta, and wine are good too. The way to my heart is through my stomach, and Argentina has already won my heart. In fact, I think I like it better here than in the U.S. I have even heard that they have free health care here. With the good food and free health care, I can say that I might not come back to the U.S.

Speaking of health care in America, I can honestly say that not reforming health care at all would probably be better than the bill the Democrats have advanced in Congress. There are not enough curse words in the English language to thoroughly convey how fucking pissed off I am about the two-party monopoly on power in the United States. The thing that pisses me off about the bill so much is the health insurance mandate. I currently don't have health insurance, and there is actually a reason for it. I've had it in the past and discovered they were so unresponsive and unhelpful, that I canceled it.

Once I went to the doctor for a regular check-up, only for the insurance company to drag their feet so long in paying the claim, that I started getting collection letters from the doctor's office in the mail. The insurance company claimed they never even received my claim, which was an outright lie. At that point, I sent only certified mail to them, so they couldn't lie through their teeth like that. It still took about six months for them to pay only about 60% of the claim. After this, I figured it was best to just not have insurance, and gamble that I never get really sick, or break a bone. If y'all think insurance companies are unresponsive and unhelpful now, just wait until you are forced to purchase health insurance. A public plan probably wouldn't be any better, since the government would probably just subcontract out to the health insurance industry anyway. I cannot accept health care reform that doesn't cut these thieving bastards out of the loop. This doesn't absolve hospitals, doctors, or the pharmaceutical industry from their culpability, but I think the insurance companies are the worst culprits. This is yet another reason I might not come back to the U.S.

On a happier note, I have recently discovered some wonderful music on-line. Now that I have access to broadband, I have actually been able to give a good listen to Vladimir Visotsky. All I can say is that I want to learn Russian, and take up chain smoking, so I can sing like him. A friend of mine also turned me on to the Plasmatics. I can't believe I had never listened to any of their music. When I listen to it, I just want to torch a cop car, and slit some pig's

throat. If any of y'all don't think that there is censorship and coercion in the U.S., all y'all have to look at is a picture of Wendy O. Williams of the Plasmatics, after Milwaukee police beat the shit out of her, while arresting her for an obscenity charge. As one music critic in the United States said, "Conservatives in America had castration anxiety, when they saw her chainsaw televisions in half." I'm convinced that there are still efforts to erase the history of the Plasmatics, as it is still very difficult to find their music. You Tube even seems to mysteriously fail, when I am trying to load their videos. This makes me even more determined to rip off the music industry. I hope all of them go down with the shit music they have been trying to force down my throat, through their control of the distribution channels. I

am so happy that I have alternate routes of music discovery, now that we have the Internet.

I was in Jujuy, Argentina when my friend told me that Farrah Fawcett died. My response was, "Who fucking cares?" Then came the news that Michael Jackson had died. To me he died about twenty years ago, but that is a moot point. I can't remember the last time people were so freaked out about a single person's death. It is like a god died or something. I suppose his music touched a lot of people, but I can't say I really care. I want to ask people if they expected him to live forever? For me Michael Jackson is far down the list of musicians who I find inspirational. However, most of us mere mortals will never achieve the immortality he has achieved through his music.

Day 634, 7-5-2009

gps: S 23°36'34.38" W 65°41'47.33"

I have not been in Argentina very long, but I love this place! I am a man of primal urges, who thinks a lot more with his stomach, than with his penis. To put it another way, the road to my heart goes through my stomach. For this reason, Argentina has won my heart and then some. This is a country that truly enjoys food. I am very seriously thinking about moving here permanently, not right away, but after I can save some more money back in Babylon.

Argentina may not have quite as much money as the United States, or parts of Europe, but I am convinced that the quality of life is better. I still can't believe it, but I ate a $2 T-bone steak last night. I have vivid memories of buying

a T-bone steak from Whole Foods for no less than $16. A homeless man can sit down after a hard day of begging and eat a $2 T-bone and wash it down with a $2 bottle of wine that rivals the quality of more expensive bottles of wine in the U.S.

There are some things I don't like about Argentina. One thing I have noticed is that they commemorate their war against the indigenous of Patagonia on the back of their 100 peso note. This is pretty much the same thing as if the U.S. government had some glorified depiction of the Trail of Tears on the back of the Andrew Jackson-twenty dollar bill. Part of me thinks that would be appropriate,

since Jackson was a murderous thug, but the other part of me thinks that no government should celebrate genocide.

In my previous post, I made a claim that Bolivia might lose a war with Paraguay. I take that back. These two countries fought a war back in the 1930s, and the then numerically and technologically superior Bolivian forces still had their asses handed back to them. The Bolivian troops, who were mostly indigenous, quechua-speaking people from the highlands, couldn't handle the weather in what is the hottest part of South America. Moreover, those fucking dumb-asses didn't have the wherewithal to hire Guarani-speaking intelligence officers to intercept Paraguayan radio transmissions. As the recent coup in Honduras should prove, militaries are a much greater threat to democracy than they are its defenders. Any-ways, enough of that. I'm going to go eat a $2 T-bone.

Day 651, 7-19-2009

gps: S 26°56'47.60" W 65°17'8.68"

I am slowly making my way down towards Buenos Aires. There is a part of me that wants to slack off, and there is the part of me that wants to make it to Brazil before long. The slacker in me got rewarded with a cold that forced me to stay in Tafi del Valle during my recuperation. Being sick made me realize that, as much as I love Argentina, I probably couldn't live here. The thing that disappointed me was that I could not find either fresh chilies, or ginger anywhere I looked. I am in Tucuman right now. It is one of the bigger cities and I still can't find these ingredients. When I am congested, I usually like to make spicy food and ginger root tea to speed up the recovery process, but I had to live without. In Argentina, it is not hard to find good meats or cheeses, but try looking for fresh vegetables that aren't regularly used here, and you will eventually have to give up in desperation.

Another negative thing that I have noticed about Argentina is that more people smoke here, and it is banned in fewer public places. I even see mothers walking down the street holding a child with one hand, and a cigarette with the other. Smoking is a nasty habit, not to mention the fact that just being around cigarette smoke gives me a nasty headache. I have been turned off from countless women on account of their smoking. It is the feeling that I just have to grin and bear it, that makes me think I might not enjoy living here.

The death of Michael Jackson has made me reflect on a growing phenomenon in Amerikkka: mediocrity. Mediocrity pervades Amerikkkan life. We have mediocre schools, mediocre health-care, mediocre politicians, and mediocre everything else. The tragic thing about this is that Amerikkka used to produce excellence. It is the country that gave the world jazz and rock and roll. Now its contribution to the world is Christina Aguilera and The Fast and the Furious movies.

Michael Jackson was the personification of mediocrity. His entire career was just one giant piece of shit in my opinion. I can't think of a single Jackson 5 song that doesn't make me want to stab chopsticks into my eardrums. Hearing a prepubescent child sing about love drives me into a murderous rage, that causes me to have dark fantasies about torturing Tila Tequila, and then stoning her to death with the severed heads of the Jonas Brothers. The only thing that could possibly be more cringe-worthy is if the adult Michael Jackson wrote a song for N.A.M.B.L.A. For those of y'all who aren't in the know, N.A.M.B.L.A. stands for the North Amerikkkan Man-Boy Love Association. Since the Jackson 5 was commercially successful, the large music companies have been marketing bands with children in them ever since. You can blame the Jackson 5 for Hansen, the Jonas Brothers, Miley Cyrus, and any other shit band made up of children. As a rule of thumb, unless the child is channeling Django Reinhardt, I don't want to hear it.

I can't deny that I liked Thriller when I was a child, but looking back now, armed with the awareness of much greater musicians, I see it for what it really was. Thriller marks a crucial turning point in the devolution of Amerikkkan music. It laid the foundation for Madonna, Britney Spears, Lady Gaga, Justin Timberlake, and any other "musician" who makes me want to kill people randomly. Looking back, there were only three songs on the album that I liked, even when I was a kid. Jack-Off made only one hit song after that album. He was too busy morphing from a black man into an alabaster freak.

Did I mention that M.J. was an overrated dancer? He had a very limited dance repertoire that consisted of the moonwalk, a counterclockwise pirouette, a right-footed kick, a right-handed crotch grab, and a few jerky motions. He was nothing compared to greats like Baryshnikov and

any of the street dancers who helped invent break dancing. In fact, I don't think he would make it past the second round of "So You Think You Can Dance." You can again blame M.J. for the prevalence of pop stars whose only qualification is that they hit the right notes, and can dance with back-up dancers. Speaking of back-up dancers, Michael Jackson was frequently upstaged by his, in almost all of his music videos.

Why does this matter so much to me? Because I am tired of being told that something that is truly mediocre is really excellent. It is this American complacency with mediocrity that gives us politicians like Sarah Palin. Can you think of a better example of someone who best epitomizes megalomaniacal mediocrity? I think she is so popular because she is mediocre just like her supporters. People want to vote for someone who mirrors them.

Barack Obama is a man of exceptional intelligence and exceptional P.R. who, nonetheless, produces mediocre results. The Audacity of Hope should have been called "The Audacity of Bullshit." I am trying to think if there is a single promise he has made, that he hasn't already broken or botched. I can't think of anything. I could exhaust myself by going down the list, starting with giving immunity to telecommunications companies that assisted the Bush administration with illegal wiretaps, but then I would be too pissed off to think clearly. To make matters worse he was all buddy-buddy with Alvaro Uribe during his visit to the White House. Obama praised the Colombian president for his "human rights" record. This is the same president who has presided over the country the entire time that homeless people were being killed and disguised as rebels, to facilitate the promotions of army officers. I guess

Barack Obama is the mediocre president that mediocre Amerikkka deserves.

Amerikkka still excels at two things: greed and gluttony. Only in Amerikkka would a man have the greed-induced chutzpah to create a $50 billion pyramid scheme like Bernard Madoff. If he had shut down the operation after only a few hundred million dollars he probably would have gotten away with it. Joey Chestnut is a new Amerikkkan hero. He is the man who has now defeated the "Michael Jordan" of competitive eating, three times in a row at the annual 4th of July Hot Dog Eating Contest. Before Chestnut came along, Takeru Kobayashi, the little Japanese guy, was dominating the world of competitive eating. As an aside I should mention that the video of Kobayashi going head-to-head with a giant Kodiac bear in a hot dog eating contest is hilarious. Despite the fact that Kobayashi has broken his own personal records in the latest hot dog eating contests, Joey Chestnut has dominated him. In the last contest Chestnut consumed 68 hot dogs. U.S.A.! U.S.A! We're number one!

The California budget crisis has brought out the anti-immigrant folks. Mirroring Proposition 187, these folks are trying to deny all state services to immigrants and their American born children. After hurling thinly veiled racist attacks on the "illiterate" hordes of Mexicans they then go around by interpreting the 14th Amendment to the Constitution in a manner that only displays their functional illiteracy. They actually believe that they can interpret, "All persons born or naturalized in the United States, and subject to the jurisdiction thereof, are citizens of the United States and of the State wherein they reside," to mean, "No wetback children!" I almost feel sorry for these folks, since they are most definitely products of our mediocre educational system.

Amerikkka is a society in decay. I will probably come back for a little while to make some money, and say my goodbyes, but my long term plan is to get the fuck off of this sinking ship. In twenty years, the dollar won't be worth shit. We already spend more money paying the interest on our debt, than even our military budget. When our debt is around $15 trillion-- it will reach that-- our foreign creditors will probably want a higher interest rate than what they are paid now. The current economic crisis is a direct result of Amerikkkan greed. I don't want to pay taxes or even spend money within the Amerikkkan economy any more. I am ready to opt out.

Day 662, 7-30-2009

gps: S 31°23'56.00" W 64°10'55.69"

Its still a little chilly, but I've been enjoying a kick-ass tailwind, which propelled me 50 kilometers into Còrdoba today in about an hour and a half. Getting sucked into the wakes of the semis keeps me moving fast. I am looking forward to the heat of Brazil. I have been reading my Austinite friends' facebook laments about 106F weather with serious envy. I will take the extreme heat of the Texas summer any day over the extreme cold of the Bolivian highlands. I hope that you are all living your dreams or, at least, enjoying life to the fullest.

Though my opinion of Argentina remains pretty high, I have noticed some more cracks in the facade. Despite Argentina's European tendencies, there is still one Latin American tradition that holds strongly here: the midday siesta. Of all the Latin Americans, Argentineans are by far the most militant siesteros. I have been in cities of half a million people where almost all the businesses, save the gas stations, close for the four hour period from 1 p.m. to 5 p.m. I am all for slacking off, but it is pretty frustrating when I arrive in a new town at 1:05 p.m. and I can't buy fruit, or anything for that matter, for the next four hours. If you want to buy something other than food or medicine, those stores don't even open until 5 p.m. I am somewhat skeptical that businesses can effectively turn a profit with such limited business hours. I also don't like how it is impossible to run any errands without being forced to wait in long lines, as everyone runs their errands at the same time. As someone who has worked mostly nights for the past several years, I'd also be annoyed by having to run errands on my days off, which for me are sacred.

Another annoyance for me is that, despite the high traffic volume between cities, Argentinean highways almost never deviate from a two-lane highway, with no shoulder design. This isn't just dangerous for cyclists, but for the many moped

drivers, and drivers in general; as people generally execute dangerous maneuvers to get around the many semis that clog the highways. It is pretty clear to me that the government already has the rights to the land, to expand some of these highways, as the property lines are consistently offset at least 20 meters from the road. The other day, the police tried to stop me when I was on one of these overburdened highways. As I knew that I did not have an alternate route to follow, and I generally don't respect law enforcement officers, I just ignored them and continued on anyway. They would have told me that I couldn't be on the highway, even though there are no signs indicating this, and I would have told them that I was already there and I needed to continue on. For this reason, I didn't see any reason in stopping for them. Let them chase me!

The difference in the prices for lodging between Bolivia and Argentina is at least five-fold, but there are ways to cut costs. Most large cities have municipal camping sites that charge between $1 and $3 for pitching your tent. These camping sites almost always have hot water and barbecue grills, which for me, is luxurious. The other day, I spent $5 for a bag of charcoal, two T-bones, and morcilla; the Argentinean blood sausage, which I have become obsessed with. This is a lot cheaper than the same meal at a restaurant.

Between the cities, the camping options are few and far between. This isn't like the Bolivian and Peruvian altiplano, where the highway traverses miles and miles of unfenced, open land. Almost all of the land is fenced off here in Argentina. I have resorted to full on homeless camping as a result. I haven't even been constructing my tent, as doing so saves me a lot of time in the morning when I am repacking my bicycle. People here are always telling me that it gets cold at night, but I always chuckle at this suggestion, since it hasn't even been freezing at night. I have slept in abandoned houses, and behind Catholic shrines to Gauchito Gil, who I suppose is the Argentinean version of La Virgen de Guadalupe.

Last night, I was awoken by police when they discovered my campsite. After explaining that the nearby campsite was closed, which it was, and that there was little time left before the sunset to choose a new campsite, the cops let me be. This happened after a carpenter, who thought I was the thief stealing his wood, approached me when I was putting down my bed. At first I was like, "Robar madera? Excuse me but I am not sure what you are talking about." After showing the carpenter my bicycle he was satisfied that I couldn't steal his wood, even if I wanted to, and he let me be. The other times that I have been discovered while setting up my campsite, I have had to turn down the families trying to offer me everything from food to letting me sleep in their house, as I carry my own food and don't want to be a burden. I just wanted to be clear that not all of my experiences being discovered are unpleasant.

I wanted to make a quick observation that, of all the female politicians in the world, President Christina Fernandez Kirchner is by far, the most feminine leader I have ever seen. While Hillary Clinton rocks the pant-suits and tries to appear as manly as possible in a male dominated world, the Argentinean president makes no pretensions whatsoever to try to conceal her femininity. The other day, I saw her on television at a church service commemorating Argentinean independence (July 9th). While all of the other congregates were dressed conservatively with dark colors, she stood out in her lavender outfit, which looked like it was designed by Gucci. I don't have any opinion on this; I just thought it was an interesting observation.

el odio es mi guia,
y el mieao mi
Alimento,

Adventures of a Ganjobicicletholic Anarcyclist in a Worldwide Fascist State

Day 681, 8-18-2009

gps: S 34°36'30.30" W 58°22'23.38"

I've made it to Buenos Aires, the southernmost point in my trip. It is starting to warm up, and I am officially sick and tired of the cold. I am looking forward to the steamy weather of Brazil. After looking at a map, I have come to the realization that my trip is almost over, as I plan to end up in either São Paulo or Rio ce Janeiro. This doesn't mean that I'm coming back to the U.S. any time soon.

On the contrary, I plan to stay in Brazil for at least a year, so I can learn Portuguese. I will also be on the lookout for a monkey skull to mount on my helmet. I have actually been reading a Portuguese/English dictionary, page by page, to familiarize myself with some Portuguese vocabulary, and to practice my pronunciation. Portuguese is a little bit harder for me than Spanish, because unlike Spanish, the pronunciation seems to be more random.

The other week when I was in Rosario, I was asking for directions to a hostel from a street juggler, who indicated to me that if I continued in the direction that I wanted to, I would be going in the wrong direction. I told him that I didn't care, because I was an "anarciclista." We both had a good laugh about that, but I thought that was a good word to describe me both politically and as a cyclist. When Argentineans cut me off, while making a right turn without even signaling, I see no reason to respect traffic laws written for people in cars. When the highway has signs that say, "Bicycles prohibited," I ignore them. The ironic thing is that the highway with all of these signs is the safest road in all of Argentina for cyclists,

as it has a wide shoulder and a median to prevent cars from crossing over to the opposite lane. When there was a deadly crash on the highway that backed up traffic for at least 50 kilometers, I crossed the median and rode on the shoulder of the opposite side, while thousands of drivers stranded in the traffic jam eyed me enviously. Strangely enough, the cops didn't give me any trouble about riding my bicycle on the highway even once that day.

The closest I got to getting in any trouble on the highway, was when I underestimated the velocity of a motorcyclist leaving an on-ramp for a highway, and cut across him. He then slowed down to have words with me and I flipped him off, since I don't like being yelled at. He then drove alongside me for a while trying to be menacing. Fortunately, he was all bark and no bite, or as I like to say, "all fart and no shit." The funny thing is I actually ran into him later, while I was eating lunch. He did the same old thing trying to be menacing, but then drove off. The funny thing is that if he actually stuck around, I would have apologized to him. Oh well, on the way back, I will try to not underestimate the speed of motorcyclists leaving the on-ramp.

Entering Buenos Aires on a bicycle is not for the faint-hearted. There was one part, where I was in the middle of the road, after two six-lane highways merged. This highway eventually morphed into a twenty-lane behemoth. When I knew that I was closer to my friend's house, I was happy to leave this monstrosity.

Despite the Argentinean government's complete disregard for cyclists, I see a surprisingly large number of cyclists on the road, many of them middle-aged women. Once you become comfortable maneuvering around the massive streets in Buenos Aires, you can actually move quite a bit faster than people in cars. I think I would go absolutely crazy if I were stuck in a car behind traffic that I could easily cut through on my bicycle.

Buenos Aires has some fantastic graffiti. Unfortunately, a lot of it is in seedier areas of town. When I was taking a picture of a fabulous demonic nun underneath a bridge, a one-legged junkie came up to me, trying to intimidate me. "Why are you taking pictures?" he barked! With a smile, that belied the "I wouldn't think twice about breaking your good knee if you threatened me," look I gave him, I just said, "It's a pretty painting." I then walked off and took some more graffiti pictures.

I have been reading a lot of the news about police abuses of power in the U.S. The Henry Louis Gates racial profiling story has finally made it out of the headlines. I am happy to see a discussion about racial profiling in the news, but I don't think that this was a classic case of true racial profiling. He didn't even get tazed, or shot in the back, while handcuffed. This is just a classic case of police abuse of power. Disorderly conduct is by far the vaguest charge a police officer can make, when arresting a person. In my opinion it is unconstitutional, as it is both "cruel and unusual," and it is used as a means of stifling the criticism of police officers, which should be protected by the first amendment.

Speaking of tazer-happy cops and racial profiling, I read with horror that police in Prince William County, North Carolina tazed a pregnant woman during her son's baptism. She was Mexican, so I guess that makes it all right. Seriously though, police in the U.S. need to follow very strict guidelines for when they can taze someone. I would start by saying that they should never taze children, elderly people, noticeably pregnant women, people on elevated platforms, and noticeably disabled people. They should also never aim for the head, heart, or anus (yes, cops have tazed people in the anus before). There should also be a very serious follow-up on tazing victims, to make sure that tazers are, in fact, "non-lethal." I have read about tazers leading to heart arrhythmia.

I have advice for anyone that encounters police officers in the United States: always be polite. Start out with, "Well sir/mam..." Then lie to their face. If you're questioned about any crime, do not speak to them without the presence of a lawyer. I've seen too many cases of people serving on murder charges, because the police coerced a confession. To summarize, do not cooperate with police, as they are not here to protect you, but to provide fodder for the prison-industrial complex.

Day 687, 8-24-2009

gps: S 34°11'27.31" W 58°37'49.25"

I have come to expect things on my bike to break but there are parts I have never seen break, even after thousands of miles on the road. This morning one of those parts broke. For those who are uninitiated in bike-speak, the derailler is the part on the back of the bike, above the wheel, that shifts gears. To my dismay, the arm of the derailler twisted and snapped off first thing this morning, bending the part of the frame that it hangs off of with it. Even though I knew that this was a problem I was not going to be able to fix on the side of the road, I couldn't help but stare at my busted derailler in disbelief for at least 15 minutes, while several trucks that could have carried me to the nearest city zoomed by.

Resigned to my fate of having to hitchhike the next 60 km to a city large enough for a bike shop that sold new derailers, I finally made a sign that said, "Concordia, emergency." The funny thing about hitchhiking is that people never seem to stop when you most need them to. Luckily, I think I appeared despondent enough that after about half an hour, some truckers with an "empty" truck bed stopped for me. I was so happy for the lift that I was able to overlook the fact that the truck was normally used to transport the left-over body parts of dead animals.

On the bottom of the truck bed, there was a piece of brain here, a hoof or scalp there, and parts which I was unable to identify, randomly strewn about. I was originally going to sit down for my trip but then I noticed that the floor was slippery with the fat of dead animals. I almost slipped and fell a number of times when the semi came to a stop. Fortunately, the trip lasted just under an hour, so I didn't have to endure the nastiness too long.

When the truckers dropped me off at the edge of the city, there was a nice supermarket owner who let me wash my hands in the back of his store, and gave me a ride to a bicycle shop, so I could beat the afternoon siesta. The mechanic at the shop appeared optimistic about bending the frame back into place. Hopefully, he'll fix my bike like new again, but I am worried that it will never shift quite the same again. I can only pray to my heathen gods that everything will be all right.

On the way out of Buenos Aires, towards the border with Brazil, I actually had to pay a bribe to some corrupt cops for the first time. This is after riding through all of Mexico, Central America, Colombia, Ecuador, Peru, and Bolivia. Anyone who has ever driven through Argentina knows that there are police checkpoints everywhere. They usually are just checking for identifying documents, but I found out the hard way, sometimes they are looking for a pound of flesh. As I approached the checkpoint, the cop indicated to me that he wanted me to stop so that is exactly what I did. He asked, "Why don't you have knee or elbow pads?" I wanted to say, "Do I look like a fucking five-year-old, asshole?" but I only said, "I have ridden over 15,000 kilometers without falling. I am willing to risk it." To my surprise he said, "Come inside so you can talk to the boss." I didn't think anything of it since I have encountered many incredulous police officers, who feigned concern over my safety before, so I went along with it. When inside, the boss immediately began talking about "fines." I protested immediately! Not only was I wearing a helmet, and had a bicycle that was almost entirely reflective, but I had ridden well over 2,000 kilometers in Argentina and passed through many police checkpoints without hearing a word about any of the traffic laws that I was supposedly violating. At this point, I should mention that a pig never uses the word bribe directly, when that is what they want. I should also mention that a bribe is negotiable. They start high and you low-ball them as much as you can. After my protest, the cop persisted in trying to get me to pay the "fine." He even showed me some bullshit law they only enforce on rich gringos, since I have seen literally thousands of cyclists without mirrors on their bikes or reflective clothing. Realizing that the pigfucker wasn't going to give up, I asked him how much the fine was, expecting some small number. My eyes popped out of my head when he told me the fine was 900 pesos. That is over $200! There was no way in fucking hell that I was going to fork over this kind of money. I would rather give my money to the Taliban, than to these inbred, thieving pigs! I told him I wasn't carrying that kind of money. "You aren't carrying dollars?" he asked. "Why would I be carrying dollars? We're in Argentina." He then pointed at a Mastercard emblem on the door and said, "We accept credit cards." I lied, "my card only works in cash machines." He said, "well, since you have a helmet and your bike is reflective we can reduce the 'fine'. How does $100 sound to you?" I said, "I can eat for a month with $100. That's way too much. I'm not carrying that kind of money." At this point, we had come to an impasse. The cop obviously didn't want to drop below $100, and I have a healthy contempt for police, so I wasn't budging either. Finally, I called his bluff, and said "I would much rather go to jail, than pay that much." He responded, "oh, we can't take you to jail for this. It is only an infraction. How much do you have?" At this point I took out the second wallet I carry: the one with significantly less cash in it that I carry for the sole purpose of having something to give thieves, if they are better armed than me. I just didn't expect that the thieves would be wearing badges. I counted out 90 pesos and said that was all I had. He

said, "how much will you give us for this infraction?" I replied, "I can only give you 50, since I need to eat," At that, a deal was struck. I'm still pissed about this, even though I talked the cops down from well over $200 to about $13. I suppose I should feel grateful that I wasn't "disappeared," since that is exactly what happened to over 30,000 Argentineans during the military dictatorship during the late 70s and early 80s. I should also mention that as much as I fulminate about tazer-happy police in the United States, cops in the developing world bring thuggery to a new level. It was just last month that a Nigerian Islamic militant died, while in the custody of police. Whenever, Mexican cops arrest some drug kingpin, they usually beat the shit out of him. This is evidenced by the black eyes and bloody noses that they almost invariably have when they are paraded before the press. American cops are models of restraint and professionalism in comparison. I remember how angry people got when a L.A. police officer kicked a suspect in the head after he finally gave up and jumped to the ground. The cop would have gotten away with it too, if this whole event wasn't captured on videotape. My point to this is that when cops abuse prisoners, this abuse is revisited upon them by the abused. Don't think that the Nigerian Islamic militants didn't take notice when their leader mysteriously died in police custody. When the Mexican cartels hire assassins to kill police and soldiers, the victims frequently show signs of torture. Restraint and professionalism is the only way cops can legitimize what they do, and it is what supposedly separates them from the criminals and terrorists.

I noticed news about the gun nuts showing up at rallies that president Obama attended. My favorite one was the man who brought a fully loaded AR-15 to the rally in Phoenix. The news article mentioned that Arizona was one of 7 "open carry" states where anyone can openly carry a gun with them for any reason. This peaked my curiosity and my Texas pride. "How could those Arizonans be crazier than us Texans?" I asked. After a quick wikipedia search, I was disappointed to find out that Texas was not one of the seven "open carry" states. We can only openly carry firearms when ostensibly hunting. There goes my lifelong dream of opening up a drive-thru gun and liquor store. Maybe I will have to move to Phoenix. I can already imagine riding my bicycle around with a fully loaded automatic rifle strapped to my back on a 120 degree day. Nobody would ever cut me off again.

*Dear reader, I am so glad you are enjoying sharing my travels and adventures.
If you would like to share in my next adventures, feel free to Venmo me using the username below. Please leave your email address and I will respond with a personal thank you letter and add you as a premium member on my next travel blog with the ability to post comments or questions....CHEERS!!*

AUTHOR NAME: Ezra Teter

VENMO DONATIONS SEND TO: @Goingnative123

Day 711, 9-17-2009

gps: S 33° 9'21.23" W 59°30'54.28"

On October 8th, I'll have been on the road for two years. I am not tired of it yet, in a good mood, though sad about the passing of my friend. I hope all is well with everyone. Yall should remember to savor every last moment you have on this planet.

I recently learned about the death of this friend through Facebook. To say that Eliseo and I were the greatest of friends would be an exaggeration, but he was a friend, and his death has dominated my conscious thoughts for the last week. When Eliseo and I lived together at New Guild Co-op, I was the cycling fanatic. He used his bicycle but wasn't half as zealous about commuting by bicycle, as I was. When he moved to New York City that changed. I know he used his bike as his primary form of transportation from his Facebook posts about riding across the Brooklyn Bridge while it was raining. This year, he wrote one of the most memorable birthday wishes for me. "May your chain never slip, your tires never puncture, your calves never cramp, and may the sun always shine on the road you're on. From one bicycle riding madman to another, happy birthday!"

To learn that he died from the injuries he sustained from getting hit by a car, while riding his bicycle only saddened me more. He held on for five days after the accident, with several moments of consciousness and false hope of a recovery. I am always saddened when a bicycle commuter gets killed by a car, but this time I wasn't separated by the normal degrees of separation that I usually have between me and the victim. Eliseo is not just another ghost bike to me; he was a real person who loved life. Getting disrespected by truck drivers, on the last stretch of road in Argentina, was even more offensive to me than normal. I am used to drivers refusing to acknowledge the deadly force they harness, with their hands on the steering wheel of several tons of steel hurling down the road, but this time it was personal. I couldn't help but glower at them accusingly each time they passed me with minimal space between me and them, even if the fault was not so much theirs as it was of the Argentinean government for not providing adequate space on the highways for all forms of transportation. This includes not just myself, but all of the poor folks who also ride bikes or ride motorcycles that seem to have lawnmower motors for their engines.

Eliseo wanted to be a writer. He would constantly post haikus on his Facebook, renewing my interest in this poetic form. I consider the fact that he had big dreams that died with him,

to make his death even that much more tragic. His death has been a reminder to me that life is too short, and can be taken from us at any moment. It can't be taken for granted. He was never able to create his opus, and this resonates with me. In his honor, and in honor of all of those who have lost their lives way too early, I plan to redouble my efforts to savor every single moment I have on this planet. I am going to make a much greater effort in conquering the last of my remaining fears that stand between me and total happiness. I know what you are all thinking: what is this world- traveling, knife-fighting, Ganjo-bicicletholic anarcyclist afraid of? I am still afraid of rejection both in romance, and in my creative and professional life. I am going to make an effort to talk to the pretty girl standing alone at a party. I will seek out more musician friends, and work more actively to perform the music I love. I will try harder to find a job that I love, not just one that pays the bills. I will no longer let my fear of rejection limit my options.

I have really been appreciating the admonition, "that you should be careful about what you wish for," these last few weeks. After riding through the altiplano of Bolivia, I was so sick of the cold, that I found myself desiring the other extreme that I am so used to, from growing up in Texas. Well, I have gotten that and then some, and now I miss the cold. It sure was nice being able to camp without constructing my tent, as there were no mosquitoes or blood-sucking gnats. I never got any of the skin rashes, which always seem to be optimally placed for maximum discomfort. I didn't have to deal with thunderstorms, though I am always mesmerized by the beauty of the lightning. I forgot about the enervating effects of the heat. At the end of the day, I am just that much more exhausted. This is all just a reminder that the physical challenges of my bike ride are not over, even though I don't have to deal with multiple-day ascents.

These last few weeks have also reminded me that there is indeed some crushing poverty in Argentina. I have seen the dilapidated houses which all seem to be concentrated in the northeast. I had also grown used to all the gas stations having Wi-Fi and cappuccino machines, but no more. I was just happy if there was shade now. Argentina cut down the majority of its old-growth forests a long time ago to make space for ranch and farm land. What remains of the forests are mostly obscene rows of eucalyptus or pine trees ready to be harvested to meet domestic wood demand. I'm happy that the Argentinean lumber industry has developed a sustainable model, but not happy that it came only after decimating almost every last natural forest in Argentina. It is really sad when poverty forces people to do things that are bad in the long term for a short term gain.

I mentioned earlier that I'm looking forward to the mental challenge of learning a new language. It is most definitely satisfying to know that I can actually hold a conversation in Portuguese, but I still feel somewhat stupid. I have gone from using mostly Spanish, which I speak pretty much automatically, to using a new language. In all fairness, I did prepare for this. I have actually been reading through my Portuguese-English dictionary and memorizing regular and irregular conjugation forms. I have made it all the way to the "I"s. There are a lot of similarities between Spanish and Portuguese, but there are a lot of differences as well. The main difference is the pronunciation which varies a lot just within Brazil. I think I am going to have to choose a pronunciation and just stick with it. I can read and hold conversations in Portuguese, but my mind does not work fast enough to follow São Paulo and Rio de Janeiro accents in rapid fire on television. I actually speak significantly more Portuguese now, than I spoke Spanish when I lived in Mexico five years ago. Welcome to Brazil. Learn Portuguese or die.

It is interesting seeing the news from a Latin American perspective, instead of my typical American perspective. The news we watch on the T.V. or read in American papers is so myopic that it drives me crazy. I am particularly irked by C.N.N. in Spanish. Not only is the news U.S.-centric but it is often inaccurate. I still remember when they had a news story about the Bolivian city of Sucre celebrating its bicentennial. The only problem with the news story, was that the stock photos they showed of the city for the news segment were actually of Potosi. I know this because I was in Potosi at the time and I had recently been to Sucre. C.N.N. also bungled the news when they showed a short headline stating that the Argentinean Supreme court had just declared that arresting people for small amounts of marijuana was unconstitutional. This is technically true, as the specific case involved several young people in the city of Rosario, who were arrested by police, after they were searched, and it was discovered that they were carrying small amounts of marijuana. It didn't however, reveal the whole truth, as the court struck down a law that refers to the possession of all drugs, not just marijuana. The court did not define the amounts considered small enough to be "for personal consumption" only. That is up to the legislature which, I suspect, will model the new law on the one that was recently signed into law in Mexico.

American media is guilty of omission when it comes to reporting on the rest of the world, and its also guilty of under-emphasizing the globaly important stories. A recent example is Colombia's signing of an agreement with the United States, allowing the U.S. to use Colombian military bases for drug interdiction. This issue is buried in the back pages of American newspapers, but its in the front-page headlines here. I was watching a televised meeting of Unasur which is kind of like a mini-U.N. composed of just South American countries. Literally every single South American president was at the meeting in Bariloche where the issue of the U.S. military presence in Colombia was the main topic of discussion. I couldn't help but notice who was noticeably absent: Barack Obama. Despite his pledges to renew diplomacy with Latin America, he refrained from making what would be the most symbolically significant way of demonstrating the United States' renewed commitment to strengthening its relationship with Latin America. He probably hasn't even met half the people that were in the room. If Hugo Chavez and Alvaro Uribe can put aside their personal enmity to share a room together, than Obama can make an appearance. He could have at least, sent his Secretary of State, who was also noticeably absent.

As further evidence that United States is quickly becoming an international backwater, Uruguay recently legalized adoption of children by gay couples. There was also an article about how every student in Uruguay is going to have their own personal laptop provided. I might have to move to Uruguay as they seem to be on a more progressive path than the U.S.

I'm Sisyphus: My Bicycle Is My Rock, Going Native In São Paulo

Day 731 (2 Years), 10-8-2009

gps: S 25°25'42.08" W 49°16'23.71"

In nature, the mama bird throws her chicks out of the nest and if they cannot fly, then too bad. I guess that is a good way to describe my immersion technique for learning a new language. It is, by far, the most effective technique of language acquisition that I know of. I am alone here in Brazil, and I do not have anyone here to translate for me. I am reading books written in Portuguese to expand my vocabulary. My goal is to try to learn twenty words every day. The problem with this goal, is that I actually already have a rather large vocabulary in Portuguese.

When I read a book I recognize the vast majority of the words. I can have a conversation and I can write in Portuguese. The thing that is difficult for me, is understanding the language when it is spoken to me. I still have to train my ear. Despite my difficulties, you would never guess that I have only been in Brazil for three weeks. I am already getting complements on my Portuguese, though I strive for perfection.

The hard physical challenges of riding my bicycle through Latin America have not ended. Apparently its an

El Niño year, so its cold and wet in southern Brazil. I've seen more rain in the last month, than in almost all of my travels thus far. Its wearing my patience thin. None of the rain gear I started with works for me any more. Northface may have a lifetime warranty, but they do not respond to emails about this. I'd recommend another brand if you are going to spend a bunch of money on gear. I spent ten dollars for a plastic rain suit, so I don't have to be cold and miserable. I am trying to camp underneath bridges when I can, and avoiding the rain in every way possible.

There are no real mountains in Brazil, but the entire southern part of the country is covered in interminable hills, so I end up climbing as much as if there were mountains here. Combined with the rain, riding through Brazil has

been no cakewalk. Rio de Janeiro is only about 900 kilometers away from where I am right now, so I do not have much farther to go.

I am in Curitiba right now, staying at the house of a friend. Tomorrow, I plan to extend my tourist visa one more time, and then I am going to disappear into the cracks here. I am pretty sure that I can get a job teaching English, especially with the 2014 World Cup and 2016 Olympics being in Rio. Once I am feeling more confident with my Portuguese, I plan to give private lessons for at least $20 an hour.

In the past I have said that I want to stay here in Brazil for at least a year. I am actually thinking of staying permanently now. I have many reasons to not want to pay taxes

to the U.S. government but the thought of an individual insurance mandate brings my disgust with the American government to new levels. There is no fucking way that I am going to be forced give my money to those thieving bastards. I might either wait for an amnesty for immigrants here in Brazil or cynically marry a Brazilian for citizenship. If I manage to obtain Brazilian citizenship I might even renounce my American citizenship. The U.S. Congress has not passed this mandate yet but I fear that it is a foregone conclusion.

11-15-2009

gps: Staying in São Paulo

I haven't written much recently, as Hotmail erased all of my old e-mails and contact information. That has actually worked out alright for me, since I have had more time for myself to get more acclimated to Brazil and its culture. It continued to rain for a quite a while after I left Curitiba, leaving me wet and annoyed. I already have a rip in the crotch of the rain pants I bought in southern Brazil, but at least the rain isn't cold, like it s in the Andes. I can get wet and not worry about frostb te and hypo-thermia, like I would in the mountains at 4,000 meters.

I am nearing the end of my journey. I have ridden through countless mountains, deserts, and jungles to get to where I am now. I have endured temperature extremes, both hot and cold. I have dealt with lots of water, and little water. I have endured weather of biblical proportions. Cycle touring is the best training available to prepare for the coming apocalypse. Rio de Janeiro, my final destination, is only 350 kilometers away from São Paolo. Many Paulistas look at me in amazement when I tell them that I am going to ride my bike from here to Rio de Janeiro. In response, I can only shrug, as 350 kilometers seems like nothing to me now. I could cover that distance in less than a week, while relaxing a lot. I have been on the road for over two years now. After traveling thousands of kilometers to get to this point, 350 kilometers IS nothing!

That being said, as ready as I am to get to Rio de Janeiro and establish a base camp, I keep on getting sucked back into the seductive embrace of São Paolo. I have always been in love with the massive cities of the world, so São Paulo is no exception. How large is São Paolo? It is the largest city in South America and one of the top five largest in the world. There are around 20 million people living in the São Paulo metropolitan area.

One of my very favorite things to do is wander around aimlessly on my bicycle. The city is filled with graffiti. In fact, I would venture to say that São Paulo is the current graffiti capital of the world. The graffiti here is unique in style, to the graffiti of other large cities in Latin America, and it is pervasive in this labyrinthine city. I am constantly discovering art that is hidden in a shaded corner or nook of one of the thousands of buildings that sprout from the ground here. Throw in the highway under and overpasses, and there is still a lot of blank space just waiting for art. Despite the pervasiveness of art in the city, I get the feeling that São Paulo hasn't even come close to fulfilling the public art potential in its walls.

There's been a number of famous graffiti artists from São Paolo. Two of the better known artists are Os Gêmeos. These identical twins, as their namesake implies, have painted art in cities all over the world. The largest of their pieces rival the murals of Diego Rivera in size, and the complexity of the work of Salvador Dali in their surrealism. They have achieved such a mainstream success that the

Brazilian national art museum here in São Paulo has a free exhibition of their work till the end of the year.

Aside from exploring all the nooks and crannies of this massive city, I have been sampling the flavors of Brazil. After being in this country for a couple of months I have begun to figure out which foods I like the most. The fresh fruits feature strongly in the food of this country. I have probably been averaging about two liters of fresh juice daily here. The juice can be as simple as fresh squeezed orange juice, or as complex as coconut water blended with fresh mint and ginger. When I get a smoothie with my meals, I have to choose from a dizzying array of choices for what I want to put in it. If you are having trouble figuring out where to get juice, you can generally judge a juice

place by the amount of fresh fruit they have hanging over their counters.

I've also developed a fondness for empanadas, which is the Portuguese way of saying empanada. The truth is every country in Latin America has their own version of empanadas, usually being quite different from the empanadas in other countries. While the Argentinean version is made with a bread dough, the Brazilian version is made with pie crust, and its like a miniature pie filled with yumminess. At my favorite empadaria, I like the shrimp empanada which is really filled with more of a shrimp étouffée, than just shrimp. I also really like the empanada just filled with palmito, which is the center of a small palm tree cooked up with butter and garlic.

São Paulo is filled with tons of restaurants of varying quality, with notable contributions from its sizable groups of Lebanese and Japanese immigrants. One can find both good sushi and good hummus in São Paulo. The immigrants' contribution to the food of São Paulo, obviously, goes beyond sushi and hummus. You can find many more obscure and authentic recipes as well.

I am completely addicted to the Middle Eastern desserts made in a restaurant, close to where I am staying. My favorite is baked in a filo dough pie crust and filled with pistachios and other nuts, and then covered in a really thick and complex tasting apricot jam. I often spend my days following my stomach to my favorite restaurants in

this city. I'm spending a lot of money at restaurants, but I'm really enjoying it.

One of the things that I try to do in every country I pass through, is learn more about its music. I have discovered so much beautiful and wonderful music in my journeys thus far. I finally had that spiritual and orgasmic experience with samba that I had been searching for, since I arrived in Brazil, when I went to a free samba show in the basketball court at O Beco do Batman, a park in the Magdalena neighborhood of São Paulo, which is a well-known graffiti gallery. Not only was the music beautiful and rhythmically complex, but everyone there was rocking out! Brazilian women seem to have a special gene which allows them to shake their booty at astonishing speed while dancing to samba. I saw an old-timer at the edge of the music, with a huge smile, singing along to almost everything, as most of the songs the group was playing were classics. The look on his face was one of complete, unadulterated joy. Up until this point, I had only experienced momentary flashes of the good samba, the stuff that foreigners know nothing about. I kept on wondering what was making the crazy monkey sound in the sambas I liked the most? At this show, I finally found out what was making the sound: an instrument called the cuica. At first glance it looks like a drum but then you notice it is not played like one. On closer inspection, one can see that the cuica is played by rubbing a wet cloth on a stick that is attached to the inside of the drum. It has quickly become one of my favorite percussive instruments.

I left the show at O Beco, armed with the name of Clara Nunes, the queen diva of samba, though that isn't the only type of music she recorded. The problem with looking for music on Youtube, is that you have to wade through a lot of muck if you just type "samba" in the search box. When I typed in "Clara Nunes" I discovered a whole world of amazing music I had never been exposed to. I have placed her in the hierarchy of my musical gods, deified after their deaths and immortalized by their music.

How important is Clara Nunez's music to me? If I had to rank influential musicians from my most favorite to least favorite, I would place her above both the Beatles and Michael Jackson. The truth is that I am not ape shit crazy for either the Beatles or Michael Jackson, but Clara Nunes rocks my world.

In my time here in São Paulo, I also had the opportunity to attend a rehearsal of one of the samba schools here in São Paulo. Rio de Janeiro is not the only place that has samba schools. The rehearsal was full of good positive energy. With percussionists numbering about a hundred, the music was a joyfully thunderous cacophony, under the bridge where the Aguia de Ouro, or Eagle of Gold, samba school meets every Sunday to rehearse for Carnival. The school itself is made up of more than just percussionists, as there are dancers and flag holders, strutting and dancing in front of them. As this is parade music, the whole samba school is mobile. Some of the dancers had the air of true divas, strutting and dancing with such confidence, that they would challenge those who just idly watched to start dancing, by dancing in front of them. My favorite thing about the samba school, is that the gay community seems to have found an acceptable outlet in the samba school, for all of their flamboyance. One of my very favorite divas at the rehearsal was a tranny who looked like she could dunk. Her six-inch heels only exaggerated her height even more. I could only sit back and absorb the atmosphere, but I am already thinking of joining a samba school after Carnival this year. Soon enough, I will be strutting around in one of the parades, like the most flamboyant of flaming queens.

I am feeling right now that my decision to live in Brazil was a good one. At this point, I think I am going to have a really good time here in Brazil. There is good food and good music here. Did I mention that the nation is populated with Amazonian goddesses, that bless us mere mortals with their presence? I am not sure that I am ever coming back to the U.S.

5-4-2010

gps: S 33° 9›21.23» W 59°30›54.28»

The first thing that I want to say about this blog is that I have not written much for it in a while. I was just trying to settle down in São Paulo. In the last blog, I said I was going to Rio de Janeiro, but I changed my mind because I already had friends here and it was almost December, which meant a lot of people weren't hiring until after Carnival. Since then, I met a girl, went out with her, and lived with her for a while, but she was crazy, so we have now broken up. We were actually going to get married, so that I could get residency, but that didn't happen. I am annoyed that I can't just work at any job, but I am staying in Brazil. I think that I won't return to the U.S. until we have a single payer health-care system, paid for by the government cutting its military budgets, and ending the drug war and all wars that are overseas. A cynic, or perhaps a realist, might say humans will be slaves to super-intelligent cockroaches before that happens.

Living as an illegal immigrant in São Paulo has its disadvantages. I can't legally work, rent, open bank accounts, or sign contracts. That doesn't mean that I can't find jobs or places to live, it just means that they rely on handshakes and cash, rather than contracts and checks. I should be able to reach my goal of falling off the grid completely in short time, as I have already began to get students who pay me in cash, and have weekly classes with me. This is in an addition to the work that my pimps give me. I am not really a hooker, I just like to imagine that my bosses are pimps laying down the law, and collecting the money. My bosses deal with bill collection and contracts and all the other headaches. I just teach English. I only accept cash when I am working for myself, because I don't relish the idea of having debtors and having to hunt the money down each month. I make about 40 Reals an hour which is actually a very good hourly rate at almost $23 an hour. In comparison to the U.S., São Paulo is a pretty cheap city to live in, so I work an enviably small amount of hours each week. Working just seven hours a week, I make just enough to survive. Fortunately, I have just begun to work about 15 hours a week, plus a Saturday night bartending gig at an illegal bar on the street where I live. The bartending job is for fun more than money. If I can keep working 15 hours a week, or add to that, I should be able to go from having the problem of not having any fun money to having too much cash to spend. The first thing I will buy is a new computer, so I can type the accent marks used in Portuguese (I am using a free Internet computer and beggars can't be choosers). I am also thinking about opening my own illegal bar, or another cash-only businesses.

Cycling in São Paulo is not for the meek. The metropolitan area of São Paulo has over twenty million people, so as one might imagine, it is filled with millions of cars, taxis, and buses. Fortunately for me, I have hardened my nerves by riding on the streets of some of the largest cities in the world, so I have no problem getting around. When I am in my ciclofaixa or 'bike lane," as I like to call the lane that is formed between gridlocked traffic going in one direction, I always have to look over my shoulders, and make sure the motoboys aren't coming up behind me. There are probably millions of motorcycles in São Paulo. The difference between the motoboys and the cyclist is that cyclist ignores all transit laws, and motorcyclists have to wait at the lights. The police in São Paulo don't really care about cyclists running red lights and going the wrong way. I think they are too busy shooting people in the periphery of São Paulo for that. Anyway, on my bicycle, I am invisible to both police and thieves, despite my white skin and obvious gringo-ness. In addition to dealing with all of the traffic, one's willpower to ride a bicycle is challenged by large hills in inconvenient places and a lot of rain. With that said, there are flat spots and down hills all over the city, where I am significantly faster than traffic. With my bicycle, I am the most punctual man in São Paulo.

There are a lot of things that a poor person can do in São Paulo to keep themselves entertained and intellectually stimulated. All of the museums, some of which are world class, are free on Tuesdays. There are always free music shows, all around town, on the weekends. São Paulo's Critical Mass is large, rowdy, and free. It is super cheap and fun to go to the samba schools when they are practicing for Carnival. One can always go to Avenida Paulista or the Galeria do Rock if you want to people-watch. São Paulo is blessed with a lot of semi-legal street vendors selling food too. I am completely addicted to the noodle stir-fry, called "Yakisoba" that a Chinese immigrant makes on the street every day, probably for the last twenty years. A large container costs about $3 and is large enough for two or three people with normal appetites to share. I on the other hand, find a large container of yakisoba to be quite satisfying, capable of sating any hunger pangs I might have. Once you get to know the terrain, you can figure out who is selling fresh coconut juice or other fruit juices for cheap. I may be poor, but the city is filled with lots of sensual pleasures that don't cost too much to indulge in.

In the short time I have spent in São Paulo, I have managed to both live in, and hear music, in buildings designed by Oscar Niemeyer. When I was living with my ex-girlfriend, we lived in Copan, which was named after a Mayan temple in Honduras. It is still the largest apartment building in all of Latin America, with 1,160 apartments and 5,000 residents. Located in the central part of São Paulo, it is hard to imagine a more convenient location. Just downstairs, I could find bakeries and video stores. I really enjoyed living there. However, I now live in the most bohemian neighborhood in all of São Paulo, so I really can't complain.

A friend of mine plays for the São Paulo Jazz Philharmonic, so I got tickets to go see them play in the theater designed by Oscar Niemeyer, in Parque Ibirapuera, which is the big park in the central area of São Paulo. It is an interesting building shaped like a white right triangle that is expanded out three-dimensionally.

The entrance is formed by a red curvy plane jutting out from the 45 degree end of the triangle. Standing in the entrance has an arresting visual effect, because the bichromatic effect of the red of white exterior continues into the interior of the building with what looks like a large red ribbon interrupting the pristine white walls. As cool as the theater was, I didn't care too much for the music, which I'll describe as samba wearing a suit and tie. I just feel that samba is a music meant to be danced to, and not to be watched passively, while wearing a tuxedo.

I am still continuing to discover the secrets of São Paulo. Hopefully, I will soon be working just the right amount, so as to not be working much at all, but to make enough money to have some fun, and continue to live outside of the Matrix!